D0240118

PUNISHING THE POOR

Poverty under Thatcher

PUNISHING THE POOR

Poverty under Thatcher

Kay Andrews and John Jacobs

MACMILLAN
LONDON

To
Adam and Callum Jacobs
and Alexander MacLeod

First published 1990 by
MACMILLAN LONDON LIMITED
4 Little Essex Street London WC2R 3LF
and Basingstoke

Associated companies in Auckland, Delhi, Dublin, Gaborone,
Hamburg, Harare, Hong Kong, Johannesburg, Kuala Lumpur,
Lagos, Manzini, Melbourne, Mexico City, Nairobi, New York,
Singapore and Tokyo

A CIP catalogue record for this book is available from the
British Library

ISBN 0-333-48721-4

Typeset by Wyvern Typesetting Ltd, Bristol

Printed by Billings Book Plan, Worcester

Contents

Contents

Contents

Contents

Acknowledgements

Many people have given of their time and assistance in the preparation of this book. In particular we would like to thank the staff of CPAG, the Disability Alliance, Youthaid, Centrepoint and Judy Foy and the parliamentary and information retrieval team at NACAB. To these, and to all the other organisations in the Social Security Consortium who scrupulously tried to secure changes to the 1986 Social Security Act that they knew from collective experience would not help the poorest people, a great debt is owed.

Mike Lewis of the University of Sussex Library located and provided many of the essential references. The staff of the Oriel and Reference Rooms, and of the Statistical Section of the House of Commons Library, in particular Richard Cracknell, Robert Twigger and Robert Clements, have been unfailingly helpful and accurate. Anyone who has worked in social security policy for a decade knows how much is owed to Julia Lourie whose superb analytical work has helped all Members of Parliament understand the most complex of policies as they have developed since the mid-1970s. Like everyone else we have profited from her knowledge and understanding of events. We are very grateful to her. Frank Field MP read parts of the manuscript at an early stage and was supportive throughout.

We would also like to thank Simon Montgomery whose expertise in the area of unemployment benefits contributed greatly to Chapter 7 on policies and practice for unemployed people. Terry Adams of the CPSA also provided helpful comments on staffing issues in the Department of Social Security.

We have also been very fortunate in our publishers and editors. We would like to thank Adam Sisman for the enthusiasm he

Acknowledgements

showed and for sharing our conviction that the book should aim for a general readership, and Brian Abraham who read the manuscript assiduously and untangled some of the more arcane passages.

The Rt Hon Neil Kinnock MP agreed to write a Foreword and gave us permission to illustrate the texts with extracts from some of the thousands of letters that were written to him in Spring 1989 by people who found that they were indeed 'losers' under the new Act. We are deeply indebted to him for that but even more so for leading the campaign against a punitive strategy of 'reform', which has been and continues to be conducted with such skill and resolve by Robin Cook MP and Margaret Beckett MP in the House of Commons.

We had personal and professional reasons for writing this book. We both share the common dismay and anger of many people who have watched as the fundamental ethics of the welfare state have been distorted for a decade, and as the deliberate policy of redistributing wealth from the poor to the rich has been legitimised by the argument that the poor must be protected from a culture of 'dependency'. In our work we have been in close contact with claimants in need who found to their disbelief and despair that they could not be helped because the rules were deliberately designed to exclude or deprive them. Many people who work with and on behalf of those who depend on social security, as well as claimants themselves, are unable to tell that story. We hope that this book will in some sense speak for them too.

Finally, although we have observed the convention that family and friends come at the end of the chronology of debts it is illogical and unfair when they have listened, argued back, contributed, contradicted and generally participated so much in the making of this book. They have all suffered from our general distraction over the past year. Barbara, Alexander, Nick and Mam know how much we owe them, but we are glad that we can thank them publicly.

Foreword

Economic efficiency and social justice depend upon one another. That is obvious to everyone who understands that unemployment and the poverty it brings are both socially oppressive and economically wasteful. The link between social disadvantage and economic performance has grown stronger over a decade dominated by an ideology which has actively promoted inequality as a means of stimulating economic growth and social independence. Equality, so the parody goes, inhibits initiative, ambition and excellence. Inequality provides the spur to self-help and prosperity. Within the wider context it means, as the Prime Minister puts it, 'that you drag up the poor because there are more resources to do so'.

The fact is that the poor have not, in that elegant phrase, been 'dragged up'. Millions of them have been dragged down by policies which could have had no other outcome because they were designed to cut central and local spending on public services and to promote unemployment. More than that. The poorest have been *held* down by policies which have required them to fund the distribution of tax relief to the richest and by 'reforms' which at nil cost required the poor to pay for marginal improvements in the incomes of those only a little poorer than themselves.

At one level therefore the Government has been supremely successful. It has created, by deliberate policy, a society which is now more unequal than ever before. In this oil-rich decade, the wealthiest 1 per cent have doubled the value of their wealth; the top 10 per cent have profited by well over 25 per cent growth in income. The poorest fifth of households have suffered real cuts in their income: 4 million more people are now living in families at or below the level of Income Support (Supplementary Benefit) than in 1979.

xi

Foreword

The most blatant link between poverty and inequality is that forged by the poll tax – designed to fall more heavily on the poor than the rich. In practice it will make millions worse off. In principle it gives offence to all.

This book focuses on the way in which the poorest have paid the highest price for their poverty. The 1986 Social Security Act was the final stage in a series of policies intended to cut the costs of welfare. It created a new class of loser – the 3.5 million people who were designed to do less well under the 'reforms' than under the old system. This April half a million people, many of them pensioners, have received no increases at all in their benefits for the second year running; another 600,000 have received an increase below the rate of inflation. Yet these were the people the Prime Minister counted as being among those who would 'gain' from the changes.

Has the strategy worked? Has punishing the poorest made Britain more efficient, more competitive? Have the incentive payments to the rich worked to stimulate the economy so that all may grow rich in time? Manufacturing investment is only now climbing back to the 1979 level. Our balance of payments this year is now estimated at £18 billion. The inflation rate is over 8 per cent. It is twice as high as the European average and increasing faster.

The verdict is devastating: Britain is both more unequal as a society and more inefficient.

This Government has made a reputation out of being economical with the truth. The gap between what was intended, what was said and what was actually done demonstrates how the strategy to 'target' help to those most in need was doomed to fail those who most need it. *Punishing the Poor* examines this gap between fact and fiction. But the significance of the book, as the authors emphasise, does not lie in statistical or policy analysis. It lies in the effects that the intention and the policies of government have had *in practice* on individual lives.

And that is the greatest test of all. The Beveridge reform was as fair as it was efficient. There were no 'losers', no accidental or deliberate victims. Yet when I and my colleagues brought case after case to the attention of the Prime Minister in the spring of 1988 she dismissed them as individual examples of that minority which would inevitably have to lose in order that others might be 'targeted' to gain.

That new philosophy – 'targeting' – holds a particular irony for those it is meant to help. The poverty that traps millions of people already targets those in disadvantage. It picks on certain regions; on women rather than men; on the old rather than the young; on those out of work and without skills; on those with disabilities. That form of targeting is the source of poverty. The Fowler reforms had the chance to build on the firm foundation Beveridge offered and the unique good fortune of oil to modernise our national insurance system for the next century.

Policies for reform – and there was need and scope for reform in social security – could have fought poverty on its own ground, as our European neighbours have: policies to increase child care and to train and retrain people out of work and returning to work. Britain has the lowest rate of publicly funded child care of any country in Europe – and the highest drop-out rate from statutory education at sixteen. In Sweden, the combined bill for high quality training and unemployment relief is less than our bills for training and unemployment benefit. They spend on training. We spend on unemployment.

Those policies matched with policies for industrial investment would lay the foundations of a competitive economy. When complemented by policies for a minimum wage and for progressive and fair taxation they would provide real opportunity and incentive to work. They would also lay the foundations of a modern employment and social security system based on flexibility at work and in retirement which could accommodate the potential for women and men to combine family responsibilities with work. That would underpin a policy for benefits which targets on need across a lifetime and which could mirror more realistically the costs of caring for children or the extra costs of disablement.

Eighty years ago, before what Margaret Thatcher called 'the right to be unequal', Matthew Arnold warned that 'a system founded on it [inequality] . . . is against nature, and in the long run breaks down'. The denigration of public values, public services and public provision in every aspect of economic and social life has, over a decade, contributed to that process of decay.

Foreword

For those who have been shut out of Thatcher's Britain, finding a way out of poverty means finding a way back into society. As the authors of this book make clear, the future can be different. It must be. I hope that *Punishing the Poor* will be read by those who share that ambition – not simply because they know that that is the way we can rebuild our economy but because they believe that we *must* work to rebuild our society into a community of equal citizens.

Neil Kinnock
House of Commons
April 1989

List of Abbreviations

ACC	Association of County Councils
AMA	Association of Metropolitan Authorities
BLIP	Board and Lodgings Information Programme
CHAR	Campaign for the Homeless and Rootless
CPAG	Child Poverty Action Group
CPRS	Central Policy Review Staff
CPSA	Civil and Public Services Association
DIG	Disablement Income Group
DSS	Department of Social Security
EC	European Community
EOC	Equal Opportunities Commission
ET	Employment Training
FIS	Family Income Supplement
JTS	Job Training Scheme
NACAB	National Association of Citizens Advice Bureaux
NAO	National Audit Office
NCVO	National Council for Voluntary Organisations
NUCPS	National Union of Civil and Public Servants
OPCS	Office of Population Censuses and Surveys
RADAR	Royal Association for Disability and Rehabilitation
RAO	Regional Adjudication Officers
SCPS	Society of Civil and Public Servants
SBC	Supplementary Benefits Commission
SERPS	State Earnings-Related Pension Scheme
SFO	Social Fund Officer
SHAC	Shelter Housing Aid Centre
SSP	Statutory Sick Pay
SSAC	Social Security Advisory Committee
UCSS	Union Coalition for Social Security
YTS	Youth Training Scheme

Introduction

'What the new definition of relative poverty amounts to in the end is simply inequality. It means that however rich a society gets it will drag the incubus of relative poverty with it up the income scale. The poverty lobby would on their definition find poverty in Paradise.'

(John Moore MP, Secretary of State for Social Security,
11 May 1989.)

Thus, John Moore, in a sweeping if selective survey of economic and social change pronounced 'the end of the line for poverty'. He invited his audience to '. . . acknowledge British capitalism's true achievements' which he said had been to wipe out 'the stark want of Dickensian Britain'.

The speech was not a success. In tone and content it revealed not only poor political judgement, it also offended common sense. By attacking government critics, ignoring contradictory evidence, and distorting language, this speech also illustrated the extent to which the government have tried to avoid serious debate on the living standards and conditions of the poorest people in Britain today. Meaningless historical parallels cannot blot out present truths. In particular, claims that policies designed to enrich the rich also enrich the poor were dealt a mortal blow in April 1988 when tax cuts for the rich and benefit cuts for the poor were seen to bring about a massive redistribution of wealth to the richest.

In the fierce debate that followed social security at last became a popular issue. For a while the media were full of the finer points of the new system of social security. 'Gainers' and 'losers' were guaranteed prime time. Not for long. Compassion-fatigue soon set in and those who had lost out were soon left to themselves. That is part of the reason for writing this book.

Government and its ministers have no problems in telling their side of the story. In Green Papers, White Papers, press releases, in countless interviews and set speeches they have made many claims for their new strategies. We have used these claims as the touchstone against which to test the outcomes of their policies. We have looked at the rhetoric of explanation and justification, and contrasted this with the reality as it has been experienced by social security claimants. The changes in policies have been accompanied by a new vocabulary in which we have all been invited to rethink the place of welfare in a leaner, more competitive Britain. We have therefore focused on the meanings of these new concepts, 'targeting', 'dependency', 'enterprise', 'simplification' and the like, and tried to show what they mean in daily life.

This new language has grown out of a new set of social values, or to be more accurate, out of a revival of a set of values which dominated social policies for the poor during the heyday of the Victorian Poor Law. To the legitimate idea of personal and family responsibility other doctrines have been added – the virtues of wealth creation, the limits of state care, the front-line role of charity, and above all the Prime Minister's insistence that 'there is no such thing as Society'. The translation of these values into specific policies gives to all the changes to dozens of benefits, and to the hundreds of rules that regulate them, a direction, purpose and coherence which add up to a major ideological shift. Our aim has been to articulate that shift and to assess its meaning for social security claimants.

As well as ideological claims, ministers have also made specific claims about the effects of their policies. We have examined these in some detail to see whether these claims are consistent with the experiences of claimants. Where they are not, we have also tried to show how the differences can best be explained, and in particular whether they are the result of honest differences of interpretation or the result of deliberate attempts to mislead or even deceive. In this respect, the book is not just about government action but also about its style, the value it places on open government and its relationship with those it governs; it is about the integrity of ministers of the Crown.

Each of these themes is pursued in the chapters that follow. Much of the first part of the book focuses on the debate leading up to the Fowler reviews, the making of the Social Security Act 1986, and its subsequent implementation two years later in April 1988. The significance of that Act and the changes it has brought cannot be understood without a knowledge of the demolition of the surrounding areas of national insurance provision, and of the betrayal of the hope that the slow progress out of poverty which had been made for the elderly, children and disabled people during the 1970s would continue. The recent history and effects of the major changes in policies affecting all the main claimant groups, families with children, young people, the disabled, the elderly and the unemployed are the subject of Part 1.

In Part 2 the focus switches from the broad sweep of policies to the detailed administration of benefits, and in particular to the small but symbolically crucial area of single payments. Only those versed in the mysteries of the old supplementary benefit system know the details of the bewildering complexity of the rules and regulations which determined whether claimants could or could not have their basic needs met, yet it is in the details of these rules that, once again, the underlying social values are revealed. These chapters have been written with the purpose of discovering these values, and the changes they have undergone in the last decade. This part of the book is a chronicle of how we in Britain have treated poor people in the affluent 1980s, and how we will treat them as we move into the 1990s. In examining this corner of the social security system we still pursue our main themes of the change in political ideology, the emergence of a new vocabulary, the intention of those responsible for the changes made over the decade, and above all the place and treatment reserved for welfare claimants in Thatcher's Britain.

Part 1

Social Values and Social Security 1979–88

1 Social Values and Social Security 1979–88

I came to office with one deliberate intent: to change
Britain from a dependent to a self-reliant society; from
a give-it-to-me to a do-it-yourself nation; a get-up-and-
go instead of a sit-back-and-wait-for-it Britain.

(Margaret Thatcher, speech to the Small Businesses Bureau,
8 February 1984)

In 1979 the Conservative government came into office with a clear
policy to cut public expenditure and to reduce state intervention.
Cutting social security expenditure and cutting national
insurance rights lay at the heart of these twin objectives.

The welfare strategy which had developed on a bipartisan basis
throughout the 1960s and 1970s had been dedicated to making
good the gaps and deficiencies of the Beveridge structure. The
Labour governments of the 1960s had, for example, grafted on
provisions for earnings-related benefits to supplement the 'short-
term' work-related benefits to cushion people against the sudden
loss of income following sickness or unemployment. Work had also
begun in the late 1960s under Richard Crossman on an earnings-
related retirement pension scheme; it continued under the Conservative government. The state earnings-related pension scheme
(SERPS) was introduced, in a modified fashion, by the Labour
government of 1974–9. The first statutory arrangements for
regular 'upratings' of benefits to protect the standard of living of
those on pensions and benefits was introduced in 1974. Family
benefits were transformed with the introduction of child benefit,
one-parent benefit and family income supplements in the early
1970s; and a start was made on extending national insurance

3

cover to the long-term sick with the introduction of invalidity benefit in 1971, and providing a range of specific benefits (such as attendance allowance and mobility allowance) for other chronically sick and disabled people.

The significance of each of these initiatives to modernise the social security system was that they were committed to extending what was described as 'the national insurance community' and, as such, they commanded all-party support. Moreover, they were based on a common assumption that welfare policies, if they were to be both just and efficient, could not be limited to relieving destitution but should aim at preventing poverty. In short, they continued that positive view of the interdependence of the individual and the community first expressed in the Beveridge Report.

At the same time, as in every other industrialised country, concern was rising about the costs of demographic and social change, particularly about the growing proportion of elderly people, the implications of family breakdown, and the rising costs of unemployment. By 1979 social security expenditure accounted for 25 per cent of public expenditure, the largest share of which went on pensions. In Britain pressure to modernise social security was compounded by the existence of a 'poverty trap' created by the interaction of low benefits and low wages, which meant that for some people (usually with large families) additional earnings could be offset by the loss of benefits. There was also the inadequacy and acknowledged complexity of the supplementary benefit system, widely acknowledged to be in need of reform, which was the subject of a major review at the end of the 1970s inspired by the Supplementary Benefits Commission itself. The review led to statutory changes in 1980 and, most significantly, to the replacement of some of the more discretionary features of the scheme by clearly laid down regulations which conferred legal entitlements on claimants.

These elements in the social security system certainly merited examination and reform. In 1979, with child benefits, earnings-related benefits and pensions in place, with work under way at the DHSS on a coherent system of income benefits for disabled people, and the reform of supplementary benefits in hand, there was every indication that the incremental progress of the 1970s would be maintained and other deficiencies made good.

This assumption barely survived the first two months of the Conservative government. It became immediately clear that the 'welfare state' was as much an ideological as a financial obstacle to achieving the government's desired change. The collectivist ethos of social security, with its emphasis on pooling risks, mutual help and mutual responsibility, posed a central threat to the credibility and effectiveness of a government committed to 'rolling back the state', and to competition, individualism and the free market. Moreover, it was argued that through 'welfare' the individual and the state were brought into a direct and 'dependent' relationship which encouraged idleness, inhibited private savings and initiative and frustrated self-help and thrift.

The tone was set by the emphasis in the 1979 Conservative manifesto on 'restoring the will to work'. The invigorating language accompanying the doubling of the numbers unemployed from 1.5 to 3 million in the first two years was matched by verbal hostility towards 'scroungers', 'strikers' and those who depended on 'hand-outs'. The policy priorities were clear: to wipe out fraud and abuse, frustrate the feckless, abolish the 'Why work? syndrome' and increase incentives to work. In particular, the reduction of benefits for people on strike and their families and the reductions in unemployment benefits in 1980 marked the updating of a principle explicitly set out 150 years earlier. Indeed, it was the foundation value upon which the Victorian Poor Law rested – that 'every penny bestowed which renders the lot of the pauper more eligible than that of the lowest-paid independent labourer is a bounty on indolence and vice'. The 'less eligibility' tests of the 1980s did not mean the denial of 'outdoor relief' or submission to the 'Workhouse Test', but they did express once more the old values by which people on benefit were judged to be fundamentally different from decent citizens who cared for their families, paid their taxes and got on their bikes.

Significantly, these new principles were set out not by the Secretary of State for Social Security but by Sir Geoffrey Howe, in March 1980 in his second budget. He stressed the 'scale and importance' of the social security programme. In the coming year, he argued, it would

absorb a quarter of public spending and cost about £20 billion

. . . which works out at no less than £1000 a year for every household in the country. Its volume has grown by 50 per cent in the last ten years. . . . Some of this growth is accounted for by an increase in the number of beneficiaries, particularly the elderly. But much of it has come about not through any conscious decision but because the level and scope of benefits have been improved in anticipation of a growth in output which has not been achieved. It is a striking example of the nation's capacity for spending money before it has been earned.

Within this statement were four assumptions which were to provide the justification and the vocabulary of policy for the next nine years.

First, that the country was spending too much money on social security – a claim which could hardly be sustained when the level of pensions, family benefits and work-related benefits in Britain was compared to the higher family benefits and pensions in other countries of Western Europe.

Second, that demographic trends were working to the disadvantage of the community by generating increasing costs which the state could not and should not be expected to plan for or fund – an argument which would emerge at its crudest in relation to the 'pensions time-bomb' and which would be deployed to justify the abolition of SERPS.

Third, that in any case the country could not and would not afford to improve the social security system.

Fourth, that there were two sets of interests and two classes of people in competition with each other, 'claimants' and 'taxpayers' – the one dependent on the social security system, the other independent of it, the one taking from it, the other paying for it.

Sir Geoffrey, who had, while an opposition spokesman on social security, supported many of the progressive measures of the 1970s, went on to describe how pensioners and supplementary beneficiaries would be fully protected against inflation. Extra help would be given to those on supplementary benefit, mobility allowance, family income supplement and on the one-parent benefit. Economies in social security would, however, be achieved in the national insurance benefits paid to people of working age, and in child benefit, which was increased by 75p that November, instead of the £1.20 necessary to retain its real value. He made his concerns clear:

> The Government and the vast majority of the British people want hard work and initiative to be properly rewarded and are vexed by disincentives to work. One of the biggest problems is the lack of balance between social security benefits and incomes in work. . . . Indeed there are people whose incomes out of work exceed what they could reasonably expect to get when in work. There is undoubtedly widespread and justified public concern about this disincentive. It is doubly demoralising; first, to those directly affected and, second, to the large numbers around them who quite reasonably enough see such provisions as unjust as well as harmful to the proper workings of the economy.

These arguments would become increasingly strident as unemployment rose inexorably between 1979 and 1983 and as it became less clear how the 'choice' not to work was being exercised in practice.

Public expenditure cuts in social security were contained in the two social security bills introduced in 1980. The 1980 (No. 1) Act was important because it brought about the codification of supplementary benefit, thereby implementing some of the reforms recommended in 1978. However, this same Act 'broke the link' between pensions, widows' and invalidity benefits and earnings. The effect of this was to peg future increases in these benefits to the rise in prices, and not, as had been the case until then, to the rise in prices *or earnings*. This was to have a major impact on the level of benefits, especially for pensioners. The Social Security (No. 2) Act 1980 was notorious chiefly because it virtually abolished strikers' benefits (leading to the triumphant statement by Reg Prentice, then Minister of State at the Department of Health and Social Security (DHSS), that 'they'd better think twice about going on strike'). Clauses 1 and 4 abolished earnings-related supplements to unemployment and sickness benefits and cut the value of sickness, invalidity, industrial injury, unemployment and maternity benefits by 5 per cent – the first real cuts in social security benefits since the 1930s.

When the bill was debated on second reading, Stan Orme,

Labour opposition spokesman, was scathing: clauses 1 and 4, he said,

> express the same contempt for the contributory principle. Those clauses select and attack the same victims for discrimination. They attack the unemployed, the sick, the disabled and those receiving maternity allowance. Both clauses reflect the two principal contributions made by this government to contemporary political thinking. The first ... is a fear of public expenditure and the second is an unsubstantiated and unproved fear that people are better off out of work than in work. If we had fewer slogans from the Chancellor and more statistics on the dimensions of this apparent problem the Rt Hon. Gentleman ... might be more convincing.

The savings in the bill were significant – £270 million in 1981/2 and £481 million in 1982/3. In fact, the cuts in social security between 1979 and 1982/3 amounted to nearly £1.5 billion. By 1985 total cuts in social security were estimated to be £8 billion. By 1987 the 'savings' from cutting the link between the long-term benefits and earnings had amounted to £12 billion.

Despite these cuts, expenditure on social security between 1979/80 and 1986/7 actually grew from 25 per cent of public expenditure to 33 per cent (an increase of £12.5 billion to £45.9 billion). Of this, two-thirds was accounted for by the fact that there were increased numbers of beneficiaries entitled to claim: retirement pensioners, single parents and, in particular, unemployed people. Significantly, £4.5 billion of this increase went entirely to the growing numbers of unemployed.

After the government had begun excavating the foundations, the structural walls came under attack between 1980 and 1983 when, for example, sickness benefit was privatised, industrial injuries benefit was abolished, and housing benefit (an emasculated and deeply flawed substitute for the universal housing benefit recommended for many years) was substituted for rent and rates rebates, bringing administrative chaos in its wake.

These were all visible changes, hotly contested, swiftly executed. They were to prove a prelude to even more fundamental changes dedicated to reducing public expenditure, redefining poverty and the role of social security, and again placing responsibility for self-help firmly upon the individual and the family.

The Great Debate on Social Security 1983–6

In September 1982 newspaper leaks indicated that the cabinet was reviewing huge chunks of the welfare state. A secret Central Policy Review Staff (CPRS) (the Conservative think-tank) report outlining the options for action was discussed in cabinet. Suggestions included ending all state funding for higher education, introducing education vouchers (with which to 'buy' school places), extending private health insurance and ending the indexation of all social security benefits. But the views expressed – and the policies they implied – were regarded as so banal that they were for the most part dismissed at the time as private obsessions, not to be taken seriously. It was reported that the Prime Minister, having condemned the report as politically inept, had backed the majority cabinet view that it would be electorally disastrous to proceed with it, and that it should be shelved.

But, as the *Guardian* reported in February 1983, the CPRS discussions had merely shifted to the cabinet. Invited to give their thoughts on a range of social and economic issues, including, for example, provision for children and families, parental rights and responsibilities, the cabinet and its advisers were still pursuing some bizarre but revealing ideals. David Howell and Norman Tebbit, it was reported thought that 'mothers should be encouraged to stay at home'. Sir Keith Joseph thought that parents should set up their own schools; Sir Geoffrey Howe's ambitions were more modest: he felt children should be encouraged to manage their own pocket money. John Sparrow, the Director of the CPRS, thought that individuals should have more responsibility for managing their own pensions. The new rhetoric was clearly focusing on self-help, self-support and self-management. Later papers to be commissioned would deal with the balance between preventing poverty and encouraging parental responsibility, assess the major influences on children, and consider individual responsibility for benefits and pensions.

Despite this activity, there was still no indication in the Conservative manifesto of June 1983 that a massive review of social security was afoot. Not until October 1983 was the term 'debate' first heard. Then, in an interview with *New Society*, the Secretary of State for Social Services, Norman Fowler, mused, 'I think we should have a great debate on the welfare state.' The assumption was that this was to be a 'debate' which would involve 'consultation' (in the full sense of dialogue and exchange) with people who knew how the system operated, what was needed to improve it and how a fairer and more efficient system might be financed and administered. The text and tone of the subsequent debate soon showed such an assumption to be naïve.

Over the next few months the DHSS was plunged into frenetic activity. A whole range of 'reviews' was announced: in October a review on pension provision, starting with 'portable' private pensions and moving on to wider areas of pensions policy; in February 1984, after widespread evidence of general chaos in the housing benefit scheme and opposition to the cuts which had come into effect almost simultaneously with the Act itself, a review into the whole of housing benefit was announced; in April a survey of disabled people was announced and two more reviews, on supplementary benefits and benefits for children. A further review on maternity provision was announced in May. The future of the death grant was also to be considered. On 16 May the membership of the review committees was published. The deadline for written evidence was set at 31 July 1984. On 2 April 1984, announcing the reviews of supplementary benefit and children and young people, Norman Fowler claimed he had set in hand 'the most substantial examination of the social security system since the Beveridge Report forty years ago'.

The reviews provoked immediate anticipation that this would indeed be a substantial reassessment of the welfare state. Fowler claimed that he wanted 'a fundamental reshaping of the system, not a tinkering at the edges'. 'I am', he announced boldly, 'prepared to hold to my commitment to meet social needs. I am not prepared to be a prisoner of the existing structure.'

The reviews were welcomed by the many organisations, professionals and practitioners concerned with the operation of the welfare state, but from the first there was deep concern about the scope, direction and motivation for the reviews. It was publicly argued by many leading organisations that to be a fundamental and progressive review of social security it would have to look not just at the benefit structure but at the nature and effects of poverty, at the fundamental reasons that people become poor and never escape from poverty, at the cycle of poverty that persists from generation to generation in some families and some regions; it would have asked why more women than men are in poverty and questioned the relationship between taxes and benefits, the hidden subsidies to the rich in the form of private pensions, mortgage tax relief, company 'perks' and subsidised health insurance, and the extra costs of being elderly, disabled and poor.

Such a review would have to examine the key social and economic changes since the Beveridge Report as they related to the provision of benefits, particularly the changing role of women in the labour market. It would have to study the costs of children at different ages. Above all, such a review would have to confront the question at the heart of all these other issues, and would have faced the real problems raised by the question of 'incentives' and poverty 'traps' for people on benefit by attempting to answer the fundamental and inescapable question: how much do people need to live on? For the first time since Beveridge it would have examined the relevance of the historic basis of the supplementary benefit scale rates to the real costs of food, fuel, transport, caring, clothing, household goods and all normal living expenses. It would have taken account of contemporary research into the meagre expectations and lives of people on supplementary benefit: that the scale rates were set at levels which meant not only that poor people could not afford holidays, refrigerators or leisure activities, but that most adults lacked standard items of clothing, half of them could not make their benefit meet their needs for a week, and many lived with chronic debt.

To present an accurate picture of poverty and an accurate diagnosis for improvement the reviews would have taken note of the picture of 'Breadline Britain' that came into focus as unemployment grew during the 1980s. This did not sit easily with the cosy picture that 'relative poverty' was somehow a distinct improvement on the 'grinding poverty' of the 1930s, a comparison popular with ministers. What it did show was that the standard of living enabling people to participate as full citizens in the community – living in warm homes, not ashamed of the quality of their clothing, able to visit relatives, to celebrate birthdays and family occasions in special ways, able to buy newspapers, keep their televisions and afford to belong to clubs and trade unions, in short to live the lives common among other people – was a remote ambition for the six million people who by 1983 depended on supplementary benefit.

The Reviews: 'Open Government' in Action

The Fowler reviews ignored almost all these issues. In particular, they overlooked the questions raised by the living standards of the poor. It was a curious omission in a 'comprehensive' review. Given that benefit levels were nothing more than the regularly updated levels set by Beveridge over forty years earlier, and given that Fowler was out to make his mark as a second Beveridge, now was surely the time for a fundamental review of the standard of living they provided. But those findings would have shattered any attempt to keep the reviews within their 'nil-cost' remit.

Parallels with Beveridge were all very well but, as Fowler said in February 1985, he was talking about poverty against a very different background. 'The world we live in today is very different from Beveridge.' The definition of 'need' said Fowler, was something that needed to be thought about 'very carefully'. No one should 'doubt that there is need', but if there now *appeared* to be more people in need they were in that situation because higher benefit levels drew more within the usual definition of poverty, i.e. the supplementary benefit line. The implications were clear: first, in the government's view, poverty was diminishing as a problem; second, the state could now concentrate on relieving the most acute forms of destitution rather than preventing poverty in the first place. The priority was to 'target' resources toward those with legitimate and deserving claims upon the community.

This limited objective could be met within a review which did not place any further burdens on public expenditure – a 'nil-cost' review. As such, it was a far cry from the commitment Beveridge had made to the 'abolition of want' and to a system of social insurance. The assumptions Fowler made about the nature of poverty and the scope of social security demanded that means-tested benefits replace national insurance benefits. Moreover, whereas Beveridge had seen social welfare as reinforcing policies for full employment, social security policies in the 1980s would complement mass *unemployment*, with means tests becoming the point of first, not last resort.

A nil-cost review did not mean, however, that there was no scope for redistribution. As Fowler said, he was 'working on the premise . . . that there are constraints, but if there are any savings in a particular area the Government clearly have the choice of seeing whether there are other areas within social security for which money could be diverted'. If 'nil-cost' was the primary objective of reform, the second objective was to 'target' benefits to those with the best case for assistance.

The third objective was that of 'simplification' of a system which was confusing and complicated, involving 38,000 staff, two volumes of rules, 16,000 paragraphs of guidance, different measures of income and capital, different qualifying levels, and total obscurity surrounding many of its provisions. 'Nobody', asserted the Green Paper with much justification, 'could be happy with the system as it stands today.'

The fourth objective was to improve administration so that it would 'owe more to desk top computers than to bulging filing cabinets'.

Finally, argued the Green Paper, to rebuild the social security system it was necessary to understand 'the relative roles and responsibilities of the individual and the state. In building for the future we should follow the basic principle that social security is not a function of the state alone. It is a partnership between the individual and the state, a system built on twin pillars.' The fifth objective was, therefore, 'partnership', with the emphasis on personal responsibility.

Each of these objectives was dressed in the rational and neutral language of policy-making – nil costs, targeting, simplification, efficiency, and partnership. For claimants and for those who administer the system the results have been anything but neutral. Given the terms of reference of the reviews, the climate in which they were conducted, the membership and conditions under which they worked and the explicit ideology which guided them, the chasm between rhetoric and reality was inevitable. Each committee was small, handpicked, and chaired by a minister. The pensions enquiry, for example, was chaired by Norman Fowler and included four other ministers, Alan Peacock (vice-chancellor of the private University of Buckinghamshire), the Government Actuary, the president of the Institute of Actuaries and the chairman of the Occupational Pensions Scheme Joint Working Group. The subcommittee of four on portable pensions included Barney Hayhoe (minister of state at the Treasury), Alan Peacock and Mark Weinberg, managing director of Hambro Life.

The supplementary benefits review team comprised Tony Newton (under-secretary of State at the DHSS), in the chair, Robin Wendt (chief executive of Cheshire County Council and a member of the Social Security Advisory Committee) and Basil Collins, chairman of Nabisco. The children and young persons review was chaired by Rhodes Boyson (Minister for Social Security) and consisted of Mrs Barbara Shenfield (chairperson of the WRVS) and T. G. Parry Roberts (personnel director of Plessey).

Not content with packing the review teams with people who, for the most part, had little experience of social security, Fowler set up an administrative process within the DHSS designed to bypass the normal policy procedures. A co-ordinating committee was created to keep the interconnecting parts of the reviews in line and the review process remained isolated from the rest of the DHSS. Policy discussion took place and policy decisions were taken under conditions approaching paranoia. As David Hencke reported in the *Guardian* on 17 January 1985, the reviews had been conducted in an atmosphere of 'unprecedented secrecy'. For example, once the reviews were finished, Fowler and a group of 'handpicked' civil servants retired for ten days to a conference at Wilton Park to decide what to do next. A press release was prepared announcing the event, but Fowler instead

decreed that the conference must remain a top secret, scuttled the press release, and put one of the highest classifications 'secret' on the conference agenda . . . Such a classification is normally used to cover background papers to foreign treaties, highly sensitive economic information and defence details. As a result most civil servants were not even to be told of the titles of the sessions. . . . Only about half a dozen civil servants were invited for the whole conference. . . . The rest were . . . to attend only for the sessions where they had a direct interest. Once the session was over they were despatched by train back to the DHSS. . . . One particularly alarming proposal on the future of the pensions scheme was read by headquarters and ordered to be destroyed immediately. Ministers have ordered all the other pension papers to be renumbered.

It had seemed at first that since Fowler had 'wanted the public to have a say in the review . . . and to be involved myself' a public dialogue was to take place. But it was clear from a very early stage that the government had no intention of publishing either the evidence to the reviews or the reports of the individual review bodies. The government would offer its own conclusions in a Green Paper, for further consultation. Despite these omens many individuals and expert organisations accepted the invitation to consider the reform of social security in its widest sense. Over the next few months they submitted a mountain of written evidence and assiduously attended the public sessions of the review committees.

When they did, however, the limited nature of the exercise became clear. In the operation of the children and young persons review (which conspicuously ignored the whole question of income support for young people over sixteen), the banality of the questions appalled those who were called to give evidence. The Child Poverty Action Group (CPAG) recalled that it was asked whether 'the sole function of the welfare state' was 'to relieve poverty'. It was clear that 'the correct answer from the review team's point of view was that it was. During CPAG's evidence, as soon as the magic words "the relief of poverty" had been spoken, the chair interrupted as he was not interested in what he saw as the other functions of the welfare state.'

The same committee displayed an open prejudice about child benefit. The essential question, as put by one of the members of the review, was: 'Why should someone who consciously decided not to have children, be expected to pay for others who decided to have a particular number?' The many hundreds of organisations and individuals who gave evidence of the importance of child benefit in preventing family poverty could not overturn the question's

15

inherent hostility to the notion that children are a collective responsibility of society.

The Green Paper, June 1985

After massive speculation the Green Paper on the Reform of Social Security was published in three volumes in June 1985. The first gave a general outline of future policy; the second a more detailed account of the background to the issues involved; the third, background statistics. The report of the review on housing benefits was published as a fourth volume.

Given the thrust of the inquiry, the tone of the review was predictable. Forty years after Beveridge 'the British social security system has lost its way'. It had become hugely expensive, confused and complicated. The objectives of social security identified in the Green Paper amplified the four concerns already anticipated by Fowler.

First, resources must be targeted so that 'the social security system must be capable of meeting genuine need' particularly in relation to families with children, 'who face the most difficult problems'.

Second, social security must be managed so that it was 'consistent with the Government's objectives for the economy' – not just in the sense that 'growth of this burden could severely damage the prospects for economic growth', but that social security was 'self-defeating if it creates barriers to the creation of jobs, to job mobility or to people rejoining the labour force'. Such obstacles existed if people were better off out of work than in work, if employers found national insurance contributions too high, and if pensions were not flexible enough to permit mobility. In short, 'If we wish to encourage individuals to provide for themselves then the social security system – public and private – must not stand in the way.'

Third, 'the social system must be simpler to understand and easier to administer . . . service for the public too often fails as the staff hunt for files in a Dickensian paper-chase'.

Each of these three objectives was in itself a sensible priority: certainly the poverty lobby had long argued for directing resources to families; likewise there was little contention that the benefit system should encourage access to and mobility in work, and should be judged as an engine of the economy rather than a burden upon it. Simplification and good administration had been the aim of successive governments. All could welcome those.

The underlying ideology of self-help was, however, also made clear in the Green Paper. The government's plans

> are not based on a grand design for a new state system but on a view of social security which allows important roles for both state and individual provision. In that respect it takes a radically different direction from some of the developments over the last forty years. We want to give greater responsibility and greater independence to the individual.

The full implications of the strategy were borne out in the detailed proposals which followed. These are described in the later chapters. The main features, however, which were to harden into the legislative proposals set out in the White Paper in December 1985, were:

(1) The burden of contributory insurance was to be reduced by abolishing the death grant and maternity grant and replacing them with means-tested benefits, and by abolishing the entire SERPS in favour of occupational and state pensions.

(2) The existing burden of social security was also to be reduced by massive savings on housing benefits, to be effected by rationalising the means test upon which it was based and at the same time making it much more stringent.

(3) Simplification was to be achieved partly by aligning the means tests for supplementary benefit, housing benefit and family credit and by introducing common rules to specify the amount of savings claimants could have before losing entitlement to benefit.

(4) The principal act of simplification was to replace supplementary benefit with a simplified system of 'income support' which would distinguish between two functions: supplying basic income needs, and supplying additional

needs for certain categories of claimant. Income support would be awarded at a standard rate (although as a novel feature people under twenty-five would receive less), and each claimant would be awarded the basic rate plus a 'premium' geared to his or her circumstances: e.g. a family premium for those with children; a pensioner premium for those over sixty, higher if over eighty; a single-parent premium; a disabled persons premium. All the differential help available to householders, to people on the higher 'long-term rate' (e.g. pensioners and the disabled) would vanish, as would all the additions for heating, laundry, diet, etc., which had largely reflected the needs and costs of sick and disabled people. Single payments to cover replacing items of furniture, heating, travel costs to work or to visit relatives in hospital etc. were to be abolished and claimants referred, in future, to a social fund, from which they might – or might not – be offered loans repayable from their benefit at fixed rates of interest. The social fund budget was to be cash-limited and there would be no right of appeal. Some grants, as opposed to loans, would be available to support people discharged into the community to avert the need for institutional care for the elderly and other vulnerable groups or to help with pressures at times of family changes.

(5)   A new principle of political accountability was to be introduced into housing benefits, which provided the rationale for some of the proposed cuts. Everyone, even those on income support, would now be obliged to pay at least 20 per cent of their rates 'so that we do not have a position in which those who make no contribution at all can demand enormous increases in local authority expenditure at the expense of other people', as the Prime Minister explained in the House of Commons. Such families would also now pay water rates and, in addition, discussions would begin with building societies to establish ending the payment of mortgage interest for those on income support.

(6)   Money saved on housing benefit and in other ways would be chiefly redirected towards a new family credit scheme to be based on net income and higher rates of benefit. This, it was hoped, would finally end the absurd trap which had resulted in some families in work losing a pound a week in benefit for each extra pound gained in earnings. It was, however, to be based on thirteen weeks' earnings (rather than five weeks' as was the case with family income supplement (FIS), which the new benefit replaced) and would last for six months rather than a year. Most significantly, however, it would be paid not by the DHSS but by the employer, and it would be paid through the wage packet by deducting it from tax and national insurance contributions and not direct to the mother, as had been the case with FIS. Family credit would no longer bring entitlement to free school meals, although there would be some compensation in the rates awarded. In future families on income support would be entitled to free school meals.

(7)   Finally, child benefit was to be retained, although there were hints that its value would not be maintained.

In conclusion the Green Paper promised that the proposals

will bring the social security system firmly back under control. Social security will be based on twin pillars of provision – individual and state – with stronger emphasis on individual provision than hitherto. The proposals will make it more worthwhile for individuals to work and to save. They will redirect help to those who need it most . . .

From Consultation to Action: the Green Paper, the Public and Parliament

The Green Paper was met with what the *Financial Times* on 21 September 1985 called a 'hurricane of protest'. There were some warm responses; Edwina Currie called on the nation to 'give thanks' for it but her appeal was not widely taken up. Minority support came from the Institute of Directors and the Monday

Club; however, as the *Financial Times* continued, 'The breadth and depth of objections, ranging from the CBI to the Church of England, from the welfare lobby to the pensions industry, and from the TUC to "large sections of the Conservative Party" had taken everyone aback.' Thirteen leading charities described it as 'no more than a half-baked mixture of means tests, charitable relief, cuts and juggling on the meagre incomes of the poor'. There was some relief that child benefit had not been abolished, taxed or means-tested, that benefits for sixteen-to-nineteen-year-olds were untouched, and the unemployment benefit had not been abolished. (In the case of the latter two benefits, however, the relief was short-lived.)

The time allowed for responses, three months, was ludicrously short, yet nearly 7000 separate submissions were received by 18 September. The vast majority were hostile. Of all the proposals, that to abolish SERPS met with incredulity and a 'near-deafening' chorus of protest, which gathered strength as it was revealed that the proposal was never seriously considered by the pensions inquiry team, while the economic and demographic assumptions on which the entire argument rested were later to be challenged by the Government Actuary himself!

Criticisms of the way in which ideology had taken precedence not merely over evidence but over the content and direction of the review process were sharpest in relation to the SERPS proposal, but they applied more generally. The worst expectations that the consultation exercise was only a charade had been realised, as indeed had the contradiction at the heart of the report: that the objectives – simplification, more help for families, self-reliance and work incentives – could not be achieved at nil-cost merely by redistributing the same amount of cash from the 'undeserving' to the 'deserving' poor. As the National Consumer Council pointed out in its response, 'improvements in simplicity, incentive and access can ultimately only be achieved by reducing reliance on means tests'. The burden of the Green Paper, through the emphasis on family credit, the social fund, and the loss of national insurance benefits, was significantly to *increase* the reliance on means tests.

A major criticism concerned the government's refusal to pro-vide illustrative figures to show how the proposals would affect real families in real situations, or how the results would distribute the social security budget between gainers and losers. In the absence of official figures, informal estimates and analyses by the Select Committee on Social Services – which expressed serious reservations about nearly all the proposals – showed, for example, that there would be losers in all groups, even among low-income families dependent on family credit and housing benefit. But of all the groups, the young, single and unemployed would lose most heavily as a result of income support changes, and the elderly home-owner would lose most from the housing benefit changes. The government had committed itself to protecting income support claimants so that there would be no 'cash losers'. It was careful not to commit itself to protecting people dependent on housing benefit.

Throughout the autumn fierce lobbying, particularly on the pensions proposals and family credit, did achieve some major changes. These are discussed in more detail in later chapters. SERPS, for example, was saved, but was to be heavily restricted for everyone except those retiring this century. The best feature of the scheme, that it was based on the 'best twenty years' of earnings, which was of immense advantage to women and to people in insecure employment, was abolished. Some concessions were also made on housing benefits, notably the decision not to impose a single, punitive taper to cover both rent and rates, which would have meant colossal cuts in the rates element of the benefit. But the main principles and proposals were left intact. The social fund remained untouched, despite universal condemnation, as did the 20 per cent contribution required of all ratepayers. Family credit was still to be paid not to the mother but through the wage packet; there were to be no additional concessions for the costs of disablement. Such changes as there had been did not satisfy critics nor did they overcome the fundamental objections to the way that decisions had been taken. It was, said the *Observer* on 3 November 1985, a 'mean-minded mish-mash of half-hearted reforms and heartless penny-pinching'.

The White Paper which followed and which formed the basis of the Social Security Bill was published on 17 January 1986. There were few fundamental changes and it met with renewed hostility from all quarters. The government had succeeded in uniting opponents across the political spectrum. Apart from the poverty lobby hostility, responses ranged from the fears of the occupational pension schemes that the bill's incentives to personal pensions would undermine their own provision to those of local authorities, which baulked at the administrative and financial costs of collecting a minimum 20 per cent contribution to rates and the losses they would suffer through the proposed changes to housing benefit subsidy. At the same time employers had no desire to pay family credit through the wage packet, and civil service unions and social workers resisted their role in the social fund.

The Social Security Bill 1986/7 had its second reading on 28 January 1986. A highly professional campaign to get key aspects of the bill changed was mounted by some twenty organisations which formed a 'Social Security Consortium' as the bill entered the House of Lords. Their aims were, *inter alia*, to restore the SERPS 'twenty best years' provision, to prevent the introduction of the lower income support rate for single childless people under twenty-five; to prevent the abolition of free school meals; to prevent the 20 per cent rates contribution; to have child benefit linked annually to rises in prices; to secure payment of family credit direct to mothers; and to prevent the creation of the social fund. They were only minimally successful. Votes in the Lords and manœuvres in the Commons frustrated their campaigns in relation to all except the rates contribution and family credit. The government was defeated on the 20 per cent rates contribution in the House of Lords on 23 June 1986, but this decision was overturned in the Commons a month later.

Commending the bill to the House of Commons on 28 January 1986, the Secretary of State repeated the claims made over two years for the significance of the reforms. They were, he said, the most 'comprehensive' since the war, based on 'the most detailed consultation ever with the public'. The new framework which had emerged

cuts through the unnecessary complexities of much of social security and concentrates on what should be its central aim – directing help to those who need it most. We have a programme which will tackle the most notorious aspects of the unemployment and poverty traps and which will give more support to disabled people as well as to . . . low-income families who too often face difficulties today. That is a programme for reform which deserves the support of the public . . .

By the time the changes were introduced in April 1988 Norman Fowler had moved on to the Department of Employment, leaving his hapless successor, John Moore, to explain to incredulous Tory backbenchers and shell-shocked constituents why some of them were losing up to £50 a week in benefits and why there appeared to be so very many more 'losers' than 'gainers'.

The following chapters examine Fowler's claims in relation to the people in whose interests the government had claimed to act. We shall look at the situation of families and young people, at elderly people on pensions and housing benefits, at disabled people, and at the unemployed and ask the question whether the policies followed were the right ones, whether the objectives of the Fowler reforms were or could ever have been met within the terms and conditions of the review process, and whether the claims made have been justified in terms of what has happened since April 1988. In the second part of the book we step back a little from recent history to look in more detail at fundamental questions affecting the living standards of claimants and at the way in which people who rely on means-tested benefits are treated.

But, whether looking at the broad political sweep or the details of life on the dole, the same images recur, of a society where, as Frank Field put it, 'I see signs in my constituency that I have not seen in London since I was a boy. I see pinched faces, shuffling feet and ill-fitting shoes, which are all the signs of poverty. It is from those people that we are taking money away.'

2 The Effects of the 'Reforms'

Our tables show that, taking the income-related benefits together, some 3.65 million people will receive *less* benefit than if the old schemes had continued.

(Michael Portillo, Parliamentary Under-Secretary of State
for Health and Social Security, House of Commons,
24 November 1987)

May I tell the Right Hon. gentleman that the overwhelming majority of people will benefit, gain, from the improved social security benefits that will come about on April 11th?

(The Prime Minister, House of Commons, 29 March 1988)

On 11 April 1988 the Social Security Act 1986 came into force. It was then that the rhetoric of the Fowler reviews could be tested against the reality of the differences they made in people's lives. The reforms had promised better targeting of resources, a simpler system and improved work incentives. In this chapter we examine what these words meant for the millions of citizens dependent on social security.

The government's official estimates of the effects of its reforms, finally published in October 1987, showed that the net effect of all the changes would be to leave *more people worse off than better off*. By its own estimates 3,650,000 would be worse off against 3,190,000 who would be better off. Among the losers were over two million pensioners, who bore the brunt of the cuts, largely due to the massive cuts in housing benefit.

The Great 'Gainers and Losers' Debate: Fudging the Figures

One of the key aims of the reforms was to 'target' help where it was most needed. In a 'nil-cost' review this carried with it the inevitable corollary that there were some people who were already getting help which they did not need and who would have it removed or reduced. The great debate over who were the gainers and who were the losers, and how many there were of each, dominated the period around the introduction of the new system in the early months of 1988.

The government's own estimates were published in October 1987 in tables which, entitled *Impact of the Reformed Structure of Income-Related Benefits*, soon became known as the 'impact tables'. These set out the estimated effects of the benefit changes in contrast to what would have happened if no changes had been introduced. However, because claimants on supplementary benefit who stood to lose under the change to income support would be protected against sudden loss of income by a transitional arrangement, the tables were presented in two forms; one, the 'cash tables', showed the estimated effects on claimants' actual cash incomes, protected by the transitional arrangements; the other showed what would have happened if no transitional protection had been given. The latter tables showed the real effects of the changes in the structure of benefits as they would affect all future claimants, and were therefore referred to as the 'structural changes'. The tables estimated the effects for three different groups of claimants: those on supplementary benefit, who would be switched to income support; working families receiving family income supplement, who would be switched to the new family credit; and all claimants in receipt of any of the benefits, whether income support, family credit or housing benefit.

The presentation of the tables in this complicated way meant that those who wished to take comfort from them could. Ministers made great use of the tables which showed the cash changes, and repeatedly told the House and the public that hardly anyone would lose any money. For example, in March 1988 Nicholas Scott claimed that: 'In cash terms, 87 per cent of pensioners, 89 per cent of lone parents, 92 per cent of couples with children and

97 per cent of sick and disabled people will be better, or no worse off, in April.' Using the cash tables, government figures showed that only 12 per cent of all claimants would be worse off while over 60 per cent would be better off. The effects of the structural changes, which showed that 37 per cent of all claimants would gain while 43 per cent would lose, were seldom referred to.

Given the complexity of the tables, confusion about the effects of the changes was inevitable. When figures were quoted it was often not clear whether they referred to *all* claimants or only to those on income support, or whether they referred to the *cash* effects or the structural effects. For example, when the Social Security Advisory Committee (SSAC) called a press conference just before the April changes to announce that the effects of all the benefit changes would leave 43 per cent worse off as against only 37 per cent better off, the *Guardian* gave the SSAC's estimates with the comment: 'It comes in shaming contrast to initial claims by ministers, which put the proportion of losers at 12 per cent.' In fact, the SSAC's figures were exactly the same as the government's own estimates; SSAC was referring to the structural changes while the ministers were referring to the effects on cash incomes. The misunderstanding was typical of the confusion created by the way in which the figures were used. Many of the government's supporters in the House were equally bemused, only to be disabused after 11 April when the sleight of hand was exposed by the mass protests from affected claimants.

Even the government's own figures showed more losers than gainers from the structural changes, but these figures were soon challenged as being over-optimistic; by independent experts, by the evidence from research on actual cases and not least by MPs' post-bags. When the 'losers' stopped being statistical abstractions and began writing to their MPs, appearing in surgeries and featuring in the press and on television, and when MPs were confronted by the evidence of huge amounts of money being taken from people who could by no stretch of the imagination be deemed to be 'undeserving', the government was faced with an irresistible revolt on its own back benches. When the thrifty elderly population of Finchley began to complain to their MP, she in turn berated her cabinet colleagues for not having warned her of the impending storm. All this led to an ignominious and hasty set of amendments only two weeks after the new Act, which had been four years in the making. (Even so, the revolt was bought off very cheaply with the promise of £100 million and still more assurances which also turned out to be largely disappointing.)

The biggest cuts in terms of the numbers affected and the amounts of money involved were those in housing benefit. These not only reduced the incomes of many pensioners but also wiped out many of the gains claimed for the new family credit scheme designed particularly to help families with children. These cuts were to provide the money for the improvements (some real, some illusory) in income support and family credit. We shall examine first the effects of the cuts in housing benefits and family credit, and then the effects of the change from supplementary benefit to income support.

The 'Reform' of Housing Benefits

The story of housing benefits is one of the move away from universal benefits available without testing means toward reliance on means-tested benefits; it is also the story of a strange form of 'targeting', which redirects money from the poor to the very poor while leaving housing benefits for the better off intact; and it is, inevitably, the story of continual cuts in the living standards of the poor.

Housing benefits have had a short and inglorious history. In 1982 the government introduced a new system of housing benefits designed to simplify the existing range of benefits and rationalise the administration. The scheme became fully operational in April 1983. Less than a year later it had attracted so much criticism that it was necessary to review it entirely. The review team reported in 1985 and its report, *Housing Benefit Review*, became the fourth volume of the Fowler reviews.

Some of the problems of the 1982 scheme were technical, and resulted from the attempt to combine two schemes into one. Some concerned the inability of local authorities to administer the scheme, which they took over from the DHSS. The chaos that followed the changeover and the distress caused to claimants have been well documented elsewhere. By 1984 there was no disagreement that the whole system was in need of reform.

Organisations with special interests in housing put forward their views to the review team. There was much agreement on what needed to be done, both as a way of solving some of the technical difficulties and in terms of more fundamental change. The review team accepted many of the suggestions for short-term improvements but paid no attention to the more fundamental changes needed as these were outside its remit. The government accepted most of the review team's technical recommendations but whittled them down in important ways. It was looking not just for a nil-cost review, but for substantial savings to finance the improvements to the other parts of the social security reforms. The result was a reformed scheme which was generally accepted to be structurally better than before, but in which all the gains of the structural reforms were more than wiped out by the government's overriding wish to save as much money as possible at the expense of housing benefit claimants.

The review team's proposals

The 1982 scheme was an imperfect combination of two quite separate schemes: one for those on supplementary benefit and one for all other claimants, principally pensioners and low-income working families. This led to problems of fairness, since the scheme for those on supplementary benefit was the more generous, even though some of the other claimants may have had incomes no higher than supplementary benefit level. It also led to problems for those whose incomes were on the margins of supplementary benefit, for whom a complicated extra benefit, housing benefit supplement, was created. This caused great confusion for claimants and local authorities alike, such that many recipients probably did not realise they were technically on supplementary benefit (an important point because it opened the doorway to all the other benefits such as single payments for emergencies). Many potential recipients failed to take up the benefit. This added to the complexity of an already baffling scheme, which had no less than six different means tests, not counting those which related to the amounts deducted from benefit for any adult non-dependants living at home, who were expected to contribute towards the rent and rates.

28

The Effects of the 'Reforms'

The reforms proposed by the review team involved using the same means test for income support as for housing benefit, which solved the problems of unfairness and complexity. Those with similar incomes in similar circumstances, whether on income support or not, would receive similar amounts of benefit.

The next step was to decide the level of benefit. Under the 1982 scheme those on supplementary benefit had the whole of their rent and rates met in full (subject to rules aimed at preventing the payment of rents deemed to be unreasonable). Those not on supplementary benefit could have their rent and rates met in full, but much more commonly had only a proportion met, depending on their income, size of family and amount of housing costs. The review team proposed that all those on supplementary benefit, and all those not on supplementary benefit *whose incomes were at supplementary benefit levels*, should have their rents and rates paid *in full*, again making for greater fairness between different claimant groups.

The next step was to decide at what rate benefit should be withdrawn as income rises. The rate of withdrawal of benefit, known as the 'taper', is the crucial mechanism for controlling the cost of the scheme or, conversely, the benefit to the claimants. If benefit is withdrawn at a high rate those in work are caught in the poverty trap, whereby a rise in wages is offset by loss of benefits. If it is withdrawn at a low rate, claimants can earn relatively high wages before losing entitlement to benefit, thus raising the cost of housing benefits. Previously the taper had been applied to gross income, which had resulted in some people losing more in benefits than they earned in extra income, after deducting tax, national insurance and benefits such as housing benefit and family income supplement. The review team recommended that the taper should therefore be applied to net income, thus avoiding this particular problem. Given this change, it calculated that the rate of withdrawal consistent with a nil-cost reform would be 50 per cent for rent and 17 per cent for rates (though it recommended a rates taper of 21 per cent).

The effect of all these proposals was that those in work whose income was at supplementary benefit level would pay no housing costs at all, but for every pound of extra income they earned, net of tax and insurance, they would have to pay 50p towards their rent and 21p towards their rates. For someone paying tax and insurance (at 1985 rates) this would mean that a £1 increase in gross wages would lead to a loss of 30p tax, 9p insurance, 30.5p rent rebate and 13p rate rebate, a total of 82.5p.

These proposals made for a simpler and more equitable system, and as such were widely welcomed. One other crucial recommendation made was that a capital limit should be imposed, so that anyone with savings above a certain level should not be eligible for benefit. What that certain level should be was later the subject of much heated debate.

The 20 per cent rates swindle

When the White Paper outlining the proposals was published in December 1985 the technical annex made it clear that the government was hoping to save £450 million by its reforms of housing benefit. By 17 December 1987 Michael Portillo stated in a written parliamentary answer that this figure had risen to £650 million. Of these savings only £430 million was used to finance the extra costs of the new income support scheme and the substitution of family credit for family income supplement. This form of targeting meant that not only had the poor paid for the very poor, but they had also contributed £220 million towards Lawsons's tax handouts to the super-rich in March 1988.

The government accepted most of the recommendations of the review team, but added some significant changes designed to bring about the desired savings. It accepted the alignment of means tests, the use of net income and the need for setting a capital limit. Crucially, it did not accept that those with incomes at supplementary benefit level should have their rates met in full, and it significantly increased the taper used to calculate withdrawal of benefit for rent, first to 60p and then to 65p. The effect of this was to save millions of pounds and to create what Robin Cook described as a 'ferocious' poverty trap.

The requirement that everyone, even those on income support, should meet 20 per cent of their rates was a completely novel idea, anticipating the poll tax. It was justified on the grounds of 'improving local accountability', though even those not prone to cynicism considered that the fact that it cut the cost of housing benefit by £340 million may have been an even more powerful justification. Out of forty-one organisations giving evidence to the review, all but three were against the proposal. The SSAC foresaw that it would lead to 'increased hardship, increased debt, or both'. (The three organisations in favour were those champions of low-incomes families, the Association of British Chambers of Commerce, the Institute of Directors and the Monday Club.)

Faced with considerable opposition from all quarters, and defeated in the Lords on the issue of the 20 per cent rates contribution, the government undertook to 'take into account the impact of this on the most vulnerable groups' when setting the levels for income support. This was later confirmed by Norman Fowler just before the election in May 1987, when he gave the explicit undertaking that

> when the rates for Income Support are set in the autumn, they will include the average amount that we expect householders who are Income Support claimants to have to meet as their minimum contributions . . . . This will mean that Income Support claimants will receive compensation in April 1988 in their benefit entitlement whilst at the same time preserving the vital principle of local accountability.

This undertaking was emphasised by the Prime Minister, who said in the House on 2 July 1987 that 'For the worst off who are on Supplementary Benefit or Income Support there will be an amount added to that Income Support or Supplementary Benefit equal to the average of the 20 per cent that they would have to pay. So they will not be adversely affected.'

These unequivocal and categorical assurances were subsequently shown to be almost worthless. This emerged from information given by Nicholas Scott on 30 October. The amount which the government added to weekly income support rates to take account of the 20 per cent rates contribution was fixed at £1 for the eighteen to twenty-four age group and £1.30 for the over twenty-fives. The 1985 White Paper had given illustrative figures for the amounts of income support to be paid. It was therefore a simple matter of arithmetic to calculate what the appropriate rates should be in April 1988; for a couple aged over twenty-five it should have been £48 (the figure given in the White Paper) uprated by the usual index to take account of increased prices, which the minister gave as £3.12, plus the £1.30 compensation for the 20 per cent rates contribution, making a total of £52.42. In fact the actual rate of income support was only £51.45, a shortfall of almost £1. For single claimants the shortfall was 50p. Nicholas Scott was later to argue that the compensation *had* been paid in full; what the government had *not* done was to uprate the White Paper figures in line with the usual index, though it had never given any indication that it would break with this convention. Either way, the claimants were *not* given the promised protection and were consequently 'adversely affected'.

The tapers

The rate at which benefit is withdrawn as income rises is the key to controlling the rate of benefit to the claimant and therefore the cost of the scheme. The government had never been slow to use it to cut costs. When the 1982 scheme was introduced the combined taper for rent and rates stood at 23 per cent, that is, for every pound of extra income the claimant lost 23p from housing benefit. It then rose at least once a year until in April 1987 it had doubled to 46 per cent. At each increase millions of pounds were saved and millions of claimants had their benefit reduced; the Shelter Housing Aid Centre (SHAC) estimates that over two million lost benefit in 1983, over a million in 1984 and a further two million in 1985. Between 400,000 and 500,000 lost all entitlement to benefit in each of these years. The annual savings were always substantial: £50 million in 1983, £171 million in 1984, £51 million in 1985, £26 million in 1986 and £68 million in 1987.

It was therefore no surprise that the April 1988 changes continued this process of attrition. The change in the whole basis of the means test meant that direct comparisons were no longer possible, but the new taper of 65 per cent on net income is estimated to be the equivalent of 55 per cent under the old scheme, representing another considerable increase over the 46 per cent then in force.

The government justified the cuts by saying that there were too many people entitled to housing benefit and that the benefit was available 'too far up the income scale'. It estimated that by 1988 there would be seven million people on the benefit, an increase of two million on the 1979–80 figure. This increase was not due to any extension of the scheme, which had been cut every year since its inception, but because more people were living at poverty levels and because rents and rates had been driven up, not least by government policies in the public and private rented sectors. The government had always justified these policies by saying that the poor were protected because of the existence of housing benefit. Now it was standing the argument on its head and arguing that because the poor were claiming housing benefit it would have to be cut.

As for the argument that the benefit was available 'too far up the income scale', official figures show that the gross weekly income, including child benefit and family income supplement, at which all entitlement to both rent and rate rebates ceased for a family with two children paying average rent and rates, was £150 in April 1987. Under the reformed scheme in April 1988 the equivalent cut-off level of income was reduced to £129 per week, which meant that, excluding income from benefits, housing benefit ceases for a couple with two small children when their weekly *gross* wage is £91, or considerably less than half the average wage.

The government had used the tapers to cut the cost of housing benefits. It had also manipulated them in a blatant attempt to deceive not only Parliament as a whole but in particular its own backbenchers when they attempted a revolt over the community charge. Warned by a loyal civil servant that the Tory MPs were at last beginning to wake up to the significance of the poll tax, Nicholas Ridley, Secretary of State for the Environment, bought off the rebellion led by Michael Mates against the unfairness of a flat-rate tax by announcing to the House on 14 April 1988 that he would reduce the taper on the rebates for the community charge. Instead of the original proposal for a 20 per cent taper it would now be only 15 per cent, thus making the rebates available to a million more people at a cost of £130 million. What he did *not* tell the House was that he and other senior ministers, including the Prime Minister, had already decided to recoup these losses by *increasing* the housing benefit taper from 65 to 70 per cent in the following year, thus completely negating the effect of Ridley's concession. Only when the minutes of the meeting at Downing Street were leaked to Robin Cook was the duplicity revealed.

The capital limit

Under the old scheme there had been no capital limit, though income from savings had been taken into account. Following the review team's recommendations the government introduced a capital limit in line with that of income support. Savings up to £3000 were ignored; between £3000 and £6000 they were deemed to produce a weekly income at the rate of £1 for every £250 of savings; and, in the government's original proposals, at £6000 entitlement was to cease altogether. As we shall see, this figure was later increased, after massive public protest, to £8000.

What the government did *not* do

It is essential to see these proposals in the context of other government policies. The government had been committed to withdrawing all housing subsidies to local authorities. These had traditionally been used to help local authorities keep their rents down, and provided a way of assisting low-income families with housing costs which was not tied to means tests. The progressive reduction of these subsidies forced councils to raise their rents, and therefore forced many tenants on to housing benefit. The progressive withdrawal of the rate support grant forced councils to raise their rates, with the same result. This substitution of means-tested benefits for non-means-tested exchequer subsidies is the housing equivalent of the retreat from the principle of general insurance benefits to specific benefits made subject to a means test.

The biggest omission of the reforms was the decision to exclude all reference to the major housing subsidy: mortgage tax relief. All the main housing and local authority organisations had stated in evidence that this exclusion was bound to leave the reforms emasculated. In 1987 mortgage tax relief cost over £1 billion more than the housing benefit for low-income tenants, yet it is given, without means tests or any deductions for non-dependants, to homeowners – who are on average much better off than those in rented accommodation. The value of this benefit was increased by the Conservatives in 1982 when the qualifying limit was raised from £25,000 to £30,000. Since more public money is spent on mortgage tax relief than on housing benefit, and since the gap between the two will continue to widen, it is sheer hypocrisy to talk of 'housing benefits' being targeted at those most in need.

One other reform was open to the government. At the time of the review only those homeowners on supplementary benefit could obtain any help towards their mortgage repayments: the DHSS paid the interest on their mortgages while they remained on benefit. Low-income working families who were buying their own homes had no similar form of help available to them. Again, all the organisations giving evidence pointed to the unfairness and suggested that the reforms should extend similar help to homeowners. Even the government's review team, while finding it outside its nil-cost remit, recommended that this issue should be 'investigated further with a view to implementation in the longer term'. The government did indeed investigate the issue; its solution was to achieve fairness not by extending assistance to homeowners but by reducing the help to those on supplementary benefit! From 1987 the DHSS met only half the cost of the mortgage interest for the first four months, thereby adding considerably to the financial problems of the unemployed.

The effects of the changes: 'The Lord giveth . . . and the Lord taketh away'

> Under the new system we will be sending out new and far more positive messages to families with children. The messages will say: we recognise the special needs of families, and are making extra help available to you for this purpose. But, in addition, this help will no longer lock you into the indefinite dependency on the state. On the contrary, you will from now on almost always be able to improve your position, and that of your family, by taking a job or by increasing your effort and earnings within one.
>
> (Michael Portillo, Parliamentary Under-Secretary of State for Health and Social Security, 23 March 1988)

> Yesterday I spent most of the time in tears and today hasn't been much better, although today I feel more angry than tearful. . . . All the adverts and press information suggested that families like ours would benefit from the changes.
>
> (A mother of three, on learning that her housing benefit had been cut by £18.74 per week in April 1988)

During the debate on housing benefit in November 1987 and in response to a series of parliamentary questions the full effects of all these changes gradually emerged. They were so devastating that they destroyed all the government's claims about targeting resources to the most needy, negated the benefits claimed for family credit, and very quickly led to an embarrassed policy rethink.

In global terms the reforms meant cutting £650 million, over 12 per cent of the annual budget, from housing benefit; one million recipients lost all entitlement; and altogether 720,000 stood to gain while 5,690,000 stood to lose. It was these shattering figures which led to the government climb-down.

The details of where the cuts fell gave the government no comfort. Of the 5.6 million losers, almost 3 million were pensioners, many because they fell foul of the new capital limit, who were therefore penalised precisely because they had done what they had been urged to do many times by Tory politicians and saved for their retirement. A further million losers were couples with children, both in and out of work, and over a million were lone parents with children. As one of the main aims of all the reforms had been to target resources at families with children these figures were lethal to the government's claims. Even among the sick and disabled the losers outnumbered the gainers by nearly two to one.

The effects of the very high tapers, and the requirement to pay 20 per cent of rates, led to astonishingly high withdrawal rates of benefits, particularly in the interaction between housing benefit and family credit. SHAC estimated that a family claiming housing benefit and family credit and paying tax and national insurance stood to lose 97p for every extra pound of income. The effects of the interaction of these benefits was clearly seen in the answer given by Nicholas Scott in February 1988 to a question by the late Sir Brandon Rhys Williams. Scott laid before Parliament a table showing the gains and losses of the various benefits for selected family types from which it emerged that not only had low income families lost almost as much in housing benefit as they had gained in family credit, but that they were generally worse off under the new scheme than under the old!

Scott's tables showed that under the pre-1988 scheme, a married couple with two children, paying average rent and rates, and with an initial weekly income of £100 had, after taking into account all the changes in taxes and benefits, a disposable income of £96. After April 1988 the same family would have a disposable income of just under £86 – a *loss* of £10. There were losses at every level of income up to £150, when there was no change in the level of disposable income. *At no level of income was this family better off under the new scheme.*

For a family with three children the position was similar, with losses at every level up to an income of £130, though after that such a family gained slightly under the new scheme. In other words, the poorest families lost under the new scheme and the slightly better-off families gained.

For lone mothers with two children the position depended on whether she worked or not; if she was on benefit and not working she was worse off under the new scheme; if she was on benefit and working part time she was better off under the new scheme; if she was not on benefit and working full time she was *considerably* worse off under the new scheme – as much as £13 a week – until she was earning £120 a week when she broke even. Again, it was the poorest women who lost most.

All these losses were almost entirely the result of reductions in housing benefit. For example, at £100 a week a working family with two children would expect to have almost £20 in family credit, but whereas under the old scheme they would also have had nearly £17 of housing benefit, under the new scheme they had nothing. For the lone working mother earning £100, her gain of almost £20 of family credit would have been offset by the loss of nearly £15 of housing benefit. For both parents, the additional losses of free school meals and free welfare foods would reduce their incomes by a further £4 or so.

After the publication of these figures it became impossible to sustain the claim that the reforms had been directed at the poorest families; it was precisely these families who had lost most by the changes. It was also difficult to sustain the claim that work incentives had improved: a marginal tax rate of 97 per cent could hardly be said to be an incentive to work when the Chancellor had just declared a top income tax rate of 60 per cent so punitive that he had reduced it to 40 per cent. Portillo's message, quoted above, was simply not true.

'Modest adjustments', or the 'transitional protection' illusion

When 11 April arrived it was inevitable that the 5.6 million people who lost housing benefit would make their views heard. MPs were deluged with letters from angry, anxious or distressed claimants expressing varieties of shock and disbelief at the sudden loss of large amounts of benefit, as much as £40 per week in some cases. Unlike for those who were to lose income support, there were no transitional protection arrangements for these losers; they felt the full effects from day one.

Manchester City Council issued a press release showing the effects of the cuts in Manchester; nearly 18,000 people, over 7000 of them pensioners, lost all entitlement to benefit; that represented one in seven of all housing benefit recipients. The vast majority of the remainder received less benefit than before. Illustrative case studies showed pensioners losing up to £28 a week, and low-income families losing over £10. The same story was being repeated all over the country, in the full glare of universally hostile publicity. The government was badly shaken, and despite the Prime Minister's vain attempts to claim that there was no need to panic, within two weeks it was forced to bow to the pressure and make some changes. As Robin Cook put it when opening the emergency debate just over two weeks after the implementation of the new scheme. 'Far from standing the test of the next forty years, the changes in housing benefit have not survived the test of the first four weeks.'

In the attempt to draw the sting of the opposition and quell the revolt of its own supporters, John Moore announced some 'modest adjustments'. The capital limit was raised from £6000 to £8000 and a new scheme of transitional protection was introduced, designed to limit the loss of benefit to £2.50 per week. Together, these adjustments cost £100 million, and were enough to ensure a government victory in the debate.

As with the 20 per cent rates contribution, closer scrutiny of the transitional arrangements showed them to offer a good deal less protection than at first sight. John Moore told the House: 'I propose to make good those housing benefit losses in excess of £2.50 per week arising from the changeover to the new scheme which have affected pensioners, disabled people, families with children and lone parents.' This meant no protection for groups other than those specifically mentioned, such as couples or single people without children. Even for the designated groups, the arrangements applied only to those already on benefit; all new recipients would receive benefit at the new lower rates.

There was to be no protection against any costs arising from the current round of rent and rates rises, which seriously undermined its effectiveness; estimates from Edinburgh showed, for example, that because of rent and rates rises people could lose up to £8 a week before qualifying for the protection.

Third, no protection was to be given against the need to pay 20 per cent of rates, which affected by far the largest number of claimants. This was a crucial weakness, and not one which was made clear during the debate in the House.

If MPs had voted for the transitional arrangements believing they would significantly ease the burdens of their distressed constituents they were badly mistaken. The meagreness of the protection was plainly visible from two simple facts; it would cost only £70 million, which, taking into account the £30 million given back through raising the capital limit, still left cuts of £550 million; and in the government's own estimate only 300,000 people would be given any protection at all, out of the 5.6 million losers.

In order to administer these hasty amendments a new DHSS unit had to be established, and the estimated cost of administering the anticipated total of £70 million of transitional protection was between £25 and £28 million. As the CPAG commented: 'We'd much rather they had listened to the critics in the first place who were predicting these difficulties so that the money could have gone to the claimants who need it and not on administrative changes to patch up the system.'

More cuts to come

The claims for the housing benefit reforms were therefore spurious. They did not target resources towards the worse off, neither did they increase work incentives. They did simplify the system, but this was of little value to those whose already meagre incomes had been further reduced.

The Housing Act 1988 contains several measures which as rents rise will undoubtedly have the effect of cutting housing benefit yet again. Before it was enacted the local authority and housing organisations all warned of the dangers, fearing more hardship, rent arrears, evictions and homelessness. But on the evidence of its behaviour to date, the government will press ahead and continue to take money away from those most in need. Unlike the great outcry of 11 April, these cuts will take effect gradually as individual tenants are denied benefits, so weakening the opportunity for effective protest. Thus the number of losers under the reforms, huge as it is, is an underestimate of the number there will be once the Housing Act takes effect.

The 'Reform' of Supplementary Benefits: 'From him that hath not . . .'

The reform of housing benefits had undoubtedly made things worse for most claimants; whether the change from supplementary benefits to income support had made matters better or worse was the subject of much controversy.

Supplementary benefits were in need of reform. The attempt to tailor payments to claimants' individual needs through a system that involved identifying which of the many additional requirements they needed over and above their basic benefit was doomed to failure as the numbers of claimants rose inexorably, reaching nearly five million by 1988. Similarly, the strain put on the administration by the need to investigate individual claims for single payments to meet the occasional emergency was creating intolerable pressures on a service which had not been given the resources to grow in line with the huge increase in workload during the 1980s as more and more unemployed and lone parents were forced to depend on benefits. The solution offered in the 1986 Act was in essence to change from a system of individually tailored benefits to ones which were paid to groups of claimants who could all be deemed to have similar needs. These were the changes which were designed to meet the aim of 'simplification', and are what are meant by the 'structural' changes, since they did indeed change the structure of benefits.

The main change involved the abolition of all the fourteen possible additional payments which could be made to claimants with special needs, such as extra heating, special diets, extra laundry costs and such like, most of which went to the elderly and disabled. In their place were introduced special premiums which went to all claimants in certain specified categories. These premiums were paid over and above the basic weekly benefit, now to be called income support. The groups qualifying for them were families with children, with extra premiums for lone parents and for a disabled child; pensioners, at two rates depending on age; and the disabled, with two rates, depending on the severity of the disability. Whether people gained or lost from the reforms would in part depend on how many of the previous weekly additions they had been receiving, and for which of the new premiums they qualified.

As a structural change it made a good deal of sense and it did simplify the administration, since now all that had to be established for each claimant was which premium, if any, he or she qualified for, instead of a time-consuming and complicated assessment of each claimant's needs to establish the appropriate mix of additional payments. What vitiated the usefulness of the reform was the need to carry it out within the overall nil-cost remit, which meant that gains for some claimants could be financed only through losses for others, and which also set very tight constraints on the amounts that could be allowed in the premiums.

There were four other significant changes which also affected the equation. Under the pre-April scheme, there was not one single rate of weekly benefit but several. There were different rates for adults according to whether they were householders or not, on the grounds that householders generally have higher expenses

41

than non-householders; and according to the length of time they had been on benefit, on the grounds that a prolonged time on benefit was likely to lead to claimants having greater needs. Those on benefit for more than a year received a significantly higher rate of benefit than those on the short-term rate; in 1987/8 the difference for a couple was as much as £12.50 a week. The only exception was the unemployed and their families, who stayed on the lower rate no matter how long they remained on benefit. With the change to income support all these distinctions were abolished and replaced by a simpler set of rates; one for couples, one for single adults aged twenty-five and over, and a lower one for those aged under twenty-five. (There was also a still lower rate for those aged under eighteen, but most of these claimants were soon to have *all* entitlement to benefit abolished completely on the grounds that they would all have a guaranteed Youth Training Scheme (YTS) place or a job.) In effect, age became the differentiator rather than householder status or time on benefit, with twenty-five as the new age of majority for social security purposes. Whether claimants won or lost by this depended on which rate they had been on and which they changed to. For example, the weekly income of a twenty-five-year-old unemployed non-householder would have risen from £24.35 to £33.40 a week; that of a twenty-four-year-old unemployed householder would have fallen from £30.40 to £26.05.

Second, under the old scheme claimants who had to meet sudden emergency payments, for example to repair a broken cooker or to meet the costs of moving house, had the right to apply for a single payment, which, if it were given at all, would be given as a cash grant. Those were all abolished and replaced by the social fund. We shall consider this in detail in Chapter 11; for now it is enough to note that the substitution of loans for grants meant a clear loss for many claimants; particularly families with children who had relied most heavily on single payments.

Third, supplementary benefit had been payable only to claimants with savings of less then £3000; the new scheme raised this limit to £6000, though any savings between £3000 and £6000 would reduce the amount of benefit payable. This change was a net gain to those claimants who had been barred from benefit because of their savings.

The fourth change was that whereas under the old scheme claimants on supplementary benefit had their rates met in full in addition to their weekly benefit, they now had to pay 20 per cent of the rates themselves. Under pressure, the government had conceded that it would protect claimants against the loss in income support by the equivalent of 20 per cent of the national average rates bill. Claimants living in areas with high rates would lose by this, while those in low-rated areas would gain.

Gainers and losers: how many and who are they?

The calculation of who gained and who lost by all these changes was very complex and depended crucially on the assumptions made about the interaction of all these factors. Leaving aside the question of the transitional protection, the government's impact tables had shown that as a result of the changes from supplementary benefit to income support 2,190,000 claimants would be better off, 920,000 would stay the same, and 1,660,000 would be worse off. This was challenged by the Benefits Research Unit at Nottingham University, which calculated that only 1,008,000 would be better off, 1,006,000 would stay the same, and 2,125,000 would be worse off. Whereas the DHSS estimates were that only 35 per cent would lose, the Benefits Research Unit estimated that 60 per cent would.

Why the difference? The Nottingham unit took into account factors which the DHSS had ignored. Even before the 1988 changes there had been some reductions in benefits which had had the effect of cutting claimants' incomes, and the Nottingham calculations included some that had occurred since 1986. The DHSS estimates made no allowance for the abolition of all single payments, or for the fact that claimants were not fully compensated for the 20 per cent contribution to the rates. The Nottingham team decided not to take certain other cuts into account even though these too had the effect of reducing claimants' incomes. This enabled them to claim that they had at all times erred on the side of caution, and they therefore believed that their figure of 60 per cent represented the very minimum estimate of the likely number of losers.

Massaging the figures

As the debate continued it emerged that there were other changes that the government had made at the last minute which had the effect of understating the real losses to claimants. What was interesting about these changes was that they suggested a calculated deviousness on the part of DHSS ministers, since at least one of the changes, that affecting housing benefit supplement, must have been engineered deliberately to massage the figures.

Housing benefit supplement was a benefit paid to claimants whose income was just above the supplementary benefit level but which fell below it after they had paid their rent and rates. It was a payment of supplementary benefit, not housing benefit, which was a very important point since it meant that recipients could qualify for any benefits associated with supplementary benefits, such as single payments for emergencies. One week before the April changes housing benefit supplement was *abolished* and the regulations were changed so that it was redesignated as housing benefit, not supplementary benefit. The effect of this was to deprive 400,000 people of the transitional protection afforded to those on supplementary benefit. They were then faced with sudden large bills for rent and rates and, with the cuts in housing benefit, many experienced substantial cash losses (see Chapter 4).

This change to the regulations was challenged when an appeal tribunal ruled it to be illegal, and upheld the appeals for four claimants. When asked in the House to extend this ruling to the other 400,000 affected claimants the Prime Minister claimed that the decision applied only to those four cases and had not constituted a precedent, manifesting what the Leader of the Opposition called 'an extraordinary sense of justice'.

The National Association of Citizen's Advice Bureaux (NACAB) issued a press release at the end of March pointing to two other 'gaps in government benefit protection'. One concerned a potentially large number of pensioners whose pensions were due to be increased one week before the changeover, for many of them lifting their income to just above supplementary benefit levels, for which they would then no longer qualify, thereby also forfeiting the right to transitional protection. The cuts in housing benefit would again mean that many of them would find themselves on

44

average about £3 to £4 a week worse off. Second, 15,000 low-paid part-time workers, mostly women and mostly single parents, who had been able to earn up to £12 a week to top up their benefit would no longer qualify for supplementary benefit if they worked for more than twenty-four hours a week, as against thirty hours under the current rules. These would be able to claim family credit instead but many would be left worse off and without transitional protection.

Finally, there was the whole question of the value of the transitional protection even for those who received it. In effect, it simply freezes the claimant's benefit at its previous level if that is higher than entitlement under the new income support. This was what ministers meant when they said claimants would be no worse off in cash terms. In saying this they had chosen their words carefully. While those qualifying for transitional protection may have had their incomes frozen at their pre-11 April level, this was not the same as saying they were no worse off. In the normal course of events claimants would have had their benefit *increased to take account of inflation*, but this year they did not, so the 1,400,000 on transitional benefit were already worse off in real terms than they would have been under the old scheme. Moreover, none of these claimants will have their benefit uprated until their entitlement under income support catches up with their current income, which for some could mean spending years on the amount of benefit they had been given in April 1987. Second, all claimants now had to pay 20 per cent of their rates; the compensation for this was given as £1 for a single claimant and £1.30 for couples. Any claimant whose rates bill was higher than these amounts was worse off in real terms. Finally, the transitional arrangements last only for as long as claimants stay on benefit. If they came off benefit, for example because they find a job, but have to reclaim again soon afterwards they will find their incomes cut in cash terms.

Gainers and losers: the effects on real people

One of several regions which attempted to predict the outcome of all the changes was Strathclyde, where one in three adults live either on or with incomes around supplementary benefit level.

Against government estimates that, overall, 46 per cent would gain and 35 per cent lose, Strathclyde's Department of Social Planning predicted from a survey of clients known to their Social Services Department that only 18.5 per cent would gain while 77 per cent would lose from the structural changes. Some of those with transitional protection would have no increase in benefit *until the end of the century*. Claiming that the changes would be 'wholly catastrophic', the Principal Social Planning Officer told the *Scotsman* in March 1988: 'We are confident our figures are accurate, though we wish they weren't. The difference so far as we are concerned is that we have calculated the effect on real people while the DHSS is dealing in hypotheses.'

After April 1988 it became possible to calculate the actual effects on real people. The Department of Social and Administrative Studies at Oxford University carried out a survey on 186 people before and after the change from supplementary benefit to income support. As they were based on real people the Department was able to claim that its findings provided 'the most precise estimates so far of the effects'. It found that 64 per cent were losers as against only 28 per cent who gained. It also found that the transitional protection failed to prevent real losses. Because of the need to pay 20 per cent of rates and water rates, and because of the failure to compensate for inflation, 78 per cent of those claimants in their sample *with* transitional protection were worse off. As if that were not bad enough, these figures were themselves an underestimate of the scale of the losses because they did not include the losses from the abolition of single payments.

Not surprisingly, there was also disagreement about which groups of claimants had gained and which lost. The government's impact tables showed that more pensioners would lose than gain, while families with children, single people under twenty-five and the sick and disabled would all generally gain. Single people under twenty-five would have more or less equal numbers of gainers and losers. In other words, the gains of the families with children, young people and the disabled were to be financed by the losses of the pensioners.

The Nottingham team agreed with the government that pensioners would predominantly be losers, but disagreed about all the other groups. In their estimates, *every group* would have more losers

46

than gainers. Parents would lose because of the loss of single payments, and in their judgement no single person under twenty-five would gain. These estimates were broadly confirmed by the Oxford study, which showed that pensioners did indeed lose, with couples losing an average of more than £5 a week and single pensioners losing £2.30. It also showed that single people under twenty-five were heavy losers, which seems much more likely than the government's optimistic claims in view of the lower benefit rates for this age group. On average young people in Oxford lost over £5 out of a weekly income of less than £31. Once the loss of single payments is added into the equation, the Oxford study showed that families with children also become losers, as they were the prime users of these benefits.

Further confirmation that the effects of the changes had left many people on income support worse off, despite the transitional protection, came in November 1988 when NACAB published the results of its own investigation into who had gained and who lost. The survey was carried out in May by bureaux covering a third of the country and involving over 500 people who had been on supplementary benefit and who had changed over to income support. It was therefore a large-scale survey conducted very soon after the April changes took effect.

Almost a third (32 per cent) of these claimants were worse off in cash terms, and were unequivocally losers. These were mostly the elderly and those without dependent children.

Of the remaining 68 per cent who gained, half did so because their income was protected by the transitional arrangements, which meant that in the longer term they would join the ranks of the losers as their benefit failed to be uprated. More significantly, the gains for many of the claimants were offset by the new requirements to pay 20 per cent of rates and to pay water rates. The great majority of them had to pay at least £1 above the £1.30 allowed as compensation for their rates contribution, and almost all had to pay at least another £1 a week in water rates; 43 per cent had to pay between £2 and £4. By the time these factors were taken into account, together with the loss of additional requirements and single payments, NACAB concluded that four out of five claimants on income support had lost in real terms by the changes. This part of NACAB's report concludes: 'Even using

47

a conservative figure of £5 per week to cover all these other elements [the 20 per cent rates contribution etc.], our survey showed that 82 per cent of claimants who transferred from SB to IS lost out in actual spending power, either immediately or over the coming year.'

This survey also provided confirmation that family credit was less effective than the ministerial claims made for it. Because of the lengthy delays in processing the claims there were only thirty-three claimants in the sample on whom full information was available, but of these slightly more (52 per cent) lost by the change than gained. The survey also confirmed, if confirmation were needed, that the losses from the changes to housing benefit were very considerable: 88 per cent of claimants lost by the changes, of whom 22 per cent lost between £5 and £10 a week and 23 per cent lost over £10.

Odious comparisons

The debate about gainers and losers became clouded by the complexity of the way in which the figures were presented, and then by the competing claims of different protagonists. It is clear that the government underestimated the effects on claimants' real resources, and that the claims made for the transitional protection were exaggerated. But the whole sorry debate is itself a distraction from the far more important question why there should have been any losers at all, or, to put it another way, why the gains of some claimants had to be paid for by the losses of others rather than by taxpayers in general. In the March 1988 budget the Chancellor gave away over £2000 million to 750,000 of the richest taxpayers; every one was an unequivocal gainer. The amount of extra money going into the income support scheme over and above what an uprating of the supplementary benefit scheme would have cost was £430 million. This means that in the spring of 1988 the government had £2,500 million to give away. It gave 83 per cent to the 750,000 richest people in the country: an average gain of £54 a week each; it gave the remaining 17 per cent to the 4,770,000 poorest people in the country – an average gain of £1.70 a week each.

Even on the government's own discredited figures, 1,660,000

claimants on supplementary benefit have lost by the 'reforms'. Overall, taking all the changes to all the benefits into account, 3,650,000 claimants were intended to be worse off. For his part in this further impoverishment of the poorest people in Britain John Moore told the nation five days after the changes that he was 'very, very proud to be able to participate in putting them into practice'.

3   Women and Children Last

Our objectives are to give individuals and their families more choice and more freedom to exercise responsibility, to raise their standards of living and to improve the efficiency and effectiveness of the welfare services.

(Margaret Thatcher, House of Commons, 25 October 1983)

What is Right for the Family is Right for Britain.

(Margaret Thatcher, *Sunday Express*, 29 June 1975)

All policies for social security, whether for pensions, supplementary benefit or disablement, bear on the quality and security of family life; none more so than those policies which are deliberately directed at supporting the costs of family life itself – children's benefits, and income support for families in and out of work. In the past decade 'the family' has achieved the highest political significance for a government which sees it as the antithesis of 'the state'. Indeed, 'the family' has come to occupy the high moral and political ground, and the virtuous language of 'care', 'independence' and 'responsibility' has taken on great political significance. The homilies quoted above are, therefore, not just statements of personal belief; they represent the highest political ambitions.

Furthermore, like many similar ministerial and prime ministerial statements about the family, they present a view of all families as active citizens, ready and able, as the Central Policy Review Staff papers put it in 1982, to 'resume responsibilities taken on by the state'. It is an attitude at once patronising and contradictory, since it presumes on the one hand a deliberate tendency for all families to shift their responsibilities on to the

50

state, while at the same time implying that all families are equally self-sufficient. It is accompanied by a view which inclines to see children not as a social responsibility, but an individual luxury. It offers a parochial view of society which excludes families in which all adults are unemployed, families in which there is only one adult to work and to care, areas and regions where wages are so low that both parents have to work, yet where there is no cheap or free child care to help them do so, families where children are physically and emotionally at risk, families in which caring for adults has become an inescapable burden, families where several generations living together crowd one another out, or families where the young have no place and no sympathy. It ignores families where deprivation and poverty have left a pattern of low expectations and inadequacy, which passes from one generation to the next.

Central to this view of society is the conviction expressed by the Prime Minister on the one hand that 'the battle for women's rights is largely won', but that, nevertheless, a woman's place is still, firmly, at home. Government policies, which have reduced the employment rights of women at work, restricted their opportunities to retrain and enter the labour market, and ignored the need for child care, help to ensure that they have no choice but to stay at home. It is a view which explains why the most serious review of the welfare state since Beveridge did not, as the SSAC put it, 'fully recognise' the changing position of women in employment and society.

At each stage of the life-cycle women carry the burden of poverty and disadvantage. They have less opportunity to work, to build up contribution records for benefits and pensions; they are the carers – and they live longer. Women are in the forefront of massive social changes in family patterns. Since 1971 the number of single parents has increased by almost 60 per cent to over a million families, with 1.6 million children. Most of those families are headed by women, and 65 per cent of those women are poor enough to claim income support. There are 6 million women caring for adult dependants. The majority of pensioners are women who depend on their husband's pension, or on their widow's pension. Sixty-three per cent of women pensioners over seventy-five are disabled. There are 2.58 million women in full-time work and 3.41 million women in part-time work who earn less than the European Decency

Threshold of £148.51 a week – women earning less than £3.50 an hour. By this definition, over 50 per cent of all women working full time and 80 per cent of those working part time are low paid. Women make up 66 per cent of the low-paid workforce. They are concentrated in the distributive trades, catering, hairdressing, and laundries, but a disproportionate number are in services such as the National Health Service (NHS) and education. Many are excluded from the contributory national insurance system for much of their lives; they have gained nothing by the cuts in income tax. In work they are low paid; outside work many, particularly single parents, have no insurance rights but must depend upon the income support system. The size of this growing female constituency in poverty over the past twenty years has perplexed poverty campaigners, women's organisations and politicians alike. The review of social security, as the Equal Opportunities Commission (EOC) commented in its response to the Green Paper, 'does not at any point, in discussing the shape of future state provision, address the particular needs of women'. These are the women who make up the alternative families which the Fowler review has left largely untouched. Indeed, women's needs are subsumed within family needs, and, as the EOC remarked, 'He' is used throughout the reviews in conjunction with 'wage earner'. Instead of promoting the positive policies which are needed to compensate women for their dual responsibilities and enable them to be self-sufficient in a real sense, the reviews did the opposite.

This chapter concentrates on the fundamental change in attitude and policy towards the family expressed in the switch of emphasis from universal child benefits between 1979 and 1988 to 'targeting' means-tested benefits on low-income families, first by way of family income supplement and then by family credit. Some of the other changes affecting women and children which have followed from the Fowler reviews are also briefly considered.

Backtracking on Child Benefit, or When is a Promise Not a Promise?

The importance of 'the family' in the iconography of Thatcherism gives Conservative policies toward child benefit particular significance. More than that, however, it commands the high ground in the political battle between universal benefits and selective ('targeted') benefits. It represents the crucial divide between those who argue that there should be positive policies for families, and that it is right for the community of taxpayers to assist with the costs of children, and those who feel that the welfare state and family policy should be confined to relieving poverty. It is the difference between those who argue that since many mothers are not 'dependent' on child benefit, those who are should be means-tested to prove that they are deserving and in need. It is not an argument which those campaigners for equity have applied to the married man's tax allowance.

Child benefit is, at present, the entitlement of every child in the country. It is the only payment which goes direct to the mother on behalf of the child; it enhances work incentives, since it goes to all families in and out of work. It provides a floor on which families can build by their own efforts. As income drops child benefit becomes more important. For the mothers who occupy the bottom tenth of the income stratum, child benefit contributes about 20 per cent of their income. But 60 per cent of child benefit goes to families just on or below average income. It is particularly effective in helping families too poor to pay tax. It raises family income and thus keeps half a million families off means-tested benefits. It is, therefore, a benefit tailor-made to encourage independence and self-sufficiency in family life. It costs £4 billion annually.

For these reasons the introduction of child benefit in 1975 commanded all-party support. Thus, Norman Fowler, then opposition spokesman on social security, quoted with positive enthusiasm the arguments of William Pitt in 1796: 'Let us make relief in cases where there are a number of children a matter of right and a matter of honour.' They were, said Fowler, 'wise words' and he took pride in the 'considerable all-party pressure' which had brought child benefit into being. Indeed, he claimed that there was a direct link between the new scheme and the Tory Party's Green Paper on tax credits in 1972, thus emphasising the ideological appeal of child benefits as a form of tax allowance.

Lurking in the background, however, was an alternative Tory view of the best way to help families. In 1974 Sir Keith Joseph, then Secretary of State for Social Security, introduced the concept of the family income supplement (FIS).

FIS was a means-tested benefit paid to families in work with incomes below a certain level. It was geared to the number of children, and it carried entitlement to a range of other low-income benefits, particularly free school meals. It was fatally flawed from the start. First, it reinforced low pay and created a poverty trap for families on low wages paying the lowest rates of tax. These families would sometimes lose as much as £1 in benefits for every extra £1 they earned. Second, whether from ignorance, scepticism or self-interest, only 54 per cent of families entitled to FIS claimed it. These were clearly the two weaknesses which any proposed reform would surely have to tackle.

It was immediately clear in 1979, however, that child benefit, the cornerstone of family policy, could not be taken for granted. As part of the first tranche of public expenditure cuts it was frozen at its April 1979 value of £4 until November 1980. Child benefit had ardent support among many traditional Tories, committed to family policies and tax credits. They were represented on the Tory back-benches by 'wets' such as Robin Squire, Sir Brandon Rhys Williams, and Sir George Young and were publicly supported by the Tory women's organisations. But a back-bench rebellion in 1979, easily put down, was to demonstrate how isolated the 'one-nation' Tories would become.

By 1984 the costs and merits of means-tested benefits for low-paid families in work, and universal child benefits for families in and out of work, had become hotly contested. Tory support for redistribution away from childless taxpayers toward families with children, on grounds of social responsibility and efficiency, were attacked during the course of the children and young persons review by the Adam Smith Institute, which argued that 75 per cent of child benefit was redundant since it went to families who were not 'in need of it . . . because they would still be above the poverty line without it'. Adopting a tone more suited to the social biology arguments of the 1930s, it went on: 'It is also strange that public policy should work to encourage parents to have children. . . . There is considerable evidence, for example, that present benefit and housing policies have led to a large increase in the numbers of unmarried mothers living on state welfare.' The notion of having more children to clock up £7.25 a week for each of them is at best improbable, and says more about the gender make-up of the Institute than it does about unmarried mothers.

Both in public and private a case was made for a change in the nature of the benefit. In public the poverty lobby was closely questioned about the continuing need for a universal benefit. In private the Treasury fought hard to secure taxation, but the DHSS fought back, arguing in the Green Paper that it would

> greatly increase the numbers of families in the poverty trap. . . . It would be very expensive to administer. . . . At higher income levels it would mean that families received no help with the cost of bringing up children. This country would be virtually alone amongst developed countries in failing to recognise that families with children had more expenses than families without children . . .

Nor would the taxation of benefits be any solution:

> The great majority of working families pay tax so that the effect would be equivalent to a 30 per cent reduction in child support. Put another way, for a family with two children the effect would be the same as reducing their tax thresholds by about £700 a year. The government's aim is to take people out of tax.

For both reasons, taxation and means-tests were politically unacceptable.

Nevertheless, a clear signal was sent to anyone still complacent about the government's commitment to child benefit when in June 1985 child benefit was increased by 50p less than the rate of inflation. The explanation offered by Norman Fowler echoed the arguments put forward that month in the Green Paper, namely that while the government believed it right to maintain child benefit for all children 'irrespective of the income of their parents, nevertheless, we have to consider its level in relation to overall priorities within social security and, in particular, with the aim to do more for families on low income'.

The Green Paper itself trailed what was, two years later, to harden into explicit policy. There were, it said, two views of child support: that it should help all families or that it should relieve child poverty. The two policies were different and should not be confused. The government made its own priority clear in the Paper: better-targeted help for working families on low incomes. 'Giving extra help where it was most appropriate – in the take-home pay of those in work – and removing the worst effects of the poverty trap.' Child benefit was to remain untouched on the grounds that it was 'the sole mechanism for providing the general recognition of the costs of bringing up children'. Since it was designed to meet the needs of families generally it was of value in itself. It was also 'simple, straightforward, well understood and preferred as it is. The case for changing it has not been made out. The government do not, therefore, propose to alter its basis or structure.'

Child Benefit Betrayed

But what did this careful language really mean? It became clear during and after the course of the election that there was in effect a distinction in the mind of ministers between maintaining the structure and maintaining the value of child benefit. A nose for nuance, and practised cynicism, were necessary to detect this, however.

Just before the election, John Major, DHSS Minister, in an interview in *Poverty*, the CPAG journal, insisted that the structure of child benefit was secure:

> We'll review child benefit each year as we always have, but I can't tell you what the outcome of that will be. But I can tell you that child benefit will continue as a non-means-tested universal payment, paid to the mother and tax-free. There ought to be no question about that.

The Conservative manifesto in 1987 followed suit, stating simply that 'child benefit will continue to be paid as now'. This, as Sir Brandon Rhys Williams warned Tory ministers in the House of Commons, 'could not honourably be held by anyone to mean either that child benefit will cease to be uprated, so that it loses its real value, or that payments to mothers in respect of their children should be deemed in future to belong after all to the father'. Yet, within weeks of the election, rumours flourished that the

56

government was about to abolish, cut or means-test child benefit. On 14 July 1987 Nicholas Scott, under pressure in the House of Commons, insisted that there were 'no plans to depart from the policy of successive governments which has been to determine the rate of child benefit as part of the annual social security uprating'.

Concern about the future value and indeed about the existence of the benefit was fuelled by fears of the coming public expenditure round, and by the transparent opportunism of the new Secretary of State, John Moore. In September 1987 in his famous speech of 'dependency' he referred to 'pools of resentment among the taxpayers who are footing the bill, often from incomes barely larger than the money benefit recipients receive. By targeting our welfare resources we will be able to provide more real help where need is greatest.'

A month later, putting principle into practice in the annual 'uprating statement' forecasting the levels of benefits for the following April, John Moore told the House of Commons that child benefit was too expensive, it did not assist the very poorest, it gave help where it was not needed. To keep pace with inflation it should have increased to about £7.50; in fact its value was to remain at £7.25 for the next financial year. On the Jimmy Young show on 28 October he was even more explicit; asked about previous pledges by Mrs Thatcher and other ministers he said, 'The world changes. People are now better off. . . . I am not going to be trapped into the position where I am helping people who do not need help.'

In the subsequent debate on the uprating of benefits the tone of ministerial macho was echoed by the junior minister, Michael Portillo, who again insisted that it was ridiculous to make a fuss about 4p a day when the government was putting so much money (about £220 million) into family credit. He argued that 'The help and support that the Conservative Party gives to the family is much more than cash support. We give vigorous moral support.' Even some on the Tory benches greeted this argument with derision. On 12 January 1988, in a major debate on an opposition amendment to uprate child benefit, Sir Brandon Rhys Williams passionately attacked the DHSS ministers for betraying the Conservative manifesto and the interests of poor families. What the minister was doing, he argued, was incompatible with the policies for which the Prime Minister has won widespread approval. . . namely her support for the family as an institution and her desire to reduce the tax burden. . . . For the large majority who draw child benefit and pay more in income tax than they draw in benefit, a cut in the real value of child benefit constitutes an increase in their relative tax burden, targeted particularly against the mothers. . .

His real scorn was reserved for the 'trick' which had been played on the 10,000 mothers 'in every average-sized parliamentary constituency': 'We are being invited now to tell those mothers "Aha. You have got it wrong." What [the manifesto commitment] meant was that it would remain at the same arithmetical figure, regardless of its real value. I do not believe we should treat 6.5 million mothers in that way.' It was a devastating attack and the minister had no answer except to insist that the words 'paid as now' meant, not that its value would continue to be maintained as it had in the past, but that it would continue to be paid as a universal benefit, tax-free and to the mother.

The opposition motion was lost, but the government's majority fell to forty-seven. Undeterred by this loss of confidence among many of his own supporters, John Moore was reported only three months later to be planning to offer the Treasury a change in the basis of child benefit payment as part of the annual public expenditure negotiations. The first internal papers circulated and leaked showed that ministers felt that they 'could not defend the present practice of child benefit payment . . . at a time when benefits were being increasingly targeted at the worst off', and that 'perhaps the time had come for child benefit to be tapered so that families over a certain level of income lost benefit, or were taxed upon it'.

Discussions on the future of child benefit have been conducted in secret. On 17 May 1988 in the House of Commons the Prime Minister merely reiterated the manifesto commitment, from which no comfort can be drawn. Recent press speculation suggests that the Treasury and DHSS have, despite John Moore's obvious enthusiasm, found both taxation and means-testing fraught with difficulties, and will not pursue them, but it is clear that the days of annual uprating are over and unless ministers now in office can be persuaded otherwise, the value of child benefits will wither away. The hitherto preferred route of laying down a universal floor to help families combat poverty and child neglect has been discarded in favour of targeting means-tested benefits on families in work through the mechanism of family credit. In autumn 1988, as Chapter 13 describes in more detail, child benefit was frozen for the second year in succession.

Mean Tests for Families

The freeze on child benefit in April 1988 saved £120 million. The government set aside £220 million for the new family credit scheme, estimating a take-up of 80 per cent as against 50 per cent on family income supplement. The scheme was given a high profile, and carried with it the government's high hopes. It was, said the minister, 'one of the most important proposals in the Green Paper'. It is, therefore, important to apply the government's own litmus test to family credit. Has it met the three criteria set out in the Green Paper? Has it effectively targeted help to those most in need? Has it simplified the system? Has it extended work incentives?

The Green Paper had been very clear about priorities. The proportion of families with children in the lowest 20 per cent of the income band had increased from nearly 40 per cent in 1971 to 47 per cent in 1982. Family poverty from unemployment was 'undoubtedly serious', but the priority was to be low-income families with children, about half of which were headed by someone in work but with an inadequate income. The government's strategy would be to 'create an effective bridge between income in and out of work for some of the poorest families in our community'.

Child benefit 'could not solve the problem' – unless the government was prepared to spend the £4 billion extra it would cost to raise the benefit to levels where it would overcome the poverty and unemployment traps. This would be 'insupportable and completely inconsistent with the object of targeting help on the areas in greatest need'. Instead 'extra support' would go 'to these families in accordance with their needs, to ensure as far as possible that they are better off in work, and to see that they can achieve improvements in family income by greater effort without losing all the benefit because of high marginal tax rates'. Family credit was to be based on net income and, significantly, 'to make employees aware of the full extent of the help they are receiving the credit will be paid to employees through the pay packet'.

There would, however, be some losses. Families on family credit would lose entitlement to free school meals and free welfare milk since it was 'far preferable' to enhance the rates of family credit instead. (The eventual 'enhancement' was £2.55 for each week of the year.) Family credit would be counted in full in the calculation of housing benefit. Given the absence of even illustrative figures it was impossible to tell whether this would really mean that rates were more generous in practice than FIS had been. And there was some administrative complication; although administered by employers, families would have to apply to the DHSS first. Finally, conditions for eligibility would be tighter than for FIS. The benefit would run for six months, not for a year, and would be calculated on income over thirteen weeks, not five (though this final proposal was eventually dropped).

Sceptics could be forgiven for thinking that, given this mixture of obscurity and complexity, the new scheme might not fulfil its promise to be more effective in helping the poorest families, more effective in reaching more families, simpler to understand or easier to administer. In particular, the proposals to pay the new benefit through the wage packet rather than direct to the mother had the unique result of uniting the poverty lobby, the SSAC and the employers in protest. As the CPAG put it, few would 'mourn the passing of family income supplement', but family credit would 'exacerbate' the problems of FIS and 'create new ones'. Non-working women would be savagely disadvantaged by this decision. At the same time, however, employers wanted no additional administrative burden.

In the event the employers carried the day. At report stage in the House of Commons, Norman Fowler announced that he would have further discussions with representatives of business, the EOC and the Women's National Commission, because 'The government will do everything that they can to avoid placing unnecessary burdens on employers and . . . therefore I am prepared to reconsider the mechanism by which family credit is paid.' The concession was announced in the House of Lords, the government having been convinced that it would not be right to introduce such a change 'if the immediate cost was undue additional work for employers who have to operate the system'.

A small victory, therefore, for women and children, even if by a roundabout route. There was still the problem of whether take-up would, as the minister insisted, be increased; few were convinced that it would. But the outstanding problem remained: how effective would family credit be in remedying the situation whereby people were trapped in unemployment or unwilling to seek a career change or a promotion because they would lose almost as much in benefit as they gained in income? The intention was that, by basing entitlement on income *after* tax and national insurance contributions, and assessing housing benefit on the same basis, the old 100 per cent poverty trap could be eliminated; similarly, by aligning income support and family credit people in work would not be worse off than people out of work. But, as the White Paper admitted,

> there is a price to be paid. In particular, the number of families facing high marginal tax rates but below 100 per cent will tend to increase. The government recognise this problem, which is unavoidable if available resources are to be directed towards those who need help most.

The final scheme was expected to reach 400,000 people (twice as many people as FIS) and to cost three times as much, despite the loss of housing benefit and free school meals. It would be calculated on the basis of a 'maximum credit' to be paid to a family whose net weekly income was at or below £51.45. (The maximum credit would vary according to the numbers and ages of children in the family.) For every £1 of income over £51.45 the family would lose 70p in benefit. This meant, for example, that a couple with two children under eleven with an income of £90 would get about £17 in family credit, decreasing by 70p for every extra pound of income.

In September 1987 John Moore was confident that family credit was a serious challenge to the notion of 'dependency'. But following the publication of the impact tables and the levels of benefit in

1987 it became immediately clear that, even in *cash* terms, the government's scheme had misfired. The interaction of cuts in housing benefit and gains in family credit meant that about 290,000 couples would gain, and 70,000 would still lose. Of the latter, 30,000 would lose more than £5 a week. Among lone parents, 90,000 would lose and 100,000 gain. Comparing the new scheme with the old scheme the picture was worse: 130,000 lone parents and 140,000 couples would lose under the new scheme, and 90,000 lone parents and 250,000 couples would gain. Thus, as Chapter 2 described, even the government's own estimates showed massive numbers *losing* among the families intended to *gain*.

In fact, as far back as February 1986 assiduous devilling in the House of Commons had already established that, for poor families in work, the combination of tax and national insurance contributions, the losses on housing benefit, water rates and free school meals, would more than wipe out the increases in family credit. But these were theoretical losses, and as such, made little impact at the time. Two years later, in February 1988, given the increase in the 'withdrawal taper' on housing benefit from 60p to 65p in every pound and increases in rent and rates (see Chapter 2) for families on low pay, the losses began to look very real. Married couples with two children on gross incomes of £70 a week, with average rent and rates, fares to work, free school meals, milk and welfare foods, who were estimated to lose £9.17 in February 1986 actually lost £11.03 in 1988. The government had constructed a scheme which had failed its first and most elementary test – to give extra help to those families in the lowest income groups, working for their poverty and living in rented accommodation. Instead it had inflicted extra losses on them.

In April the Social Security Consortium wrote urgently to the minister pointing out that:

one in three recipients of Family Credit (generally seen as the most advantageous of the new benefit schemes) will not gain or will be worse off in real terms. Those losses will be immediate for the vast majority since they are due to cuts in housing benefit which is not covered by transitional protection. Many of these families will be amongst the lowest paid, who were intended as a 'target' for additional resources: as many of those under £75 a week gross will lose as will gain.

(These figures do not include the two out of five families whom the Government estimates will not claim the family credit they are entitled to and who will lose from the freeze in child benefits.)

The Consortium added that it 'was difficult to see the logic' of the suggestion that restructuring means-tested benefits would reduce 'dependence', arguing that although the 'extreme version' of the poverty trap would be removed, spreading the net of means-tested benefits for those in work would make it *more* difficult for many claimants to 'move towards greater independence' and 'assume greater control over their lives'.

As the 'reforms' took effect in April 1988 MPs were deluged with letters from bewildered, disbelieving, angry and upset constitutents. Many showed just how much more difficult it had become to 'move towards greater independence'. For many families the loss of school meals and the loss of housing benefits far outweighed the 'gains' from family credit; far from gaining control, they felt that they had lost it. They were particularly angry that they had been misled. The distress and disappointment caused to those who had been told that they were the low-income families to be helped is best expressed in their own words. A single parent from Hampshire wrote:

> I am a single parent with three children, aged ten and twins of seven. I fully support the children myself with no maintenance from my ex-husband. I work part time as a theatre nurse and receive Family Credit. Under the new rate I get an extra £13.50 a week which sounds really great. But now my children have lost their free school meals which was worth £10.50. . . . I have also lost all my Housing Benefit, my rent has increased by £25. I was paying £10.37 per week, but now I have to pay £35.36. I felt so sick to my stomach when I found I was going to be so much worse off. . . . I could have stayed at home and lived off social but I prefer to work and try to help myself. But I'm now beginning to wonder if it's worth it. . . .

A working couple with two children and a weekly income of £85 wrote:

Before the changes made to 'benefit' we were receiving £11.00 a week FIS and getting free school meals for our two children. We were so pleased when we saw our new Family Credit would be almost £25.00 and thought at last the government are keeping their promise and actually doing something for us. But a few days later we had a letter telling us that our rent rebate has not just been slashed (as we were warned) but wiped out completely. Before we were paying £10.00 rent and now we will have to find £35.00 . . . and with the loss of school meals we will be £17.00 worse off. I understood that school meals were being taken away and replaced with money so we would get extra all year round and not just in term time. Why then has this been swallowed up in paying more rent? Incidentally, we have absolutely no savings so this cannot be the reason for losing our rent rebate. The other night on the Radio 4 programme 'In Committee' Nicholas Scott said that no one on a low income would be worse off in real terms or indeed in any terms. What then happened to us?

A self-employed single mother with three children aged fifteen, nine and eight described how the scheme destroyed the 'incentive to make the effort to work':

I have worked extremely hard since 1983 to establish a small retail business. That seemed to be the only way of working that was possible for me as I can work from home. However, I find that since Monday 11 April I am going to be even worse off than I would be if I claim Income Support, and earn £15.00 per week. I studied for 15 months and put all my savings into the business. I took advantage of the Enterprise Allowance scheme but still find it has been a struggle to pay my bills. I am now extremely disappointed to discover that I have lost virtually all my Housing Benefit and also have to pay for two lots of school meals. . . .

Finally, and most eloquently, a family bringing up four small children on an income of £100 a week;

Before this appalling Act we received £20.70 per week in FIS, £20 rent rebate plus free school meals for 3 of our children and free milk tokens for the fourth. All the adverts and press information suggested that families like ours would benefit from the changes, or at least not lose out. The Government insisted that the changes were necessary in order to channel the money to those who really needed it and to give people an incentive to work as opposed to being unemployed. We thought that the Government might be right when we received our Family Credit book which gave us benefits increased by £14. . . . For nearly two weeks now I have prepared sandwiches and drinks and yoghurts for the 3 of them and told myself I didn't mind . . . £10 a week for school meals is just too much to pay for my convenience alone and anyway the children seem to prefer sandwiches to school meals.

I was quite happy really . . . when yesterday the letter came. . . . I had to read it several times before I could believe what I was reading. It was from the Treasurer's Department and I read that we were no longer entitled to any rent rebate and that our rate rebate would be £1.76 a week. No apology. Just figures and facts which spell out all too clearly that our weekly income had been cut by nearly £20.

It is difficult to describe how I felt then, but I can honestly say that never have I felt so completely lost and distressed as I was yesterday morning. . . .

After much delay and many complications, some of these families and others in similar situations were helped by the concessions on housing benefit that were introduced in May. But what of the families now claiming for the first time, or reclaiming? All the problems identified and the losses described bear on them as harshly or more harshly. Their situation is best described in the words of one mother who wrote: 'If the people it [the extra money] was designed to help are £17.00 a week worse off, then I pity the rest.'

Women and Children: Making them Pay

The principle of concentrating help on the most needy families was reflected in other aspects of the Fowler reviews, namely, the restructuring of income support, the abolition of free school meals for low-income families and changes in maternity grant and maternity allowances.

The proposed changes in income support for families were largely welcomed. The essential change was the introduction of a family premium and a lone-parent premium on top of the basic allowances for adults and children. The family lobby approved of the explicit recognition of family costs, though without knowing the level at which the family premium was to be fixed it was, said CPAG, 'likely to be modest, if not meagre'. The SSAC gave it a warm welcome, seeing it as particularly helpful to lone parents and to unemployed families on the traditional 'short-term rate' of benefit. It was not a view shared by lone parents, however, many of whom depend on income support because they cannot work and for whom, therefore, all the problems inherent in the social security system are so much worse. Their problems had been recognised in the award of the higher rate of supplementary benefit once the parent had been on benefit for a year. For the first year on supplementary benefit a lone parent with two small children would have received just over £51; on income support she would receive nearly £60. (However, her benefit would then remain at that level, whereas under the old scheme her £51 would have risen to £59 after a year, so that gains were only in respect of the first year on benefit.) The White Paper reported that 'the principle of continued recognition of the need for specific further help for lone parents on top of that provided by the family premium has been welcomed'. This did nothing, however, to help the single parents trying to support themselves in work, many of whom, although eligible for family credit, were to be hit by cuts in housing benefit and other changes in income support which would make it too expensive in child care costs to work.

But the supplementary benefit changes also brought further hardship for women who have always been heavily dependent on single payments, especially for clothing and household essentials. From now on they will have to apply for loans from the social fund. For some women, the consequences are particularly grave. Those who are forced to leave home because of domestic violence have been heavy users of single payments to establish themselves and their children independently. As the EOC made clear in response to the Green Paper, 'It will not be possible in such extreme circumstances for women to repay loans from their weekly benefit without undue hardship to themselves.'

Just as the measures were silent on so many aspects of women's poverty, and have indeed extended it in specific ways, so they ignored the key question relating to children: how much does a child cost, and how much should be provided?

Traditionally, supplementary benefit has allowed different rates of benefit for children of different ages, thus reflecting in theory the increasing costs of children as they grow older. Originally, the Green Paper had proposed restructuring the children's rates with the increases coming at ages eight and thirteen rather than eleven and sixteen, in an attempt to meet increasing costs at those ages. The proposal was later dropped. But the real problem of the adequacy of the 'children's scale rates' was, once again, neglected. The difference between the benefit rates and the real cost of children can be judged by updating the classic study made by David Piachaud in 1979 on how much it cost to provide for children and comparing it with the actual money available for children of different ages. Thus, in 1987 a child aged two would cost about £11.40 a week; at eight £15.70; at eleven £16.80; and at thirteen £30.10. These rates are hardly generous; indeed, when the original study was published they were described by Tony Lynes as 'frugal to the point of inhumanity'. Nevertheless, comparison with benefits for children show how far short these fall in providing adquately for the costs of bringing up children. Child benefit (£7.25) is worth less than half the weekly costs for all but the youngest; for older children less than a quarter. Compared with the age-related children's additions to supplementary benefit – under eleven, £10.40; eleven to fifteen, £15.60; sixteen to seventeen, £18.75 – the inadequacy is equally apparent. As CPAG commented, there could be no substitute for a 'general overall increase in the children's scale rates, particularly in the case of larger families who are most vulnerable to poverty'.

Another change designed to help some unemployed families was the increase in the 'earnings disregard', that is, the amount of money which they were allowed to keep from part-time work before losing any benefit. On supplementary benefit the unemployed were allowed to earn only £4; under income support this rose to £5 until the claimant has been on benefit continuously for two years, in which case it rises to £15. For single parents the change is one which, like so many of the changes, looks fine at first sight but on closer inspection turns out, because of other changes, to be a loss in reality. Under supplementary benefit rules they were allowed to earn up to £12; on income support this rose to £15. The catch is that whereas under the old scheme all work expenses and child-care costs could be claimed for and set against earnings, under income support they cannot. The National Council for One Parent Families cites many instances in which lone parents on low incomes lose half their income in costs. Once again, the capacity for self-contradiction means rules which for some people will simply abolish the incentive to work.

As we have seen, the brunt of 'targeting' benefits on the most needy not only misses the target because take-up is so low, but the burden of payment has been borne by those families who are not quite so needy, namely all families who are not on income support. Thus low-income families who did not qualify for family credit but who had been eligible for local authority discretionary schemes for providing free school meals found that they too lost entitlement. In addition, about 200,000 families receiving free school meals, free welfare foods and help with school clothing under the discretionary powers of the local authorities also found that these were abolished without warning. No compensation was given. Families on family credit received compensation of 66p a day, but recent surveys of school meal prices show that this sum will not buy a meal in half the education authorites in England and Wales. The Association of Metropolitan Authorities denounced the decision to abolish the powers of local authorities to help poor families as 'a disgrace' – an act 'that has nothing whatever to do with the government. It must be fully within the right of the elected representatives of the community to decide what help the children of that community require.' Pointing out that the service ensured that every schoolchild in the country could have at least one 'hot, nutritious meal a day', it added: 'in successive moves this government has set out to destroy the service. Now it intends to price any sort of school meal out of the reach of thousands of those most in need.'

One of those families described the difference it would make:

Before this . . . became law I was getting . . . £16.25 a week school meals. . . . I'm a disabled miner who will never work again for the rest of my life . . . my wheelchair gets me out a bit and my disabled car . . . but what money I got to make life a bit better is all gone now because I got to pay for my childrens' clothes and shoes, also school meals.

Finally, the Green Paper put forward radical proposals for maternity benefits and maternity allowances. First, it proposed the abolition of the universal maternity grant of £25 (unchanged since 1969) as it 'has outlived its usefulness and makes only a minor contribution in most cases to the expenses of confinement'. Contribution conditions for the grant had been abolished in 1982, which was particularly welcome for those mothers with no contribution record. It was proposed that a maternity benefit of £75 would be paid to families on income support and family credit. The DHSS assessment of essential items for a new baby came to £121 in 1985 – excluding a cot, pram or carry cot. As the EOC pointed out, £75 'will not even match the amount received in 1983 by those mothers on supplementary benefit who received single payments of £60 or more in addition to their £25 grant'.

Not only was the level of the benefit too low, it would, as the SSAC pointed out, create its own 'trap' since many families would not find themselves on either benefit until after the baby was born. In the event, the amount of maternity benefit available to those on income support or family credit was fixed at £85, a ludicrously low amount, and even this is only for those mothers with less than £500 in savings; other mothers on the means-tested benefits receive no extra help.

The maternity allowance, then paid at a rate of £27.25 per week to expectant mothers with an adequate contribution record, was to remain, but conditions for eligibility were to change and the contribution record replaced by a 'test based more upon recent work and contributions'. No further details were given. In principle, this was yet another attempt to concentrate resources upon the most needy families, the effect of which was to exclude some mothers from benefit altogether.

The key criticism of both proposals is that they underlined the complete and historic failure of government to take seriously the need to support mothers during and after pregnancy. In 1980 a review of maternity benefits (which had led to the abolition of the contributory conditions to maternity benefit) did not properly examine the role they might play, the importance and the cost of a good diet during pregnancy, or the initial costs of a new-born baby. Like the death grant, the value of the maternity grant had been eroded over nearly two decades to the point where it no longer fulfilled its original task. This, instead of justifying a national policy which would, as in Sweden, have met the sudden and often incalculable expenses of a new-born child, was used instead to justify abolition.

Conclusion

The government's policies for the family were ambitious. The White Paper insisted that it was time for action:

> Social security is failing to give effective support to many of those in greatest need. All the evidence shows that low-income families with children need particular support. This applies to families where the parents are unemployed and to low-income working families. . . . The need is not for trimming but for proper reform.

As we have seen, the reforms have come nowhere near providing 'effective support'. In the case of hundreds of thousands of low-income working families, 'targeted' for special help, their incomes have actually been reduced. No wonder that figures published in September 1988 showed that only three out of ten eligible families took up family credit – far below the government's worst estimates. Ministerial appeals to show more spirit, independence and self-sufficiency have rightly shocked families who were told they would be better off, and have ended up worse off.

The argument, as Nicholas Scott put it in *The Times* on 8 March 1988, that the government 'is committed to strengthening and supporting family life and values' is hardest of all to reconcile now with the hostility to child benefit and the determination to freeze its value. Any switch to family credit will mean at best more families pushed on to means-tested benefits at a greater administrative cost to the state, and at worst that many if not most will simply not claim the help to which they are entitled. More than that, recalling his own experience as a social scientist looking at the effects of means tests in the 1930s, Professor Hans Singer in a letter to the *Independent* in November 1988 described how means tests reduce self-respect: 'Something is lost in the process, the value of which, though hard to assess, is considerable.' That loss of self-respect is something which women, in particular, will suffer as they apply as single parents, pensioners or widows for additional help. For all women, however, the social security reforms put a stop to the gradual improvement in principle and in practice that were won during the 1970s. The Green Paper contained but one reference to equal rights for women in social security, and not one attempt to build upon equal rights provisions or to use the European Commission's general commitment to equal rights in a positive way. This is hardly surprising, since the changes in social security which have affected women are only one of a number of related policies – spanning income support, employment and training – that have reduced opportunities and support for the least privileged women.

'Rolling back the state' has meant not only pushing people off national insurance benefits. It has meant that maternity and employment rights have been reduced as the conditions for part-time work have been made more stringent, as training opportunities have been reduced with the abolition of the Training and Opportunities Scheme (TOPS) and the Community Programme, that assistance with child care is vanishing in the inner cities in particular as cuts bite ever deeper into local authority provision, and as the powers of local authorities themselves are ever reduced. It means that the beginnings of pay equality, a proper regard for child health and maternity provision, the growing sense of the rights of lone parents and carers which had begun to emerge, albeit slowly and against much indifference, at the end of the 1970s came to a full stop and then went into reverse. At best, as the Fourth Report of the SSAC put it, the reforms failed to offer a comprehensive analysis

> of how the benefit and contribution systems ought to respond to social and economic change in this area; how to reconcile greater participation in the labour force and expectation of

equal treatment with the undoubted fact that women remain the principal carers, and because of the interruption in their working lives find their earning capacity reduced long after caring responsibilities have ceased.

Without that analysis and the strategic policies for social security geared to interrupted earnings, for maternity and child costs, for the child care, training and employment opportunities that need to be provided before earning and independence can become a reality, there is no hope of springing the poverty trap for women who cannot obtain or keep work or who are stuck in work at levels of low pay just below family credit limits – a situation guaranteed to entrench poverty. In child care family benefits Britain trails behind other European countries. Child care is left to market forces on the principle, as Edwina Currie put it, that 'parents who go out to work . . . should make appropriate arrangements and meet the costs' and only 2 per cent of children aged 0–4 are provided with private or public nursery places. Other countries do things differently.

In Denmark it is assumed that women *want* to work and a range of supportive services, including appropriate training and child care, are provided. In France there is a minimum guaranteed income for single parents, fixed at about 90 per cent of the minimum wage excluding child benefits. The majority of EC member states have some form of universal benefit which recognises the additional costs of pregnancy and childbirth, the necessity for a good diet and for good antenatal care. It is significant that, after many years of steady improvement, infant mortality figures in the UK are still among the worst in Europe.

Due to the government's failure to do anything other than try to improve income support, or to enforce maintenance as now seems likely, the future for single parents will be as bleak as the present, unless and until a new commitment is made to focus on the poverty of children in Britain irrespective of whether the parent is single from choice, death, divorce or separation. Universal maternity provision, geared to maternal and child health, would be the first and most obvious step towards welfare equality from birth. But if poverty is not to be handed down from one generation to the next comprehensive policies are required for employment, health, housing and child care. That means a new approach to family policy which focuses not simply on finding a better benefits system, but on tailoring opportunities to train and work, providing child care not merely in the community but tax-free at the workplace, developing new working patterns which accommodate the fact that men and women want to spend time with their families and find a new way of sharing family and working lives. That would ensure that the 1990s really do become 'the decade of working women'. Otherwise the words of one single mother, quoted in the *Observer* in April 1988, will be all too prophetic: 'I was brought up poor. I never thought it would go on for ever, on to my children and maybe now their children's children.'

4 Young People: 'Back to Mother' or 'Underneath the Arches'?

The preceding chapter dealt with the way that government policy has reflected views of family life, the relationship between work and family, the concept of 'incentives' for poor families in work and support for children in families out of work. This chapter looks at what the present government has done for and to young people, how they fit into the notions of family life and the need to 'target resources' and increase work incentives. The argument falls within the wider, important scope of the nation's need for a skilled, competent and qualified workforce.

It is hard to escape the conclusion that the young have been deliberately selected as easy targets in the assault against benefits. Unemployment, poverty and homelessness have become, for a minority of young people, tragically linked as their rights to independent income and housing benefits have been lost. In their place they have been offered policies that reflect not only an idealised notion of family life which for many youngsters simply does not exist, but an interpretation of their lives and motivation which puts them in the wrong from the start.

The official view is that young people must be specifically protected from absorbing the ethics of the 'benefit culture' and that this demands special measures. Those measures were prompted by the very increases in unemployment which forced up the cost of young people out of work. Thus, as the number of unemployed sixteen-to-eighteen-year-olds rose, from 148,000 in 1979 to a peak of 368,000 in 1984 (16 per cent of the total cohort) so successive cuts were planned and made in entitlement to benefit. The YTS was devised as a direct response to this, but also as a permanent training programme. It was recast in 1986 to last for two years and, simultaneously, a guarantee of a 'place' (not a specific place) was offered to pave the way for measures which in effect have made it compulsory in the sense that full-time and part-time work is discouraged. As the numbers of unemployed increased, from 3 per cent in 1979 to 10 per cent in 1985 and 15 per cent in 1987, so YTS was extended. By 1988, with the introduction of compulsory YTS, unemployment for the age group had fallen to 9 per cent.

The objectives of training and benefit initiatives in past decades have therefore not only been inextricably linked, they have proved mutually supportive of an objective to reduce the number of young persons on the unemployment register and eligible to claim benefit: an admirable objective had it been accompanied by training policies that had attempted to address the fundamental weaknesses in the provision made in Britain for youth and adult training, and for people in and out of work. There is a growing crisis in many manufacturing and service areas for technical, technological, engineering, educational and managerial skills. But as a series of recent reports from academic and national bodies confirm, YTS is neither meeting the acute skill shortages of today nor will it meet the future demand for qualified men and women. In effect, the training being offered risks tragically reproducing the cycle of low skills–no qualifications–low pay which has been the pattern of the past. It is a massive missed opportunity to challenge the known failures of the past, and it will give those nations which do things much more purposefully and successfully even more advantages.

In response to this deep and vexatious problem the response was not to challenge the culture and the cycle of industrial decline, but to 'blame the victim' – the unemployed worker. Rather than working with the best of industry, building up good practice and insisting upon jobs that carry training as a prerequisite, the easy, cheap way out has been the preferred option; YTS, the Job Training Scheme (JTS) and now Employment Training (ET) have been discredited by the failure to require a floor of educational and training skills upon which employees can build up their 'added value' and stay employable. Many young people, and now older workers, are coerced into jobs which specify 'training' but do not insist upon relevance, quality or standards and which carry no career plan or job guarantee. When one adds the assumption that the natural tendency among those out of work is

75

to stay out of work, the result is a set of policies that fails the nation as surely as it fails the individual.

The facts suggest that even at the height of unemployment only a minority of sixteen- and seventeen-year-olds were unemployed – and it can safely be assumed that most of them did not make poverty their first choice. The choice of what is 'best' for the individual is notoriously complicated. In 1986, before the introduction of compulsory YTS, 45 per cent of sixteen-year-olds were in some form of education, 26 per cent were on YTS, 19 per cent were employed and 10 per cent unemployed. For seventeen-year-olds the pattern was similar. The problem of how to raise incentives to ensure that all young people are motivated to do well has concerned successive governments since the early 1970s.

Rising unemployment in the late 1970s sharpened the issue of how to provide necessary financial help for young people out of work without reducing the incentives to stay on in school or to work. The choice between school after sixteen, further education, unemployment or low-paid work in turn raised complex questions about independence and maturity as well as family responsibility. It reveals the notoriously complicated area of overlapping rights and benefits, characterised over the past two decades by confused, sometimes contradictory political objectives. Supplementary benefits for those out of work, training allowances for those on YTS, child benefits, a random scatter of educational maintenance allowances for those in school to the age of nineteen, discretionary grants and statutory student grants for further and higher education are all available under different terms and conditions. Apart from a general determination to separate educational support for students from income support for young people out of work there has been no unifying or consistent principle or policy objective which would have imposed a definition of independence or which would have established rights to benefits and secured equity of status and income.

The confusion over benefits and training has been bleakly mirrored by the use of young people as a source of cheap labour. The Low Pay Unit has demonstrated how relative earnings have actually declined between the mid-1970s and 1988. Young men's wages, for example, fell from 40 to 36 per cent of the adult average wage over the same period.

By 1983, therefore, there was a long history of attempts to think through the tangle of provisions, and some thwarted initiatives (particularly the 1975 attempt by then Secretary of State Shirley Williams to introduce a pilot scheme of educational maintenance allowances) at reform. More urgent, however, and highlighted by acute unemployment for young people, was the need to reform a system which actually prevented them from taking up opportunities for further education and training.

In this critical area the Fowler reviews were a massive disappointment. They not only kept a complete silence on these fundamental issues but limited their initiatives to a new principle which would at one and the same time increase young people's dependence and reduce their living standards. The reviews proposed that those under twenty-five needed less benefit than those over twenty-five, couples with children included. This chapter examines some of the policies targeted on young people, and some of the consequences for them of the Fowler reforms.

Young People and Unemployment

In September 1988 the age of entitlement for state assistance (income support) was raised for the first time since 1948, from sixteen to eighteen. It was the final stage in the erosion of entitlement to unemployment benefits which began in November 1980. By May 1987 Youthaid, the charity specialising in assisting young people, estimated that in the previous seven years benefits paid to young people had been cut on fourteen separate occasions, producing a total saving of £200 million.

The first cut in benefit, in November 1980, had deferred the payment of supplementary benefit for school leavers until the start of the new academic term, affecting 500,000 and saving £29 million. In April 1983 and April 1984 the addition paid to young people to pass on to their families with whom they were living was abolished, first for sixteen- and seventeen-year-olds, then for eighteen-to-twenty-year-olds. Some 460,000 families lost over £3 a week. Another cut in housing benefit came in 1984 when the 'non-dependant deductions' (i.e. an amount deducted from housing benefit to represent money theoretically coming into the family from a young person) was raised for sixteen-to-twenty-year-olds, and 30,000 families each lost about £3 a week, saving £43 million. In 1985 more cuts followed when the new 'board and lodgings payments' were introduced. These are discussed in more detail later.

Compulsory training has effectively removed remaining rights to benefit for those under eighteen. It was first proposed in 1981 by then Secretary of State for Employment, Norman Tebbit. The case was lost at first, however, not just because both employers and trade unions argued that it would defeat the purpose of training, but because the Manpower Services Commission (MSC) itself argued that linking compulsory training to the abolition of benefit was both unnecessary and undesirable. Government gave in but Tebbit laid down a marker for the future, saying: 'We still believe that these young people should not be entitled to supplementary benefits in their own right.' In response to this threat, in 1982 and 1984 the SSAC made its case against the loss of benefit forcibly, insisting in the latter report that

> an independent right to supplementary benefit remains a necessary support for 16 year olds. We acknowledge the Government's belief that families should take more responsibility for supporting teenage children who are not yet in work but in the midst of the current recession we are very conscious that many families would find this a considerable strain.

The Green Paper on the Reform of Social Security was introduced at the same time as government plans to reform YTS and to extend it to two years. No changes were proposed to the eligibility of young unemployed people for supplementary benefit – to the disappointment of some Tory MPs. Ralph Howells, who had popularised the notion of the 'Why work? syndrome', urged the government to 'offer young people the discipline of training or national service' and 'take away the option of receiving benefit and doing nothing'. The absence of a work test was, he said, 'the reason why the cost of supplementary benefit has got totally out of hand. . . . What is wrong with compulsion? Each child over the age of five is compelled to go to school. Why is compulsion so evil when a person becomes sixteen?'

The argument for compulsion was undermined by the fact that the existing regulations gave the Secretary of State considerable power to reduce benefit to young people who chose not to take up a YTS place. In practice, the numbers who had their benefit reduced were tiny. Between December 1983 and May 1987, 25,697 people had lost benefit under the existing regulations for refusing the offer of a place for no good reason; of those, 23,453 were 'early leavers', that is, they failed to complete the course. Only 2244 had actually refused an offer of a place. As the Social Security Consortium commented,

> During this same period more than one million young people entered the YTS. There are no indications that these regulations are not being implemented. In the light of these figures the all-encompassing scope of this legislation (which affects an age group including around 1.4 million young people) seems totally out of proportion to the size of the problem.

The two most common reasons for not going into YTS given to the Youthaid Survey 'Nothing Like a Job' were the low level of the allowance and the fear of exploitation by employers. When asked what would change their mind, the most common reply was 'the guarantee of a job'.

Such evidence did not, however, fit the stereotype that, given a chance, the young would opt for idleness and poverty, as Industry Secretary Lord Young made clear in May 1987 when he emphasised that the state could not be expected to pay benefits to young people who 'lay in bed' after consistently refusing places on YTS. The Conservative manifesto made it clear that it would offer a carrot in place of benefits – a guaranteed YTS place to every school leaver under eighteen who was not going directly into a job – and, consequently, steps would be taken 'to ensure that those under eighteen who deliberately choose to remain unemployed are not eligible for benefit'. This would save about £95 million in a full year, some of which would be offset against increased expenditure on the YTS and by extending child benefit for four months after the school leaving date to allow young people not wanting to move on to YTS to take a job.

When the Employment and Social Security Bills were published in autumn 1987, a punitive tone had become strident. The changes, said the DHSS, were 'designed to avoid the damaging effects of young people moving straight from school into the benefit culture', and the Department of Employment continued: 'The only option which is being taken away from young people is the option to spurn the offer of a training place and live on benefit. That is not a good option. With the growth in the number of jobs and the guarantee of a YTS place for every unemployed school leaver, that option is no longer necessary.'

Given the dedication with which the government has kept to this policy it is legitimate to ask whether the two-year YTS scheme will in fact offer the high skills and qualifications British industry is now demanding with increasing anxiety. Will it solve the problem of skill shortages in the short term? In the long term will it raise the technical competence and utility of the British workforce? Does it provide the real incentives to employers faced with a shrinking labour pool of school leavers to make training an automatic part of every job offered – whether that training takes a place in colleges of further education or on the shop floor or in the office itself? Does it reward the good employer by increasing its reservoir of company skills, or give the bad employer an opportunity for job substitution and cheap labour? It is legitimate to point out that no additional money was put into a scheme which now lasts for two years, not one; that both placement and monitoring of schemes are notoriously haphazard; that no particular care has been taken to determine the specific skills or training needs of young women or ethnic groups; that employers are free to mop up young unskilled labour without any formal requirement to train them – and, as demography works for the employer, that will become an increasingly powerful trend.

The outlook is not optimistic. Recent reports confirm serious reservations about the quality, effectiveness and relevance of the training on offer. The key criticism is that YTS is offering sporadic training in low-level skills, with only a 'handful' of people trained to craft level and with no route to the qualifications, skill mobility and career choice that individuals, companies and services really need. Given that the other routes to qualification have been closed this presents a grave diagnosis for the future. The estimated ten thousand sixteen- and seventeen-year-olds who are studying part time for 'A' levels or a Business and Technical Education Council Diploma under the '21-hour rules', which allowed them to study for up to twenty-one hours a week and still be deemed available for work, are now disqualified from doing so. Thus, while there is still no educational incentive to stay in school, the practical educational disincentive to part-time study has now increased. Youthaid and the British Youth Council argued:

This is an important option for young people from low income families where the cost of maintaining the young person in full-time education can be prohibitive. Removing this option by making unemployed teenagers ineligible for benefit will reinforce the financial disincentive for some young people to stay in full-time education.

The SSAC itself has said that 'the benefit system is not fully geared to helping young people make the right choices in this area'. Similarly, Youthaid stated that: 'For young people whose families cannot afford to keep them in full-time education, and who want to study for A levels or equivalents, the option of studying on the dole is an essential one. Removing it would impair, rather than improve, the chances of teenagers finding work.'

Will the YTS scheme help young people find jobs? Again, the answer is – it depends what jobs you mean. As demography works to create demand for school leavers over the next decade it will become easier for the teenager to drift into work straight from school – but with no guarantee of training. Traditionally, the teenage job market is extremely volatile and exploitative. Young people under eighteen, for example, are more than twice as likely to become unemployed within any three months; one in four teenagers in work is in a part-time job, half of which are temporary. All these people, starting work at sixteen and losing or changing jobs before they are eighteen, now run the risk of disqualification from benefit. The Low Pay Unit has expressed its fear that the disqualification will merely serve to 'turn the young into a conscript army of cheap labour, either because they will take jobs without prospects immediately on leaving schools rather than go into YTS, or because, rather than looking for jobs with prospects and training they will go into YTS where training will be inferior and often irrelevant'. Finally, was it necessary to abolish these rights to benefits in order to restrain abuse? The position before the Act came into effect was quite clear. A school leaver who refused a place on YTS without 'good cause' could be disqualified from claiming unemployment benefit and would then suffer a 40 per cent reduction in supplementary benefit for up to thirteen weeks. As we have seen from the figures already quoted, this had already proved an effective deterrent.

Board and Lodgings

Apart from finding work, the key issue for most young people is finding somewhere to live. The present housing market's extremely high entry point excludes the majority of young people; but for a minority the question is not when or how to get on the housing escalator, but where to find and how to pay for the most basic shelter – a bed for a night or a week or, crucially, a period long enough to look for a job. These young people have joined those who are by temperament and tradition the displaced persons of urban life. As unemployment and poverty have fractured families the ranks of those looking for temporary housing have swollen. In London 51,000 people between sixteen and nineteen are estimated to be technically homeless: 1000 are in hostels, 1800 in board and lodgings, 2000 squat, 900 are in short-life properties and 45,300 live in other households and want their own home.

Of this group, those who seek board and lodgings are in a particularly vulnerable minority. While there are no national statistics it has been estimated that 15,000 people were living in bed and breakfast accommodation in 1986, most of them young and single. Technically they are eligible for weekly 'board and lodgings payments' but in the past five years this entitlement has been reduced along with rates of benefit.

Before 1983 board and lodgings payments were awarded on the basis of what was considered 'reasonable' for the local area, including an allowance for meals and expenses, with an element of discretion where charges were higher. Since 1983, as changes in supplementary benefit and housing benefit rules have taken money away from 'non-householders' and 'dependants' so that they have become less able to meet family housing costs, and as regional unemployment has forced more and more young people south – particularly into London – controlling board and lodgings costs has become another test of the government's ability to cut public expenditure, deter the 'work shy' and control abuse. The problem is that the cost of board and lodgings, which spiralled from £52 million to £166 million between 1979 and 1982, has been fuelled primarily not by the increased demand from young people, although that has risen, but by the huge increase in the provision and the cost of private residential homes for elderly people, which have traditionally been governed by the same regulations.

There was clearly a case for preventing profiteering in the private sector and, equally clearly, there was exploitation within some of the special hostels provided for young people. But within the general mythology of the 'Why work? syndrome' a special place was reserved for the young 'work shy', who were felt to be enjoying endless seaside holidays, being supported at rates far higher than they would have enjoyed had they stayed at home.

In November 1983 the DHSS made a fatal error in replacing the local offices' discretionary powers to meet costs with official 'maximum limits' for nursing homes, residential homes and board and lodgings in general. The result was immediate and dramatic: charges predictably rose to meet the maximum, resulting in a threefold increase in the costs of the residential sector. The following November, claiming increasing evidence of abuse and an increase of 60 per cent in the number of under twenty-fives receiving board and lodgings payments, a consultative document proposed two national limits for residential care and nursing homes and six area limits for ordinary board and lodgings.

There were other new sanctions. Couples who had been receiving twice the single person's rate would now receive only one and a half or even one and a quarter times it; young people under seventeen would not be eligible for board and lodgings payments if they stayed within their 'local area' but would be treated as 'non-householders', thereby getting a very much lower rate of benefit, one that would certainly not enable them to live independently. Unemployed people under twenty-five without dependants who claimed benefit outside their local area would be able to claim only for two, four or eight weeks, depending on where they claimed, after which they would move to another area or receive the lower rate of 'non-householder' benefit.

The second sanction reaffirmed the notion of 'dependence' by making it unrealistic for many youngsters to leave home at all and was the initial step toward withdrawing benefit for all sixteen- and seventeen-year-olds; the third reintroduced the concept of 'parish boundaries' and 'parish responsibilities' powerfully reminiscent of the Victorian Poor Law.

The assumptions and the proposals set out in the consultative document were greeted with a storm of protest. The SSAC received 500 submissions, the majority of them hostile, protesting that rising costs were not the fault of a new and feckless generation of young scroungers but the result of cutting housing investment and building, the decline of rented property, rising house prices, selling council houses and rising youth unemployment. It was also pointed out that the estimated percentage increase in average payments for board and lodgings charges had been just 9 per cent in 1984 – hardly enough to justify major cuts. Forcing sixteen- and seventeen-year-olds back upon their families was likely in some cases to be catastrophic. The SSAC itself argued that the regulation would create 'a class of homeless and rootless young people who are unable to return to the parental home and who cannot remain long enough in any one location to find permanent accommodation or a job'. Finally, the time limits on benefits outside the local area would inevitably make it difficult for people to find and keep a job.

The final regulations established 132 local 'board and lodgings areas' within six national 'limits'. In Greater London, for example, the limit was £70 a week; in Torquay it was £50. The time limit for claimants under twenty-five was eight weeks in Greater London, two weeks in seaside resorts and four weeks elsewhere.

In July 1985 the High Court ruled that the government had exceeded its powers in creating local areas and setting time limits to benefit. The DHSS was forced to suspend the operation of the time limits. It tried again. This time the Statutory Instruments Committee of the House of Commons cast doubt upon their legality. In November 1985 new regulations were introduced, this time legally, but in December the earlier judgement was upheld on appeal and all those who had been denied board and lodgings benefit between April and November were reimbursed.

If the DHSS had created problems for itself, it had created many more for young claimants. Apart from the fact that the local limits had been set unrealistically low in relation to real market rents, so that by 1986 65 per cent of hostels below the limits had no vacancies, the policy, designed to increase work incentives and discourage the 'work shy', had made it even more difficult for young people to find jobs. A NACAB report commissioned in July 1986 showed how the short-stay time limits made it almost impossible for young people to find jobs in the time allowed. The South Tyneside CAB, for example, pointed out that the chances of finding work in a borough which had one of the highest unemployment rates in the country verged on the 'impossible'. Given that there was little work within reasonable travelling distance, young people were forced to move away; moving from one area to another after four weeks helped them neither to find work nor to maintain any stability within the community. The Letchworth CAB reported:

> We have had enquiries made by young people affected by the new regulations. They find themselves in the position of having to leave lodgings where they have been able to settle with a caring landlord and landlady following family upheavals. Unable to return they will have to move to another area where they may know no one and from where they shall have to move again within a few weeks.

'We all accept', said NACAB, that 'there are people who abuse the DHSS, but why do these young people have to be treated in this abhorrent manner?'

It was not as if many of them could return home. One Scottish bureau observed that in almost all the cases referred to it, young people had left home 'because all the adult members were unemployed' and the atmosphere was intolerable. NACAB observed that in general such young people 'have moved from the parental home in order to begin an independent life free from a violent, overcrowded, fraught or unhappy home'. The option to return home was 'neither feasible nor wise'. That evidence was confirmed by a combined report from many of the groups concerned with homelessness among young people published in *Enforcing Vagrancy* (West End Co-ordinated Voluntary Services, July 1986). This survey found that 12 per cent of young people making use of the groups' services had been in care; 55 per cent had no homes to which they could return; 34 per cent were from broken homes or had no contact with living relatives or no relationship with their parents. Such people 'would have been most unwelcome if they had made any attempts to return'. Five months after the sample had been taken, 14 per cent were still homeless. Danger, lack of privacy, lack of information about their rights to exemption from the legislation, appalling conditions, all were catalogued, as were the options 'being forced on more and more people – squatting, or sleeping rough'. The survey concluded: 'The assumptions lying behind the legislation can be seen from this survey as from others, to have been simply wrong. The young people who were affected are shown to have had no other choice open to them but the accommodation from which they were so unceremoniously removed.'

A more recent survey conducted by the Centrepoint Night Shelter among those using the shelter confirms that the 'push' factors (pressure or compulsion to leave home) accounted for about 44 per cent, while the 'pull' factors – looking for a job or wanting to live in London – accounted for 52 per cent. Of those who were 'pushed' nearly half were told to leave home or were evicted. Forced into vagrancy these young people were, according to Citizens' Advice Bureaux (CABx) across the country, at risk from 'criminality, prostitution, unwanted pregnancy'. Put at its most graphic, the Scunthorpe CAB described a vagrant army of young people, modern journeymen for the most part but without the skills to sell, tramping on every four weeks to another town, and another set of lodgings:

> a pitiful cycle is emerging. People from Grimsby forced from hard-found lodgings leave for Scunthorpe to search for lodgings, passing their counterparts moving the other way, knowing that within months the migration will be repeated. Surely in administrative terms this cannot be cost-effective and in human terms is sad beyond belief.

The DHSS had committed itself to monitoring the regulations. In June 1986 DHSS minister Tony Newton announced that there would be no general increase in the financial limits, but the limit for couples would be restored to twice the single limit, and those people under twenty-five who had been in ordinary board and lodgings before 25 November 1985 would be indefinitely exempt from the time limits. New claimants would, however, continue to observe them.

April 1988: Board and Lodgings and the Social Security Changes

Enforced vagrancy has become a way of life for many young people since November 1985. But according to the Board and Lodgings Information Programme (BLIP), which includes voluntary bodies such as the Central London Social Security Advisers, the Campaign for the Homeless and Rootless (CHAR), the housing campaign groups for single people, Shelter and others, the board and lodgings regulations have not encouraged young people to remain in the parental home; nor have they forced hotel prices down. The numbers of young people homeless in London have steadily grown since 1985 and in 1985–6 only fifteen hotels in London offered a single room below the DHSS maximum of £7 a night. Thus 'rather than remaining in overcrowded intolerable parental homes or wandering from one board and lodging area to another, homeless people in London are electing to remain in London'. Many people, according to BLIP, have simply 'disappeared'.

More recently, however, another twist to the no-home, no-job spiral for young people has actually added to their problems. Among the relatively minor administrative changes consequent on 'tidying up' social security in the Social Security Act 1986 was a change from paying board and lodgings in advance (so giving the young person cash in hand for a bed for the night or the week) to paying in arrears. This has had a devastating effect. In June 1988 the plight of one group of young homeless people at the Centrepoint Night Shelter in London came to public attention when it was revealed that there had been a 36 per cent increase in calls for night shelter places since the change in April. Few landlords are prepared to risk taking on a new lodger on the promise of money to come, so now many young people cannot even get into the few places that are prepared to take them. Knowing the problems they will face, young people are reluctant to move out if they have secure accommodation, and gradually, the options decline.

On 7 June 1988 in the House of Commons Neil Kinnock asked the Prime Minister whether she would change the regulations to ensure that young people could receive money in advance to obtain lodgings. Her answer was instructive:

> It is true that a number of young people are leaving home who would not have done so in previous circumstance. . . . the Government are indeed doing a great deal to tackle homelessness. The total support for housing is very much larger. . . . We also have a hostels initiative with 14,700 places approved since April 1981 to benefit young single homeless and others.

Kinnock replied:

> That answer can only mean that the Prime Minister is willing to see huge numbers of young people at risk from crime, prostitution and even hunger. Does she not realise that in London alone there are 50,000 young homeless people without secure accommodation, that the hostels are packed and that there are one million fewer places to rent than there were at the beginning of the decade? Is she willing to see a new generation of street people increasing, or will she answer the first question I asked and change the regulations to revert to the original position so that these young people can get money, lodgings, jobs and look after themselves?

Prime Minister: 'No Mr Speaker . . . there are now 1.6 million more housing units than there were eight years ago.' This response – in effect that there was housing for those who could afford and obtain access to it – satisfied very few. However, such was the publicity given to the absurdity of the new regulations that they were slightly modified – to enable benefit to be paid not two weeks but one week in arrears.

In the autumn of 1988 came further changes when the payment of £10 per person per night made by the DHSS to the London overnight shelters was threatened with abolition. The campaign to ensure that this vital income for the hostels was not lost was led by Centrepoint, which stood to lose 30 per cent of its income. It emphasised that in caring for 1000 sixteen- and seventeen-year-olds each year it was not only sheltering them in emergency, it was actually helping them establish themselves with employers and placing them in training – thus assisting the government to fulfil its guarantee that everyone should have a YTS place. To lose 30 per cent of its income would mean that the shelter and others like it would close, leaving young vagrants with nowhere at all to turn to. The Prime Minister replied that there was a YTS place for everyone, and that 'special hardship payments' were also available. The first assertion was challenged by the fact that in November 1988 there were 4000 young people without YTS places in Scotland alone and, throughout Britain, a possible 20,000 who had not been placed. The second assertion was qualified by the fact that young people had made only 1200 claims for income support 'special hardship'. Of these, 802 had been awarded, indicating that claims had been justified. The Prime Minister did not agree that a special advertising campaign should be mounted to ensure that young people knew of their entitlement to special hardship allowances.

The Fowler Reviews and the Under-twenty-fives

To appreciate the full significance of the specific campaigns for compulsory training and enforced dependence, they must be seen as part of the broad campaign to reduce the benefit levels of those under twenty-five. Forty years after Beveridge, the tangle of principles governing the range of income support for young people had reached baroque complexity. Two 'key issues' for the review team considering children and young persons were age limits and entitlement, and how to introduce rational principles and equity into the award of benefits to young people of the same age but not in work. As the House of Commons Social Services Committee put it, the Green Paper was 'surprisingly quiet about the sixteen–seventeen age group, particularly considering that one of the Reviews was specifically considering the benefits made to young people above school leaving age'. The only specific proposal in the Green Paper was that everyone under twenty-five should receive a lower rate of benefit. This was in part a direct consequence of the decision to abolish the distinction between householders and non-householders, on the grounds that it was increasingly difficult to administer the rules on household status, and that in practice the majority of people under twenty-five were not householders whereas 90 per cent of those over twenty-five did live independently.

As a result of this change, since April 1988 single young people under twenty-five receive £7 less than their equivalents over twenty-five, and those who are householders receive a minimum of £4 less. This final change in status and entitlement marks the logical conclusion to the twin policies of reducing or abolishing income support and housing benefits for young people, reflected in the policies described above. The original proposal had been even more brutal; that *all* young people under twenty-five, including couples with children, should receive the lower rate of benefit. This proposal was greeted with disbelief and, as the White Paper later conceded, 'widespread criticism'. Among the government's most severe critics was the Social Services Committee of the House of Commons, which pointed out that:

> The proposed over 25/under 25 divide seems to reintroduce the householder/non-householder distinction. The choice of the age of 25 . . . is inevitably arbitrary. Mr Newton pointed out that the 'vast majority' of under 25s now receive the lower non-householder rate, many of them with dependants; they represent 30 per cent of all 18–25 year olds receiving supplementary benefit. Under the proposals as they now stand a parent aged under 25 with children would get less in total than a parent aged 25. . . . There is no evidence that their needs are any fewer . . .

In a similar vein the Fourth Report of the SSAC argued with some acerbity that 'the benefit system cannot duck the fact that householders of all ages do have genuine additional responsibilities which the present arrangements attempt to recognise financially. Pointing out that 32 per cent of people aged between eighteen and twenty-four were householders, and that this proportion rose to 50 per cent for those aged between twenty-one and twenty-four, and to 58 per cent for all twenty-four-year-olds, it added that it could see no justification for regarding twenty-five 'as an adequate proxy for the assumption of householder status and responsibilities'. The clinching argument was that this distinction would prejudice the welfare of children in young families, and was hardly in line with the government's concern for the family. It was also inconsistent in that the higher rate of benefit would be available to single parents under twenty-five.

The government backed down, acknowledging the overwhelming arguments against the proposal. It was not, however, prepared to do any more for those youngsters who might have special needs. Youthaid estimated that there were about 10,000 vulnerable young householders, including some 8000 who had left care to move into independent accommodation. It suggested a special 'young householder's premium' for them, arguing that these claimants 'would come from those young people who were forced to live independently because of abuse or violence they had experienced in the family home, or because they had had no family home in the first place'. Such a premium, it was estimated, would cost about £3 million a year. An Early Day Motion attracted all-party support from over a hundred MPs but was rejected by the government. Youthaid commented that its proposed premium would fit the government's often stated purpose of its social security reforms, by giving 'extra money to vulnerable young householders who lived independently because they had nowhere to go . . . surely they would accept the need to protect the position of young people brought up in care, or other vulnerable groups, whose independent accommodation is all that they have?'

The government refused Youthaid's appeal. There is no young householder's premium, and as the latest changes on board and lodgings show, young people who cannot or will not stay in the family home are finding it more and more difficult to find places to live. The policies have made it harder for young people to leave home and mean, therefore, enforced dependence upon families in the most unsympathetic and ultimately destructive ways. In the experience of one single parent:

. . . when my son reached eighteen and managed to get a job (£50 a week less tax) the council said he had to pay them £10.60 a week. He already had to pay me £20 a week (the amount DHSS stopped for him). He couldn't afford it – so he had to leave home and live rough for a while. Can you imagine what it was like to throw out your own son. It nearly killed me. . . .

Now the April changes have stopped his rent allowances. He pays £33 per week board and lodging, minus £10 fares and is left with £3.60 a week. I've told him to go on the dole. But he wants to work. So much for an equal society. But if Poll Tax comes into force think of the effect on thousands like him. People will be made homeless as others won't take in lodgers for the amount of Poll Tax. There's enough homeless already.

There's no future for the ordinary person under this Government.

At the same time, particularly for young people who have known little family life at all, a life of enforced vagrancy with no hope of independent, affordable housing actually robs them of their rights as citizens. As NACAB put it:

these citizenship issues include losses in respect of
- contact with family and friends
- useful job contacts
- family GP and other local medical services
- part-time and evening education
- access to children of separated parents
- council waiting list allocation
- eligibility to vote.

Again, the striking impression of this part of the Fowler reviews is that of an opportunity wilfully and disastrously wasted. Instead of a positive search for ways of extending opportunities for further education, qualifications, and independent housing, young people have been subjected to a punitive philosophy and to the practical consequences of cuts in housing investment and in housing benefit. Indeed, young, single people have been deliberately excluded from transitional protection concessions on housing benefit. It has been said of the First World War that it was the revenge of the old men on the young, and there is an unmistakable flavour of a similar vindictiveness in the policies for youngsters implemented by successive ministers. Youthaid sums it up:

The results of this are not difficult to imagine. Rent and rates arrears will grow; more young people will turn to loan sharks to dig themselves out of a deepening hole; housing single childless people will become a very unattractive proposition to local authorities and housing associations and young people unable to manage on inadequate benefit levels will face eviction proceedings for unpaid rent and rates. Presumably the Government imagines this will mean back to mother. More likely it will mean going under the arches.

In March 1989, prompted by public concern at the growing numbers of homeless young people, the government finally took action to help the small group of teenagers 'genuinely estranged' from their parents by extending income support to them at the rates awarded for eighteen-to-twenty-four-year-olds – but only for 12–16 weeks after leaving school. Their entitlement will then cease on the assumption that they will have found a YTS place or a job. Young people in night shelters will be given automatic consideration under the severe hardship provisions.

Although this was a welcome decision to put right one wrong, the cycle of poverty, unemployment and homelessness is hardly challenged by minor modifications to the benefits system. As the Association of County Councils, providers of emergency help, recently put it in evidence to the Social Services Select Committee the overwhelming need is 'to provide adequate benefit'. Many young people on YTS placements are forced to seek local assistance because they cannot survive independently on YTS allowances. They are more fortunate than those who appear to be 'sans home, sans work, sans everything'. In their destitution these young people bring the images of Victorian London to life again – and, in doing so, provide another and more grotesque representation of Victorian values.

5   Poverty and Disability 1979–88

I warn you not to fall sick.

(Neil Kinnock, Bridgend, 1983)

In any barometer of need the chronically sick and
disabled and those who care for them must stand near
the top . . . We do have a special responsibility to them
and it is a responsibility we shall meet.

(John Major, Conservative Party Conference, 7 October 1986)

In September 1988 the government received the unwelcome news
that the number of disabled people in Britain was not three million
(the previous estimate based on Amelia Harris's survey in 1971)
but six million – 14 per cent of all adults living in private
households. The Office of Population Censuses and Surveys
(OPCS) survey, the most detailed ever made, presents a stark
picture of poverty and disability increasing with age. The majority
of those in the survey, particularly the more severely disabled,
suffer from more than one type of disability, of which the most
common are difficulties with walking, hearing and personal care.
Seventy per cent of all disabled adults were aged sixty or over, and
nearly half were seventy or over. In the two most severely disabled
categories, 64 per cent were aged over seventy. There are more
disabled women than men, not merely because women live longer
but because they are more likely to be disabled than men. The
question is: What will the government do? The answer, on the
experience of ten years in office, is: very little that will help.

In the rhetoric of Thatcherism people with disabilities have
been awarded a clear role at the apex of the 'deserving' poor. It is
not a distinction which they or those who represent them have

sought or welcomed. At the same time however, the emphasis on self-help, self-sufficiency and getting on suggests that government policies for disabled people would concentrate on policies which would promote skills and increase opportunity, access to work, and income at home or in work. The Conservative manifesto promised as much when it made clear that the aim was 'to provide a coherent system of cash benefits to meet the cost of disability so that more disabled people can support themselves and live normal lives. We shall work towards this as swiftly as the strength of the economy allows.'

This has proved to be hope betrayed at the highest level. In practice, the political rhetoric has borne a double insult. Invocations of self-help must bring a particular despair to those who would give anything to be able to help themselves, but these strictures have been made worse by so often being accompanied by appeals to political responsibility which have served to underline the loss of benefits, rights and services, all of which have been reduced. In July 1982 Hugh Rossi, Minister for the Disabled, made the priorities clear: 'There were simply not the available resources for major improvements in benefits and services for disabled people. Nor could [they] . . . be entirely sheltered from the effects of high unemployment.' The changes which followed this highly ambiguous, and as it turned out, ominous statement are the subject of this chapter. To understand their significance a brief account of the benefits available to disabled people is necessary.

Poverty and Disablement

The deficiencies of the system lie deep in its architecture. Because disabled people find it more difficult to find and keep work they are bound to be poorer. Because a disabled child or adult needs care and attention in the home, there is less opportunity for other members of the family to work; because disabilities bring extra needs – for heating, diet, laundry, help in the home – they bring extra costs. Because elderly people are more likely than younger people to be disabled, they are at greater risk and in greater need. That none of these key features which link disablement with poverty is properly covered in present policies explains both the problem of the current system of dealing with disabilities, and the urgent need for reform.

Inefficiencies have accumulated over the years as attempts have been made to fill the gaps and strengthen the structure. The result is that seeking compensation for sickness and disability has been described as 'like playing roulette with a loaded wheel'. Employment, age, marital status, sex, cause of disability, degree of dysfunction – all can affect entitlement and amount of benefit. In particular, the means-tested benefits, such as mobility or attendance allowance, and those which depend on assessment of severity of disablement, such as the severe disablement allowance and industrial disablement, abound with Jesuitical definitions that cause irrational and arbitrary decisions. How far, and how easily, can a person 'walk'? What governs this 'disability' – physical or mental incapacity? What is the meaning of 'attendance' during the night? How much is the loss of a little finger worth? How competently or how easily can a woman cook a meal? These and many other questions and the answers to them have dominated and ultimately determined the lives of those who for whatever reason find themselves on benefit. Despite every help, claiming can be a humiliating and unsuccessful process. And many who are entitled do not know the range of help available or the best choice to make.

The scope and complexity of the system can be measured by the range of benefits available. Some are 'contributory' (i.e. national insurance benefits such as invalidity benefit, paid to people who are in work). Some are non-contributory (e.g. severe disablement allowance) and go to people who are chronically sick and unable to work. Some are long-term benefits (e.g. disablement benefits), some short-term (sickness benefits). Some are awarded according to the cause of the disability (e.g. war pensions, industrial injuries benefit, criminal injuries compensation); some are for special purposes and are means-tested (attendance allowance, mobility allowances, invalid care allowance). Some measure disability on a percentage basis and assume a related degree of incapacity (e.g. industrial disablement benefit); others are related to age; yet others are paid at a standard rate. Underlying the system are the income support provisions (formerly supplementary benefit) upon which millions of people rely in whole or in part. The result has been an unstable tower of overlapping benefits and layers of assistance, with each new benefit or condition threatening to overload the system.

Latest figures suggest that about a million people receive invalidity benefit; 128,000 are in sickness benefit; 261,000 receive severe disability allowance; 641,000 receive attendance allowance, 541,000 receive mobility allowance; 184,000 receive industrial disablement pension; 203,000 receive war pension. 300,000 long-term sick and disabled people under pension age are on supplementary benefit; and just under a million disabled pensioners claim income support.

The distinctions made between cause of disability and degrees of disability have led to a massive range of incomes between people in virtually identical conditions. War and industrial injuries have traditionally commanded higher benefits. On balance the OPCS estimate that the main benefits for disabled people provide an income of about two-fifths of average earnings.

Until 1942 even those with legitimate expectations of state assistance had only limited, uneven and often arbitrary assistance. The Beveridge Report provided universal coverage for those in work, a guaranteed system of flat-rate contributions and preferential benefits for industrial injuries and sickness benefit, but it also maintained the link between need and 'cause' and linked the loss of faculty to a percentage scale of benefit fixed in steps from 20 to 100 per cent. This 'marked a departure not only from the basis of workman's compensation but also from the principles still followed today in industrial injuries schemes in nearly all other countries'.

A fundamental weakness of the scheme was the lack of provision for those who were outside the labour market. Women, in particular, are placed at a disdvantage in a contributory system, and for disabled people there were no rights for those who could and would never work for whatever reason, whether because they were themselves chronically sick or disabled as children or as adults, or because they were carers. There was no provision for those who were 'long-term sick'. Once sickness benefit had expired claimants passed directly on to means-tested benefits. Finally, none of the available help provided for the additional costs of disablement.

During the late 1960s and early 1970s, inspired in part by the evidence of Amelia Harris's 1971 *Report on Handicapped and Impaired People in Great Britain*, which identified three million disabled people, a start was made under the Labour government and a new Minister for the Disabled on extending the national insurance scheme to the long-term sick by way of an 'invalidity benefit' based on the government's White Paper *National Superannuation and Social Insurance*. It was based on entitlement to sickness benefit, and was accompanied by an earnings-related sickness benefit scheme. Invalidity benefit was designed as a long-term benefit which would carry dependency additions for children and spouses and which would transfer, on the age of retirement, to an invalidity pension with an earnings-related addition. The plan was implemented by the incoming Conservative government in 1971, together with an attendance allowance for severely disabled people who needed a great deal of care in the home.

At the same time, steps were taken to bring out-of-work disabled people within the 'membership of the national insurance community'. In 1975 a non-means-tested benefit for people of working age but incapable of work was introduced, the non-contributory invalidity pension (NCIP). The implicit goal was to reduce the number of long-term sick and disabled people dependent on supplementary benefits. In due course this benefit was extended to disabled housewives. In 1975 the mobility allowance was introduced to help meet the costs of personal transport, and in 1976 the invalid care allowance was established to meet the needs of those who gave up work to care for disabled people. The significance of these changes was not only that they commanded all-party support but that they reinforced the national insurance basis of the benefit system, recognising the rights of disabled people to belong to the 'national insurance community'. A start was also made on identifying the particular needs of carers and the costs of disability. But the complexity of the range of benefits and, in particular, the means-tested benefits brought many new problems. They made only a modest step towards what was increasingly seen as the overwhelming case for a rational, comprehensive disability income. Work had already begun on developing such a scheme when the Conservative government came into office in 1979.

The 'Disastrous Years': 1980–3

Conservatives have singled out the disabled for priority
within the social security budget.

(Conservative Research Department, *Politics Today*,
February 1979)

A year before the 1979 election, Patrick Jenkin expressed the hope
that the Conservative manifesto would 'point the way towards a
more rational pattern of help for disabled people, with a central
aim of helping people to help themselves, wherever possible'. In
1979 he became the first Secretary of State for Health and Social
Security and the chief axeman of the social services. He was
assisted in this by the first Conservative Minister for the Disabled,
Reg Prentice, who on 19 March 1980 had assured the House of
Commons that, 'when asked whether I am in favour of a general
disability income, I give the emphatic answer "Yes" '. One of his
first acts in office, however, was to stop work in preparation well
before the election, on a comprehensive new benefit. The reason?
'It would raise false hopes if we entered into detailed discussions
now on the format of an allowance which could not possibly
materialise for some years.' Disabled people could not escape the
new economic realism. While a disablement income was 'still our
aim. . . we cannot start planning the way forward until we have
achieved our first objective which is to beat inflation and revitalise
the economy. There is simply no money available at present to
introduce any new benefits or allowances or to alter the qualifying
conditions for existing ones.' Instead, in 1980 people on disability
benefits found that their existing benefits, far from being
increased, had been targeted for cuts.

There were several related strategies carried within the two
social security bills introduced in 1980, each designed to make
savings and reduce national insurance coverage. First, the basis of
'upratings' whereby benefits went up in relation to movements in
prices or earnings was changed. Whereas before 1980 the
increases in the long-term pensions, for retirement or disability
for example, had risen in line with average earnings, henceforth
this link was broken and future increases were to be in line with
prices only. Second, the 'earnings-releated additions' – the extra

payments for the first six months of sickness, injury, unemployment and maternity benefit (the 'short-term' benefits) – were abolished. Third, it was made more difficult for people to move from the lower short-term rates of sickness benefits to the higher long-term rates of invalidity benefits.

There were some compensatory moves; sick and disabled people not required to register for work would be entitled to draw the higher long-term rate of supplementary benefit after one year rather than two; the invalidity trap, which had kept people off the higher long-term rates of supplementary benefit, was abolished, and the mobility allowance was increased. But these moves were designed to improve access to means-tested benefits; they could not compensate for the losses of national insurance income.

Those who suffered most were the 650,000 people on invalidity benefit, the key long-term national insurance benefit linked to retirement pension, who, together with retirement pensioners, have lost considerable sums of money each week as a result of the failure to increase benefits in line with average earnings. By 1989 a single person was losing over £11 and a married couple over £17 *per week*.

These were losses which would accumulate each year, but for the 'short-term sick' there was a more immediate drop in income. The Social Security (No. 2) Act 1980 introduced the '5 per cent "abatement" ' on short-term benefits: a novel term for a 5 per cent cut in the value of benefits, which went up in November 1980 by 11 per cent and not by the full rate of inflation, 16 per cent. People on unemployment, sickness, injury and maternity benefit were all affected. Invalidity pension was also cut, thus present and future living standards for the long-term 'contributory' sick suffered a double blow. A single person on invalidity benefit lost £1.40 a week in 1982; a couple, £2.25. The explanation offered for the cut was that it was merely a prelude to taxing the benefit, even though 400,000 of the 650,000 people on invalidity benefit had incomes below the tax threshold.

The savings from the 5 per cent 'abatement' amounted to £140 million. Under considerable pressure the 5 per cent was eventually restored in 1985. It has *never* been taxed. The cut to the basic invalidity pension was made good in November 1984. By then the cumulative losses amounted to £354 for a single person and £560 for a married couple. There was no compensation.

Finally, the earnings-related supplements to the short-term benefits, which provided valuable additional income for the first few months of incapacity, were cut from January 1981 and abolished in January 1982, on the grounds that, with more generous redundancy payments, they were 'much less needed'. This saved £360 million a year at an average cost to people on sickness benefit of about £12.50 a week.

The 'linking spells' of sickness which enabled people with intermittent illness to become eligible for the higher rate of invalidity benefit were cut from thirteen to eight weeks, saving £20 million.

By 1983 total losses from these cuts were estimated at £330 a year for a couple with two children. That excludes the losses from the abolition of the earnings-related supplement.

The effects of these cuts in income were made more severe by the massive cuts in local authority budgets, which led to increased charges for services such as home helps and meals on wheels and the cuts and closures in old people's homes, day care centres and training centres. By 1983, said the Disability Alliance, these policies had 'made the lives of disabled people harder to bear than they were in 1979'.

Paving the Way for Fowler

While living standards were being crudely cut, in 1980 a more subtle political process had already begun to reduce the national insurance rights of people in work and, at the same time, to reduce the opportunities available for people out of work to qualify for benefit. First, progressive steps were taken to abolish industrial injuries benefit and trim disablement benefits under the guise of 'targeting' help to the most severely disabled. Second, privatisation of benefits would begin as employers were required to administer a new scheme for statutory sick pay. Third, non-contributory benefits were 'simplified' with the introduction of the 'severe disablement allowance'.

In retrospect it is clear that the reduction in national insurance rights at work was part of the overall assault on employment rights and security which ranged, between 1980 and 1983, from the loss of maternity rights and the reduction in employment protection for part-time workers to the abolition of the wages councils. Each of these had a predictably savage effect on those at the sharp end of the labour market: the young, the ethnic minority groups, the low-skilled, those in part-time, casual and unskilled labour, women workers and disabled people.

Industrial injuries benefit was an obvious target. Originally designed to compensate for the pain, injury and suffering of those injured at work, the benefit was paid on top of other benefits for the first six months and, most significantly, unlike sickness benefit did not require any contributions to have been paid. It was paid at a higher rate, although this premium had been eroded with time from a 70 per cent increase on the basic sickness benefit in 1948 to 12 per cent in 1980. After six months, those with permanent disability as a result of work injuries could obtain disablement benefit, assessed according to the severity of injury or disease, or a lump sum benefit. The degree of disablement was assessed as a percentage, e.g. total blindness and absolute deafness both count as 100 per cent, the loss of a hand, 60 per cent, the loss of a little finger, 5 per cent. Additional allowances were also paid, particularly special hardship allowance, available if a person could no longer follow his or her regular occupation, an unemployability supplement if he or she became incapable of work and likely to remain so, and an industrial death benefit for widows and other dependants.

Despite the protests of the TUC and the Industrial Injuries Advisory Committee, industrial injury benefit was abolished in 1983. There was some compensation in the fact that disablement benefit would be made available after fifteen weeks, but it was made clear that people injured in industrial accidents in work would now have to 'look at their employers for payment during the first eights weeks of incapacity and will only qualify for national insurance benefit thereafter' (a reference to the simultaneous introduction of statutory sick pay). The abolition of the benefit would save £25 million a year. (One retrogressive by-product of this change was that industrial injuries would no longer be recorded.)

This was a prelude to a second strategy – to abolish the lower rates of disablement benefit in order to target resources on the 'most severely disabled'. It was a strategy entirely consistent with the theme of 'targeting' being pursued by the Fowler reviews, then in full swing. In December 1985 the government issued another consultation paper, developing earlier proposals for further changes to the scheme to focus it more clearly on the most severely disabled and 'help to improve the balance of support for disabled people as a whole'. This involved ending *all* payment of disablement benefit for disablement below 14 per cent; replacing the special hardship allowance by a 'reduced earnings' allowance, offset against any additional pension and frozen at retirement age; abolishing industrial widow's benefit (55p more than the ordinary widow's benefit); and replacing unemployability supplement by invalidity benefit.

Some of the proposals had been anticipated in the earlier White Papers, but the proposal to abolish all entitlement for people with less that 14 per cent disablement was new and draconian. Between 80 and 90 per cent of all claims for disablement fell within this category – 180,000 successful claims a year for people with common conditions such as occupational asthma, back strain and dislocation, or injuries to the hands or feet (including loss of fingers and toes). Most of the lump sums awarded were between £1000 and £2000.

As Andy Stewart, Labour MP for Sherwood, pointed out during the debate on the consultative document on 20 May 1986, 'At Sherwood's ten collieries it is normal to have five serious accidents a week per pit, making 50 in all ranging from 1 per cent upwards with 80 per cent of those accidents under 14 per cent. If my Hon. Friend insists in this course of action those who have suffered such injuries will receive no industrial benefit.'

Significantly, these changes were presented not as a separate bill, which would have been fully justified given their significance, but as new clauses to the bill introducing the Fowler reforms. Savings were estimated to be £55 million.

Sickness Benefit Privatised

If the abolition of industrial injuries benefit and the savings on disablement benefit savaged the national insurance principle, the introduction of employers statutory sick pay (SSP), the other wing of the pincer movement, was to exemplify, as the Green Paper on social security reform put it, 'principles which accord entirely with the approach to this Green Paper. The overlap between state and private occupation provision has been rationalised by the new statutory sick pay scheme.' It was argued that the majority of people were in fact already covered by employers' sick pay schemes and would not be affected. Sickness benefit was to be abolished for the first eight weeks and replaced by sick pay, paid as wages, by the employer. Three rates, related to earnings, with no dependants' allowances, would be payable. It would be taxable. The employee would have to prove entitlement. The objectives were clear; it would save £400 million; it would reduce the number of civil servants; it would bring 90 per cent of sickness payments into taxation; it would abolish the overlap between the state and occupational provision. Above all it would put into the practice the principle that 'The state should, wherever possible, disengage itself from activities which firms and individuals can perform perfectly well for themselves'.

The effects were predictable, and applied equally to every argument for the privatisation of national insurance benefits; those who needed the protection of such benefits would be precisely the people left out of the scheme. Although 90 per cent of all workers now have some sick benefit, DSS statutes show that only half of all private firms offered even short-term sick benefits. Those not covered by such sick pay schemes were people in part-time, unskilled, low-paid and insecure employment. Many would be eligible for the lowest rates of SSP, and, since they were often in the least secure employments, would run the greatest risks of receiving none at all, or being threatened with dismissal if they insisted on pursuing a claim. Women, the least skilled, disabled people, the youngest workers, the poorest paid – all would be at an immediate disadvantage. At that time, a man earning just above the statutory level for national insurance contributions, with a wife and two children, who would have been entitled to £41.05 under the old scheme, would have been entitled to £27.20 for himself and nothing for his wife or children under the new scheme.

For unscrupulous employers, given the lack of powers taken by the DHSS to regulate practice, opportunities for defaulting were legion. There would be many opportunities to make up stringent conditions, to victimise those who were liable to chronic or intermittent sickness, such as multiple sclerosis or arthritis. There was nothing to prevent employers dismissing workers in order to avoid payment. There would be no appeal against those who would not pay.

These objections carried little weight. The objections of private industry, and in particular of small businesses, appalled at the administrative implications, were more effective. Their initial hostility was suppressed by an agreement that all sick pay given under the scheme would be reimbursed.

The government has claimed that the scheme is a 'great success' and extended its operation from eight to twenty-eight weeks in April 1986. For many claimants the reality has been very different: a loss of £155 million to employees in the first year of operation. The DHSS saved £90 million and employers gained £95 million. In 1987 the Disability Alliance reported a pattern of 'private insecurity', with some employees being forced on to means-tested benefits, firms refusing to operate the scheme or pay some workers, and other workers being sacked or being encouraged to declare themselves self-employed.

In April 1987 there were yet more changes when the government 'merged' the two lower rates of SSP, making an effective cut of 18 per cent in the rates of benefit for 400,000 spells of sickness, and saving another £19 million a year.

Caring for the Carers

Since 1979 such progress as has been made in the award of benefits for those who stay at home to care for sick and disabled people has been inspired not by any sense of ordinary justice, by a desire to compensate for the costs saved by the community, but by the fact that European law requires that basic human rights of non-discrimination are observed. In 1975 the Labour government recognised the need to award some benefit to those who gave up work to care for others, though with predictable chauvinism it was argued that, although many married women would undertake to do this voluntarily, 'they may be home in any event'. Married women were, therefore, deliberately excluded from the scope of the invalid care allowance, and despite pressure, not least from the Equal Opportunities Commission, there is little doubt that they would have remained excluded had it not been for Jacqueline Drake's appeal to the European Court in February 1985.

The European Communities Council Directive of 19 December 1978 clearly required the 'progressive implementation of the principle of equal treatment for men and women in matters of social security'. In February 1985 Jacqueline Drake, a married women looking after her husband, applied for the invalid care allowance. The government argued that the directive did not apply to third parties involved in looking after a sick person. The Advocate-General of the European Court rejected this interpretation and found that the exclusion of married women was discriminatory. After first insisting that it was not 'binding' the government announced in advance of the final judgement that it would accept the ruling. It did so by way of a new clause in the Social Security Act 1986. By 1987, 89,000 married or cohabiting women had received this new benefit and 10,000 were still waiting. The total cost to the government in 1987/8 was £164 million.

The European directive was also invoked in 1984 when the government agreed to abolish the iniquitous 'household duties test' attached to the housewives' non-contributory invalidity pension. Designed specifically to provide an income for disabled housewives it was a degrading and arbitrary test of lack of domestic competence. When the disabled housewife had proved that she could not shop, cook, dust, make beds, etc. without severe difficulty, she was awarded £20.45 a week – 60 per cent of the contributory invalidity pension. Many thousands of disabled housewives failed the test.

The problem facing the government was how to devise a new test which would cut down the numbers of claimants without falling foul of European law. The solution was the severe disablement allowance, which, ministers argued, would go to 20,000 more housewives. According to the later Green Paper it would also bring 'a move towards a more coherent system' – to be achieved by imposing not one but two tests of disability. To qualify, a claimant had to prove, first, that she had been out of work at the age of twenty or over and, second, that she was at least 80 per cent disabled. Inevitably, the same people – largely married women – who had failed the previous household duties test found themselves caught by the twin tests of work and incapacity.

According to the disability organisations, the new benefit was quite simply 'a disaster'. But their views were irrelevant for the Health and Social Security Bill 1983 was published virtually simultaneously with the government's decision. It was, said the Royal Association for Disability and Rehabilitation (RADAR), 'unprecedented for such a significant change to be introduced without prior consultation'. The percentage test, based on industrial disablement, was totally inappropriate for a benefit supposed to be paid precisely because of incapacity for work. In any event there is no necessary link between degree of disablement and capacity: in some cases 100 per cent disablement does not impair a person's capacity to work; in others 20 per cent disablement can mean that a person can never work. Adjudication, said RADAR, would prove 'a nightmare' and for people with, say, 78 per cent disablement there were 'no consolation prizes'. The result would be more people pushed on to supplementary benefit, and the further complication of an already confused system. Far from simplification and rationalisation it was, said Peter Large, chairman of the Disablement Income Group, 'a step further away from what we have consistently sought. It is a step towards further confusion.'

Fairer or Fowler?

> Overall, disabled people on low incomes will benefit
> significantly from the proposals.
>
> (Norman Fowler, 16 December 1986)

Given the ambitious objectives and the historic antecedents called up by Norman Fowler, it remains surprising that the opportunity to establish more rational and coherent policies for disabled people was not taken in 1985. Instead, the ambivalence of the government's attitudes toward thorough reform was very clear. On the one hand, a radical review would have to wait until the information from the survey on disabled people was available. On the other hand, not having that information was no handicap when it came to devising reforms which, directly and indirectly, would affect disabled people. The Disability Alliance argued in vain that under these conditions 'any new policies are likely to be defective from the start'. That organisation, representing over a hundred organisations working with disabled people, rejected the entire ethos of the review, and in particular the government's attempt to drive a wedge between the 'deserving' and the 'undeserving' poor. It argued that the concept of 'losers' and 'gainers' for those at the lowest level of subsistence with the highest level of needs could 'not be allowed by the government to form part of the agenda'.

The Green Paper, published in May 1985, confirmed worst fears. Like so many other pressure groups and professional organisations which had acted in good faith, setting out a strong agenda for reform, the disability organisations were appalled by many of the proposed changes to pensions, family and housing benefits. Their carefully argued case for a single disability income was shattered by the discovery that the government had come up with a scheme for income support which actually abolished all the additional requirements available to meet the special needs of the disabled, *precisely* those parts of the supplementary benefit system which were most effective in helping disabled people.

In 1988 there were fourteen different additional requirements, of which ten were in some way related to the costs of ill-health or disability. The most comon additions were for heating, diet and laundry, but there were others to cover the wear and tear of clothing, special clothing, domestic help, attendance costs, the need for extra baths, an addition for blindness, hospital fares, storage of essential furniture, boarding out fees and certain hire-purchase payments. In 1986 it was estimated that over 300,000 disabled people received additional requirements and a marked increase had been evident since 1980 (reflecting in part the increase in the numbers of disabled people on supplementary beenfit) in the take-up of each of the disability additions, e.g. bathing needs up 433 per cent, laundry up 250 per cent and clothing 131 per cent. In 1983, 117,000 people received more than £7 a week and 17,000 more than £10 a week in these additional benefits. Most important, 2000 people received domestic assitance, £44.90 for essential domestic help. It seemed to many that it was precisely the popularity and cost of these necessary benefits that had marked them for abolition.

The Green Paper proposed that, instead of these additional payments on top of the basic supplementary benefit, disabled people would have a basic income, plus a specific 'premium' for claimants eligible for one of the standard invalidity benefits. In principle the concept of premiums was commendable. The key point was, at what level would the premiums be fixed and how were the highest costs of disablement to be met? The wide variation in individual needs and costs made the levels of benefits crucial. Simplification, fraught with problems for every client group, could, if judged wrongly, prove a real disaster for disabled people. The lack of illustrative figures made it impossible for the effects of the changes to be judged accurately, but the disability organisations recognised immediately that the loss of additional and single payments would mean 'a picture of increasing poverty, misery and degradation. As well as cutting the weekly income of disabled people the proposals will strip away their legal entitlement to payments which they presently have as of right.'

It was clear from the structure planned and from the minister's own words that it was 'highly unlikely' that 'any premium rate for the disabled could be set at a level which meant that the maximum conceivable amount of additional payments obtainable under an extraordinary case . . . would be compensated for by the rate of premium under the income support scheme'.

Once the illustrative figures were published some calculations could be made. For example: a young person with a congenital illness, living independently but with help in the home, and receiving attendance and mobility allowance would lose £58 a week; a pensioner couple with one receiving attendance allowance and additions for heating, laundry, baths and domestic help would lose £42 a week.

These were not extraordinary cases, but the ordinary, predictable and recurring costs of certain types of disability. Other drawbacks with the premium system reflected and reinforced the very weaknesses which demanded reform. In some cases they made those weaknesses worse. For example, premiums would be available only to people in receipt of disability benefits, thereby excluding all whose disabilities did not fit the 'classic structure'.

Second, the costs of disabled children were, once again, omitted. Any family with a disabled child would not receive a special benefit recognising the rights and costs of that child, but an additional family premium. To qualify, a child would have to be on attendance or mobility allowance; but the age bar on both benefits would mean that children under two would not qualify while, at the same time, many over that age would fail the tests of incapacity. For these people Fowler's proposals retained and extended the rules for exclusion and discrimination.

For those who cared for disabled dependants the proposals were actually retrogressive. Previously, carers had been able to claim the higher long-term rate of supplementary benefit, an indication that they were not 'available for work'. But nothing in the new premium structure recognised either the rights of carers, their special situation or their income needs. The minister explained that the premiums were designed to compensate for the loss of additional requirements; thus, logically, there was no reason for carers to receive a special premium. It was left to the House of Commons Social Services Select Committee to point out the moral turpitude of such arguments. In its view, 'the fact that carers are neglected at present is not a good reason for perpetuating the neglect under income support'. At the very least, argued the disability organisations, the government had to stop dragging its feet and extend the invalid care allowance to married and cohabiting women.

Overall the disability lobby was adamant that the effect of the changes set out in the Green Paper would be

> to impose significant losses on thousands of people with disabilities who already have inadequate incomes. . . . The scheme will lack the flexibility of the existing system of additional requirements and will be completely unable to respond to varying needs of weekly requirements within each of the client groups. . . . We must stress that the Green Paper proposals cannot in any way be regarded as a constructive move towards the sort of comprehensive disability income scheme that we have been campaigning for for the past ten years.

But of all the changes which would hit disabled people the social fund provoked the greatest anger. Dependent upon 'single payments' for essential furniture, bedding, household goods, etc., it was clear that many disabled people would be at the mercy of the social fund's loan arrangements and the arbitrary discretion of its officers, who might or might not recognise the costs of disability. The idea reduced the most patient of lobbying groups to open fury, the reasons for which will be discussed in detail in Chapter 11. In great anger the Disability Alliance concluded that it was

> totally unacceptable. . . . It is difficult to comment in a temperate manner on the social fund, so pernicious are its likely consequences. It will divest social security claimants of legal rights, income and any last vestiges of dignity. The Disability Alliance demands that the government abandon this obscene proposal.

Although the government took virtually no notice of the 'intense criticism' of the principles of the new scheme, the White Paper did contain what it called some 'significant improvements for less well off disabled people'. Among the concessions revealed were an extra family premium for every child receiving attendance or mobility allowance and more generous treatment of part-time earnings. But every attempt by the disability organisations to persuade the government toward more flexibility was rejected on grounds of cost. One significant victory was forced on the government. Both the SSAC and the Social Services Select Committee, while they agreed that the highest costs could not be used as the basis for general assessment, argued that they were not extraordinary but 'constant' and 'recurring'. They suggested a two-tier premium system with the higher rate linked to the receipt of benefits reflecting severe disability.

The government still resisted. It took a defeat in the House of Lords on an opposition amendment to secure the final concession of a higher rate of disability premium for people living on their own, to be paid on top of the ordinary disability premium. But, pusillanimous in defeat, the government made the conditions of entitlement so stringent that it is hard to imagine who will qualify, for they require almost total destitution and isolation. The severely disabled person must live alone, be very severely handicapped, and have no one receiving or eligible for the invalid care allowance on his or her behalf. Even on the government's estimates only 10,000 people are likely to be eligible for a benefit which will be paid at the same rate as the invalid care allowance, and will cost no more than £12 million.

The Independent Living Foundation: Privatising Help

Not until October 1987 could the scale of the disaster for disabled people be measured. The 'impact tables' showed that 60,000 'sick and disabled people' would lose because of the changes. These figures were based simply on those people under pension age eligible for a disability premium under income support; as such they were a gross underestimate of the numbers of sick and disabled people actually affected by the changes. The Disability Alliance estimated that 500,000 sick and disabled people would directly lose out; if all pensioners were included this would rise to 'almost a million' people.

In particular, all the proposals put forward to protect the living standards of those who would lose most because they needed most additional requirements had been rejected. The Disablement Income Group calculated that about a thousand people could lose up to £80 a week. Replying to a final exchange with the disability lobby in October 1987 the Minister of State, Nicholas Scott, was unmoved; he claimed that the administrative considerations were insuperable:

> It has proved extremely difficult to produce solutions which would avoid either a very high cost on top of the extra financial support we are already planning, or major difficulties in defining eligible groups and operating the detailed rules for help. . . . We may disagree on this issue but I remain very much open to any further suggestions and comment you may wish to make on support for disabled people.

The 'extra financial support' built in through the disability premiums on income support was estimated to be only £60 million. As for the suggestion that the government was still open to persuasion, 'Comment', said the Disability Alliance, 'seems superfluous.'

Limited concessions were, however, made. In February 1988, following continuing adverse publicity, the government was forced to take additional steps to help those who did not fit into the 'classic structure'. On 9 February 1988 the minister announced that an 'Independent Living Foundation' – a trust fund of £5 million, to be administered by the DHSS in co-operation with the Disability Income Group (DIG) – would be set up. It was designed for those who needed extra help, 'to permit severely disabled people on low incomes who need personal care or domestic assitance to enable them to live independently in the community'. Few people will qualify; only those who live alone or whose partner is incapable of providing them with the help they need. Such people will have to be poor enough to qualify for income support before or after paying for domestic help and receiving attendance allowance.

The fund has split the disability organisations between those who reluctantly agreed to co-operate (DIG) and others who see it as 'scandalous' and a 'tragic abdication of responsibility by the government' (Disability Alliance). Whereas the severe disability premium will go to thousands, Nicholas Scott estimated that the beneficiaries of the Independent Living Foundation will be 'numbered in hundreds'. It marks a further shift away from individual rights and community support towards reliance on charity, calling for judgements to be made by people who will need the wisdom of Solomon to discriminate between people who are all in the greatest of need.

April 1988

> Yes, we have had structural changes. Yes, they were meant to retarget the money spent so that disabled people, families with children and those in low paid work are better off. In cash terms transitional protection of income support means that 97 per cent of sick and disabled people . . . get more or the same.
>
> (Prime Minister in response to Neil Kinnock, 31 March 1988)

Given these positive assurances that only 3 per cent of disabled people would lose cash (no mention was made of the overall differences the structural changes would make), the numbers of people who were to lose immediately – and the scale of the losses – came as a shock to the claimants, their advocates and politicians alike. For example, two surveys (NACAB and Strathclyde) on the loss in income comparing the existing system with the post-April system, made at the end of March 1988 in respect of existing claimants, found that 84 per cent and 83 per cent, respectively, would lose.

But even those were theoretical losses. The letters which poured in to newspapers and to the House of Commons told the inescapable truth of sudden, totally unexpected cuts in benefit. Three types of casualties arose from the April changes. First, the 'accidental victims', those disabled people who have lost because of the changes in housing benefit, particularly the new requirement to pay 20 per cent of rates, the loss of the 'non-dependant deductions' for family members living at home, or the fact that the industrial disablement pension now counts as income in the calculation of housing benefit. The majority of these cases are elderly people. Second, there are those who have been affected by changes in the rules governing income support, including the '24-hours rule' which disqualifies claimants or partners from working more than twenty-four hours a week. Third, there are *new* claimants who simply receive less under the new scheme than under the old scheme.

In the first instance, as the OPCS survey, the evidence of campaigning organisations, MPs' letters and newspaper stories have proved, there is an inescapable link between age and disability which has made the impact of housing benefit cuts particularly devastating. Testimony is best given in the words of those who have suffered. As every MP could verify, many cases could be cited. The following story illustrates what it means to someone suddenly to have to find 20 per cent of their rates for the first time. A lady from Wolverhampton wrote:

I am a Registered Disabled Lady, with no family whatsoever. I have never had to pay any rates as my only income is £20 per week maintenance from my ex-husband. . . . I have now lost all my special additions, i.e. diet, heating, laundry. I am also now having to pay £11.30 a month water rates. I have also lost my

114

long-term high rate sickness benefit. There is no way that I can pay 20 per cent Poll Tax (what from?).

I am 57 years of age. . . . I already live on porridge and roast potatoes four days a week to try to pay for some heat.

My savings are £300. Dear Lord. Is suicide the only answer?

Another case shows how the loss of 'non-dependant deductions' for young people living at home has affected one already severely disabled person:

Andrew, my eldest son, has Crohn's disease. . . . He is and has been on severe disablement benefit. It was, before Maggie got her teeth in, £47.80. The rise from the budget added £2.00 exactly. So now he gets £49.80 a week.

My younger son, Stephen, is at the moment on sick pay. He broke his leg in a fall. He gets £30.31 a week. When his leg is fully mended, unless he can find work, he will go back on supplementary benefit. . . .

I, too, am on Severe Disability pension. I am blind and have got myself an ulcer. My pension before the budget, if that is what it was, was £48.63. I had a rise of £1.30.

Our rent/rates to the Council . . . was, before the rise £2.60. . . . The council informed us that we have to pay £13.70 a week and that we were as from the budget almost £80.00 in arrears. . . .

The Thatcher Government gave the three of us, between us about a 2 per cent rise of less than £5.00. Our rent/rates have gone up from £2.60 to £13.70 – a rise of over 500 per cent. . . .

The other major change in housing benefit as it affected disabled people was caused by counting industrial disablement pension as income in the assessment of housing benefit. The couple writing the following letter, with a total income of about £96 a week, suddenly found themselves £21 a week worse off.

My husband and I are two pensioners who are absolutely stunned by the drastic cut in our income under the new system. . . . The Prime Minister, when approached, just glibly quotes figures and statistics. How do we break through the arrogance of her to make her realise we are not numbers on the electoral roll but living human beings. . . . We have been fortunate in having a rent and rate rebate and have been paying only £8 plus per week. This week we have the pension increase, but also a rent rise (the second one this year). Under the old scheme the Council made a discretion in our rebate because of my husband's disablement pension. We have never made any application for any help monetary or otherwise from the social services. We look after each other. We have paid ourselves for our spectacles and teeth. . . . We live carefully. . . . We have never ever been in debt. . . . We feel we try to help ourselves without imposing on the State. The Government imply we are sponging off the State. Please tell us, what do you think? The bombshell for us is the rent has gone up . . . we must now pay £29.

Other disabled people lost their free school meals:

My husband is only 36. He is disabled with chronic asthmatic bronchitis, sciatica and a dislocated knee cap. We receive Mobility Allowance and our Invalidity Benefit is going to £91.35 a week. Out of this we pay £10.15 rent and its going up. And we have just lost our free school meals. So now we pay £7 a week school dinner money. The DHSS reduced me help to buy a gas fire for my room as its got a radiator in it. I have large electric bills for the electric we burn as my husband must be kept warm with his condition. . . . We also had to buy a machine to help my husband to breath – £120. . . . I have two sons aged nearly 11 and 7 to keep. And a housebound mother.

But compared with a lot of my friends, family and neighbours we are a lot better off financially than they are. . . . Everyone I have spoken to are at least £2.50 a week worse off and they can't afford to be.

The housing benefit lossess have been modified by the changes in the rules introduced in May 1988 when the government was forced by the hurricane of protests to introduce transitional protection for some of those on housing benefit, though as we have seen in the previous chapter, the protection still left the vast majority of losers with heavy losses.

Finally, the most severe change to income support, affecting about 15,000 people, was the '24-hour rule' which disqualified from benefit those who, or whose partners, were working more than twenty-four hours a week. Mrs Felicity Godden suffered from multiple sclerosis, which left her barely able to walk. She had three small children at home, a brain-damaged elder son, and was dependent upon constant attendance allowance and on the £47.74 a week domestic assistance addition for help in the house. Because her husband worked full time she lost that addition with the introduction of the '24-hour rule'. The *Mirror* put it graphically: 'If he is forced to give up work to care for his wife, the outlook is simple. No house, because the clean little bungalow in Bristol comes with the job, no wage, and no marriage.' Mr Godden, who chose to work rather than claim social security and care for the family himself, was, as Robin Cook pointed out in the ensuing debate, 'precisely the kind of person Conservative members tell us they want to support – people who choose to work rather than go on the dole'. Government ministers handled the case disastrously, insinuating in the House of Commons that, as the Goddens were able to afford a holiday, the family were not as badly off as was made out. This provoked an angry response from Robin Cook:

I shall never forget the reception that her case received in the House yesterday. It was received on the Government benches with laughter. . . . They found it the biggest joke of the day that a disabled claimant had taken her children on holiday as if people on benefit should be under a kind of house arrest. . . . Yes, all right, the Goddens had a holiday. It lasted six days and it ended 12 days ago. They went to Plymouth to see Mrs Godden's relatives. Mr Godden is a caravan salesman. His company gave him free use of a caravan for a week. They parked it in a farmer's field at a rent of £12 a night. That, and the petrol from Bristol was the entire cost of the holiday that Conservative members found funny.

John Moore responded by pointing out that the total income of the family was £247 a week for a family of five with no rent and rates and a working-age son at home. Neil Kinnock observed that half that income 'was the price of a mother having multiple sclerosis', leaving a weekly income of about £120 a week, or £17 a day for five people.

There were other categories of claimants, already receiving income support, who were supposed to be protected in every way but who still found themselves losers, largely because their new rates of benefit did not compensate for increases in rates, water rates and other housing costs. On 26 April the Royal National Institute for the Blind (RNIB) appealed to the DHSS on behalf of three people, who, despite transitional protection, had found that they were worse off. In one case a diabetic single parent with a twenty-year-old son suffering from cerebral palsy, whose previous income under supplementary benefit had been £116 and whose new entitlement was £97, had received transitional protection compensating for the loss – but increases in rates, water rates and repairs and insurance left her over £6 a week worse off. In another case a single woman with arthritis of the spine would have suffered a weekly loss of £25 given the calculation of income support. She received transitional protection but was still £1.15 a week worse off – because her rates and water rates had increased more that the transitional protection. And she was at even greater risk, as the RNIB pointed out:

> Because of her medical condition there is a high risk of her being hospitalised. If her stay in hospital lasted more than six weeks she would lose her transitional addition. On returning home she would be £27.99 a week worse off. She does not qualify for the severe disability premium and she would not be eligible for payment from the Independent Living Fund. In the past, the cases we have presented to you have of necessity been hypothetical. These that are annexed to this letter are real and require an immediate response.

Because they had been covered by the transitional arangements none of these people was regarded by the government as a 'loser'; they were all officially unaffected by the April changes. Moreover, none will receive an increase in benefit until the new rates catch up with his or her existing benefits. Unless the rules are changed they will live on a declining real income for years.

What is compelling about these personal accounts is the way they illustrate the vulnerability of disabled people and their families, the margins of expenditure upon which they live, and the sheer variety of ways in which they have suffered losses. What is even more impressive is the dignity with which they describe their personal distress. Some of these individual cases should have been eased by the transitional protection conceded on housing benefit. For many of the newly disabled, especially those who are not sufficiently severely disabled to receive one of the qualifying benefits, there will be only losses.

What is striking about the process of events is that each concession had to be wrung out of ministers who, against the best advice, still appeared unable to comprehend how the slightest shifts in income could push those on the margins into even greater dependency and despair. But as the Disability Alliance put it, when reviewing the first year of the Act ('at best . . . an appalling failure'), 'It gives us no pleasure at all to say to the Government, "We told you so." '

Since April 1988 a fresh blow has been levelled at people with disabilities. Not only will millions of them be worse off as a result of the poll tax itself, they will also lose the rebates which were available to disabled people under the rating system.

Thanks to the OPCS revelations, the government now has all the evidence and the opportunity it needs for radical, progressive change. But, although crucial, change must not simply be built on a more rational benefits system. Other European countries see rehabilitation and support for those in work as the key agents of economic independence for disabled people. If that assumption were built into the strategy for reform most recently put forward by the SSAC which reiterates the need for a single coherent system of benefits, a fundamental change would occur in the view taken of people with disabilities. For, as long as disabled people are seen as dependent and therefore different and as long as those who care for them are seen as expendable within the community, the double gates of discrimination and poverty will never be smashed.

6 Pensions and Poverty

I warn you not to grow old.

(Neil Kinnock, Bridgend, 1983)

It remains the Government's firm intention that pensioners and other long term beneficiaries can confidently look forward to sharing in the increased standards of living of the country as a whole. This has always been the intention and the achievement of Conservative Governments. It remains the intention of the present Government.

(Patrick Jenkin, 13 June 1979, House of Commons)

The year 1988 marked the eightieth anniversary of the Old Age Pensions Act, which established for the first time a universal national pension for people over the age of seventy. It was a modest innovation, the fruit of a decade of agitation from trade unionists, early socialists and philanthropists. Destitution and starvation in old age and repugnance for the workhouse, that physical embodiment of Victorian values in the field of social security, created not only a coalition of politicians and philanthropists, but also provided an important focus and *raison d'être* for the early Labour party. The first pension was worth five shillings (about £10 at today's rates). It was subject to a test of means and even of character, since recipients had to show that they had not needed support from the Poor Law in the preceding two years, but these conditions were secondary to the fact that, for the first time, there was an alternative to the workhouse. It proved to be a turning point in social reform. The old age pension was not simply a universal payment as of right, it was also a statement that social justice and economic efficiency could reinforce each other.

Many were opposed to the pension, notably the Poor Law authorities themselves. They argued that it would discourage thrift and encourage idleness; that it was too expensive a burden on the population; that it would impoverish and threaten private insurance. They lost the argument in the face of popular demand, common sense and a well-organised political campaign. In 1942 the Beveridge Report replaced the concept of an old age pension with that of a contributory pension based on retirement from work.

The history of the pension is worth recounting because the same arguments have informed, explicitly and implicitly, the present government's policies for security in old age. After several decades of incremental improvements – the most important of which were placing the annual uprating of pensions on a statutory basis, linking it with the rise in earnings or prices, whichever was the higher, and the improvement of the provision for elderly women through SERPS – the direction of policy was fundamentally changed in 1979. The link between the rise in pensions and the rise in average earnings was broken and only that with rising prices was retained, annual increases were again reformulated to reflect historic rather than 'forecasted' prices, and in the Green Paper on social security the government tried to abolish SERPS. It failed to do so, but nevertheless managed to inflict serious damage on the principles of the scheme. This was followed by successive assaults on housing benefit, of particular importance to the generation of pensioners with smaller personal or occupational pensions which lifted them off means tests but brought them within the scope of help with rates and rents. In April 1988 pensioners found themselves the direct target of savings in housing benefit. As Chapter 2 describes in more detail, 2.5 million lost some entitlement to housing benefit; 700,000 people lost benefit altogether; 400,000 had their entitlement to housing benefit supplement summarily abolished.

Pensioners are in the forward trenches of the ideological battle. The government has argued that the spread of occupational provision and savings has enriched the whole generation of pensioners to an extent that those who are still dependent on the

121

basic pension are in a dwindling minority; furthermore, the ground has been prepared for the spread of private pensions, for the extension of personal risk-taking and 'independence'. Only this, it is argued, will prevent the pensions 'time bomb' from exploding in the face of the next generation of working people, placing an intolerable contribution burden upon them.

The fact is, however, that this construction is only one version of the truth. The government claims that since 1979 there has been a real increase of 23 per cent in pensioners' incomes, twice that of the general growth of incomes. These figures mask wide differences. The top 20 per cent of retired households, for example, have an income of over £10,000, based on a state pension (£2180) with the balance made up of occupational pensions, while the bottom 20 per cent live on about £3300, consisting of the basic state pension and means-tested benefits. This divide is growing as increasing numbers of pensioners are receiving the additions from SERPS, in 1988 an average of £6.33 per week for the newly retired. It is ironic, therefore, and not a little misleading, for the government to claim credit for the largest single element in the growth of pensioners incomes – under a scheme which it tried very hard to abolish.

While there is a growing number of elderly people fortunate enough to have occupational pensions and private pensions to supplement their basic pension, two-thirds of pensioners rely on the basic pension. Two million of them live on supplementary benefit (income support), and their circumstances are often pitiable. A further million pensioners, the saddest instances of all, are eligible for income support but fail to claim it. Only two out of three pensioners, therefore, claim what they are fully entitled to, due in part to ignorance of what is available; another reason, however, is often pride, and the fear of being questioned about income and savings. Another three million pensioners have incomes which are only 40 per cent above the income support line.

The effects of poverty among the elderly are manifest in many ways. As the OPCS survey mentioned in the preceding chapter shows, many are also disabled. These are among the most elderly and the majority are women. The link between poverty and mortality is equally clear. In 1988 the King's Fund Research Institute found that men aged sixty-five have a shorter life expectancy in Britain than in twenty-one other countries, including Sri Lanka and Uruguay. Women of the same age have a longer life expectancy in sixteen other countries, including Greece, Spain and Portugal. The explanation for Britain's appalling standards is given as 'severe poverty and disadvantage among a substantial minority'.

The pensions policy devised in the Green Paper ignored the poor half of the population. By breaking the principle of linking pensions with earnings to keep them in line with national standards of living and with personal earnings as a whole, it effectively locked this generation and the next out of any real rise in national prosperity. This chapter concentrates on government policies for the basic state pension, for widows' pensions, and for the state earnings-related pension. It does not offer further details of the impact of housing benefit changes, other than by illustrating what, in individual terms, those changes meant for elderly people. Because the majority of pensioners become disabled with increasing age (often with more than one disability) and because the majority of them are women, much of what has already been described in Chapters 3 and 5 also applies to the elderly.

Two Nations in Old Age

In 1985 there were 9.3 million pensioners in Great Britain. In 1995 it is estimated that there will be 9.8 million; in 2005, 10 million. Every decade after that will add another million pensioners. The first three decades of the twenty-first century will therefore see three million more pensioners, while the number of contributors will be reduced from 2.3 per pensioner in 1985 to 2.0 by 2015. About 70 per cent of disabled adults were aged sixty or over. In 1981 it was estimated that 43 per cent of unfit dwellings were occupied by a 'retired' household. Only 26 per cent of married couple pensioner households own a car and 4 per cent of single pensioner households. Individually, pensioners spend about twice as much as the rest of the population on fuel. In January 1984 the total state pension in Britain was worth 26 per cent of average earnings, compared with 60 per cent in France and Belgium and 50 per cent in West Germany.

The government has developed three strategies to deal with

what it sees as an intolerable burden on the economy and the community: first, to keep down the level of the basic pension; second, to reduce the costs of SERPS; and, third, to cut housing benefits. Of these, the value of the current pension is the most immediate and most emotive issue.

In his speech quoted at the beginning of the chapter the first Secretary of State for Social Services of the Tory government, Patrick Jenkin, while promising that pensioners would share in the increasing prosperity of the nation, revealed that the government intended to 'break the link' between pensions and earnings. There was no indication of this in the 1979 Conservative manifesto. The link with the higher of earnings or price rises had been introduced during years of high inflation in 1974–5 as a guarantee to pensioners that their standards of living would not fall below those of people in work. It was a vital commitment. Between 1974 and 1979 the value of the retirement pension rose by about 150 per cent for married and single pensioners; prices rose by 109 per cent and earnings by 118 per cent.

The statutory obligation to maintain the pension in this way was, said the government, simply 'not sustainable' in the long term. According to Jenkin, the only guarantee that really mattered to pensioners was that 'against rising prices'. The savings to the government were to be huge, for 'breaking the link' was not confined simply to the basic pension, although this was the most significant element; it affected all the 'long-term' benefits.

By November 1981 the decision hd already resulted in a cut in the single rate of pension of £1.23: it was estimated to save £500 million in 1982/3. Compared with what they would have received, by April 1989 single pensioners were each losing £11.20 a week and married couples £17.55. Savings in the year 1988/9 alone were estimated at £5 billion. Accumulated losses on pensions and related benefits are now too complex to calculate, but there is no doubt that breaking the link has proved and will continue to prove one of the richest sources of savings for the government. Both in principle and practice the implications are equally serious for all pensioners. Without abandoning its statutory commitment the government has seriously limited its responsibility for maintaining pensioners' living standards. For the more elderly pensioners, and for women and unskilled workers unable to build up an occupational pension record or ineligible for one, the consequences are grave.

In effect it means the steady erosion of the one secure element in the pensioner's income and a recourse to means-tested supplementary benefits. In October 1982 the Select Committee on the Age of Retirement concluded that: 'some sort of assistance for older and poorer pensioners is inevitable . . . future governments will have no choice but to regard this as one of the first calls on additional resources'.

The SSAC has called several times for the restoration of the earnings/prices link. In 1983 it pointed out that if earnings consistently kept ahead of prices, periodic upratings of pension levels above minimum prices would be necessary to maintain pensioners' standards of living. As the SSAC was again to point out in its Fourth Report, in 1985, maintaining a link with prices means the steady erosion of the comparative value of the pension. In November 1978 the basic single pension was worth 20.4 per cent of all male average earnings; by November 1985 it had dropped to 19.2 per cent. It would then continue to fall to 15 per cent by 2000, to 10 per cent by 2025. As the SSAC pointed out in its Sixth Report, it would then be 'significantly less than the relative value at any time since 1948'.

The tide had already turned, however, and despite a well-organised pensioners' lobby it was clear by the June 1983 election that the government would not return to linking pensions with earnings. Pointing out that half the working population were covered by occupational pensions, the Conservative manifesto pledged simply: 'We shall continue to protect retirement pensions and other linked long-term benefits against rising prices.' There was no question, however, but that only this minimum committment to uprate the basic pension would be maintained. Thus, the Green Paper was quite clear on the state's minimum obligations to pensioners: 'The proper role for the state is the provision of the basic retirement pension. The Government remain entirely committed to this and will continue to ensure that it retains its value.' However, it also suggested that, by making cuts now, 'Governments will in the long term be in a better position to choose whether to improve the basic position as national wealth increases and so to raise the living standards of all pensioners, not just those who have retired more recently.' This suggestion that improvements could and would be made was quietly dropped and did not subsequently appear in the White Paper.

The current basic pension is fixed according to inflation based on the previous year. Thus in April 1988 pensioners received a 4.2 per cent increase – £3.29 for a married couple. By January 1989 inflation was rising at the rate of 7.5 per cent and earnings by 9 per cent.

For pensioners the contrast was even more grave. As one wrote:

Out of this money we have to pay the following increases;

14% rate increase
20% first time rate payers
7.5% council house rents
6% gas
25% rail card
12% electricity
7% meals on wheels 4.14% home helps
7.8% TV licence
13% water rates.

What shall be our answer when we cannot pay the increases. Do 10,000,000 pensioners protest by going to prison?

The Attempt to Abolish SERPS

Today's pensioners are thus slipping further behind any increases in the standard of living. Tomorrow's pensioners, unless they have extremely good occupational or private pensions, will be significantly worse off. This is no accident. It follows from changes to SERPS, which, though saved from abolition, is now a very anaemic version of what it once was.

The Beveridge scheme of flat-rate pensions for flat-rate contributions was already regarded as deficient by the late 1950s. It has been complemented by the growth of occupational pension schemes and by the introduction of additional, earnings-related pensions funded by national insurance. For twenty years after the Second World War the number of occupational schemes grew rapidly. The larger the firm, the higher the earnings, the more pension was generated. By 1967, 12.2 million people were covered by occupational pension schemes. Although this had fallen to 11.1 million by 1983, the proportion of the workforce covered has remained around 50 per cent – but with enormous variations between industries: only 23 per cent of agricultural and 37 per cent of construction employees, compared with 53 per cent in manufacturing. Very few part-timers have occupational pensions.

Earnings-related pensions were first introduced in 1961 by way of the graduated contribution pension scheme. In the 1960s and 1970s accommodation between state and occupational pensions was sought under successive Labour and Tory governments, and earnings-related rather than flat-rate benefits were introduced. Beginning in 1968, in a scheme of stunning complexity, Crossman had proposed an earnings-related scheme which allowed for 'partial' contracting out of the state scheme and/or abatement of pensions. This was overtaken by Sir Keith Joseph's scheme, which was a flat-rate pension paid for out of earnings-related contributions complemented by an earnings-related state reserve scheme. In May 1974 Joseph departed and in the following September Barbara Castle set out her proposals in *Better Pensions*.

These proposals had three objectives: to reduce poverty in old age by improving the value of flat-rate pensions; to provide good cover for that half of the workforce not in occupational pension schemes; and to improve occupational pension schemes in relation to inflation.

The key innovation was that the flat-rate pension would be supplemented by an additional state earnings-related pension based on 25 per cent of earnings over the 'best twenty years' of earnings. The advantages to those with an incomplete or sporadic work record were obvious. Women out of the labour market for a decade, people in casual or seasonal work, those who had qualified late in life, people with intermittent or chronic sickness – all would benefit significantly. The new scheme had other advantages for women. It proposed to abolish the 'half test', which since 1948 had required women to have contributed for at least half the weeks between marriage and retirement to qualify for any pension at all. In addition, it provided that widowed mothers and widows over fifty would inherit the whole of their husband's earnings. Widows between forty and fifty without children would also receive an

127

age-related proportion of the total. For the first time, widowers would also obtain benefits. It was therefore a pensions scheme genuinely 'targeted' on need and on sexual inequality in provision for old age.

After a decade of confusion and argument the foundations were laid for a partnership between public and private pensions. After a somewhat grudging start, the scheme which had commanded the support of the pensions industry eventually won the support of the Conservatives – not least on the grounds that future pensions planning should be politically stable. The political consensus achieved in 1975 was, therefore, welcomed on all sides.

The first suggestion that this consensus was under threat came in an interview with the Prime Minister in the *New York Times* in which she referred to a 'pensions time bomb'. In 1982, in the twilight years of the CPRS the 'think-tank' had also been charged with a major study on pensions. The terms of reference reflected the government's two major preoccupations: to cut down on public expenditure, and to encourage labour mobility and self-reliance. As Tessa Blackstone and William Plowden, then working for the CPRS, record, the study started with four premises: 'the state pension cost too much; it did not focus enough on the genuine poor; there was too little scope in the pensions system as a whole for the individual to look after himself; the system of occupational pensions was rigid and acted as a disincentive to career change'.

The first paper prepared suggested that SERPS was inadequate because it benefited the better off. It suggested that it should be phased out and the basic pension raised to buy off 'some of the key hostile reaction'. The second paper made recommendations on the development of personal pensions as a credible alternative. The papers went to the Prime Minister, closely followed by John Sparrow, the fourth and final head of the CPRS. Blackstone and Plowden recorded the outcome of the meeting:

He returned visibly shaken by the response. The problem was simple. Mrs Thatcher was contemplating going to the country in the near future, although the CPRS could not have known this. Most people were predicting an autumn election and she saw the report as an electoral liability. Sparrow was directed to recover the report from departments to ensure that all copies were destroyed. The second paper on portable personal pensions seemed to have been given no consideration at all.

The Green Paper and SERPS

When asked in an interview in *New Society* in October 1983 whether the government would give 'an assurance that the earnings-related scheme would be preserved in its present form', Norman Fowler replied: 'We've got no plans to take it away.' There was, therefore, no public proposal for changing SERPS, and no mandate for change was sought in the 1983 manifesto. In the light of what followed this was an indefensible silence, given the gravity of the changes proposed. But there was a plan and it was largely of the Prime Minister's making. As *The Times* reported on 6 May 1985, the cabinet discussion of the future of SERPS was 'pre-empted' by the Prime Minister's insistence that occupational and private pensions should replace SERPS. As *The Times* went on: 'The Prime Minister has effectively bounced the Cabinet and the Treasury out of any alternative in spite of her insistence yesterday that . . . Cabinet is considering it.'

The Green Paper in June 1985 argued that social security had achieved one of its basic targets, the improvement in the living standards of pensioners between 1951 and 1981, and indicated the signs of increasing prosperity among pensioners, notably the fact that half were owner-occupiers and 'have a self-sufficiency and independence denied to their predecessors'. This and the anticipated costs of the pension were the two major planks in the argument for the abolition of SERPS. The costs of SERPS would, the Green Paper assumed, rise to £4 billion by the turn of the century and, thirty years later, to £25 billion – half the total cost of the pension bill. Moreover, the Green Paper went on:

We should not be deceived about the nature of national insurance today. It is not the same as private insurance, and owes little to normal insurance principles. It is a pay as you go scheme. Today's contributors meet the cost of today's benefits. As for tomorrow the most we can do is create a liability to be met by our children.

Coming to the point, the Green Paper warned in apocalyptic tones:

> The certain and emerging cost of the SERPS should give everyone, of whatever persuasion – pause for thought. The twenty year postponement of the full implementation of the scheme had nothing to do with building up a fund. There is no fund. The postponement was based on the hope that the scheme could be afforded from 1998 and go on being afforded thereafter. The hope was based on the assumption that the rate of unemployment would be two and a half per cent and that the growth in real earnings would be three per cent a year.
>
> . . . there are few who would now defend those assumptions and even fewer who would say with confidence that the commitment can be met. There are central questions, therefore, about whether the present scheme is a sensible way of planning and whether it is fair to the future working population to hand down such a bill.

There was also the question of the disincentive SERPS posed to building up an occupational pension. The responsibility for meeting 'all our financial expectations in retirement' could not in all conscience, it was argued, be laid on our children. 'Instead we should ensure that everybody is able to save and invest for his [sic] own additional pension.' SERPS was, therefore, to be abolished, the basic pension was to be enhanced, and all employees would have to contribute to an occupational or to a personal pension.

But the alternative to SERPS was not to be the extension of occupational pensions. Rather, pensions, like home ownership and share ownership, were to be another expression of popular capitalism and to enable the

> people in this country to take a more direct share in their own future and in the future of the economy. The Government's proposals on pensions respond to that desire by giving greater freedom and greater choice to individuals. They will replace the two nations in old age – those with their own pension provision and those dependent on the state – by a nation in which everyone is saving through their job for a better retirement.

Reaction and reconsideration

The proposals to abolish SERPS provoked the strongest and most effective reactions of all those contained in the Green Paper. The opposition parties, the pensions industry, the trade unions, pressure groups concerned with pensioners and the SSAC all rejected the proposals, using in many cases virtually the same arguments to demolish the demographic and economic assumptions made. Some of the alarmist figures could be exposed quite quickly as totally misleading, for example, the fact that future pension costs were presented in cash terms. As the TUC said: 'this presentation distorts and exaggerates the impact of future pension costs . . . [and] ignores the ability of the next generation to meet future costs out of higher future earnings'.

Any calculations of future costs would obviously vary depending on the assumptions about growth, unemployment, fertility and mortality. In both its economic and demographic forecasts the government appeared to have taken the worst possible case. To begin with, the Green Paper implied that the demographic findings were new and that it would be irresponsible of any government to ignore them. They were in fact the *same* demographic assumptions on which SERPS had been based in 1975. Indeed, the Government Actuary, feeling that his professional reputation had been compromised, was stung into a public defence of the assumptions made in 1975. SERPS, he said, 'was introduced in full knowledge of the likely costs'. Second, in its projections, the government chose to take the 'worst case' by basing the increase in costs on the 2030s, the 'pensioner peak' years caused by the baby boom of the 1960s. At this point the 'dependency ratio' – the ratio of people in work and contributing to the numbers of pensioners – was at its lowest. After that, as the government itself admitted, the ratio would improve . Third, the government chose to assume that the economy would grow by only 1.5 per cent a year (compared with a yearly average of 2 per cent over the previous twenty years – in 1985 it was actually forecast to grow by 3 per cent). Finally, casting doubt upon its own confidence in its economic strategy, the government forecast unemployment stabilising at 6 per cent, compared with 5 per cent over the previous twenty years.

The SSAC in its Third Report summed up the flaws in the government's case succinctly:

> We do not feel it would be justifiable to make pension scheme changes now in anticipation of a demographic problem in fifty years time. We consider that it would be more sensible to wait until the turn of the century when not only will the likely ratio of elderly people to workers in 2030 have become clearer but the longer term prospects for economic growth through into the next century will be more apparent.

Indeed, the whole notion of the 'dependency ratio' and its significance was questioned by independent experts who emphasised that the critical factor for the contribution rate was not simply the pensioner–worker ratio but the profile of employment and unemployment in general. Thus, Professor Bernard Benjamin of City University argued that: 'Even on the extreme assumptions . . . the overall dependency ratio will not be much larger than it was in 1951. . . . Claims that further demographic changes will be economically intolerable do not seem to be founded on past experience or on the facts.' As the Union Coalition for Social Security (UCSS) later pointed out, there had been a bigger increase in the proportion of pensioners to the population of working age since the 1950s than was expected to occur in the next century, and yet in that period pensions had risen significantly without undue hardship to people in work.

The argument was endorsed by the SSAC, which also implied that the government in its ideological enthusiasm was massaging the figures. No case had been made, it said, 'which would justify revision of any of the key features of the scheme established with such care in 1975 . . . it is premature to make alterations now'.

Most significantly, the government did not provide figures showing how contributions would have to rise to pay for SERPS. The Government Actuary's report on the bill eventually showed that tying pension rates to prices and abolishing SERPS would mean an increase in the joint employer's and employee's contribution rate from 17.65 to 18.5 per cent by 2033. If SERPS were maintained and the basic pension raised in line with earnings the joint contribution rate was projected to rise to 27.3 per cent – 10 per cent above its 1986 level. As the UCSS pointed out, 'Compared with the increases in contribution rates imposed by the Government in the last few years . . . an increase of 10 per cent over a period of nearly half a century does not seem particularly alarming, especially bearing in mind that this level of contribution would be needed, in all probability, for only a few years.' Even the Institute of Fiscal Studies, which had at an early stage been sceptical of the cost of SERPS, estimated that it would cost at most 5 per cent of the wages bill by 2020 and, as such, was indeed 'affordable'. In any case, as was pointed out by many of the hundreds of submissions received on the Green Paper, the abolition of SERPS and the introduction of private pensions involved an increase in national insurance contributions whether contracted in or out of SERPS. Irrespective of how pensions were provided, they would have to be paid for by the working population in some form.

The ideological significance of personal pensions, a particularly hazardous form of personal risk-taking, in the overall strategy of 'popular capitalism' became clearer when it emerged that the review committee itself had not even considered the option of abolition, and that the government in turn, in its zeal to rush to abolition, had not considered the alternative methods of saving money by modifying rather than abolishing the scheme. Moreover, not only were the administrative costs of private pension schemes far higher than SERPS, it was also evident that the compulsory minimum contribution of 4 per cent would not only be a higher contribution but that the level of benefits would be far lower. Finally, the 'money-purchase' alternative, based on unpredictable and high-risk investment returns, was a poor alternative to the more secure option of final salary schemes.

By promoting private pensions the scheme was also making a deliberate attempt to undermine occupational pension schemes which, because they were often earnings-related, money-purchase or index-linked, were seen by the right-wing Centre for Policy Studies as a subtle form of socialism. Such schemes did not, it was argued, create that feeling of direct participation and involvement in the wealth creation of the nation. Only private pensions could do that. The '2 per cent' incentive for people leaving their company occupational pension schemes to take up private pensions was, therefore, an explicit attempt to undermine occupational pension schemes, with their built-in guaranteed minimum pension equivalent to SERPS. The SSAC summed up in its Fourth Report the significance of what the government was proposing: 'Taken together with the abolition of earnings related supplements to maternity, sickness and unemployment benefits, the implied abandonment of earnings relation as a matter for the state sector marks a fundamental change in social security philosophy.'

The White Paper and the Bill

The government was stunned by the unity and the consistency of the response to the proposals to abolish SERPS. The White Paper insisted that it stood by the objectives of reform, which were supported by bodies 'such as the Institute of Directors and companies like the Save and Prosper Group'. However convincing such impartiality was, the government recognised the 'substantial body of opinion which favours modifying SERPS rather than abolishing it'. This included 'bodies representing employers such as the CBI . . . and pension interests'. Few attempts were made to defend the economic or demographic arguments. The weight of expert and political opinion had made it clear that it would have been politically inept, possibly fatal, to force it through.

Instead, the White Paper, like the Green Paper, proposed no change for people retiring this century, but instead of abolition there would be a modified SERPS scheme coming fully into effect by 2010 which, designed to look like major concessions, placated the pensions industry and the employers while significantly reducing the scope and effectiveness of the scheme.

Briefly, the main provisions in the White Paper were:

(1) To calculate the SERPS pension not on 25 per cent of the 'twenty best years' but on 20 per cent averaged over a lifetime's earnings. Special protection would be built in for women who had breaks in work to bring up families and for those who became disabled and for those looking after them.

(2) Survivors' benefits would be cut to a half of the earners' pensions for deaths after 2000.

(3)   People would be allowed to opt out of both their employers' schemes and SERPS and buy individual personal pensions from insurance companies, banks and building societies; the occupational pension schemes contracted out of state schemes would be responsible for inflation proofing their guaranteed minimum pensions by 3 per cent a year (an erosion of the previous requirement since the state had previously been responsible for all post-retirement inflation proofing); an extra subsidy of 2 per cent national insurance contributions would be allowed for new contracted-out occupational pension schemes and personal pensions.

(4)   The additional pension for people in contracted-out money-purchase or personal pension schemes would be calculated as if it were on the earnings-related formula. That would be deducted from their SERPS pension, regardless of what they were actually receiving, on the assumption that the employer would make it up.

The effects of the 'reform' of SERPS

If SERPS were now fully operational, it is estimated that the average SERPS addition for newly retired people would be £23.85. That, as the TUC put it, 'would provide for a significant improvement in the living standards of pensioners without creating an unsupportable economic burden. It would also dispense with the need for pensioners to apply for means tested benefits to survive'. The full impact of the government's plans emerged during the debate on the Social Security Bill. As with every other aspect of the reforms the government was extremely reluctant to provide figures which would illustrate the effects of its proposals. Finding out what effect the full SERPS cut would have on future pension levels involved, said the UCSS, 'a good deal of detective work'. Basic information to the Standing Committee on the Bill was blocked by 'inexcusable delays' and 'in one case a blank refusal'. The effects of the bill were eventually deduced by comparing the figures in the technical annexe to the White Paper with figures obtained by way of parliamentary questions.

A fundamental point was that the full implications of the government's proposals involved a *permanent* break in the link between pensions and earnings. In other words, future pensioners would be much worse off than they are now, in relation to the incomes of working people. From a parliamentary answer on 6 February 1986 it was possible to compare the difference in the value of a pension if (a) the basic pension were related to earnings and SERPS were retained in full with (b) a pension linked to prices only and cuts in SERPS. Using these data, the UCSS showed that the effects of the Fowler proposals would be that the pension expectations of a young person leaving school in 1988 and retiring forty years later would be *halved*. A sixteen-year-old male embarking on a career of low-paid work would be worst hit. With a full SERPS pension, on lowest earnings, he would receive a pension of £128 per week, based on the government's assumptions that average earnings would be £411 a week. The modified SERPS pension would be £64 a week – exactly half. Compared with average earnings at retirement age the value of the pension would fall from 31 to 15.5 per cent. A sixteen-year-old female in a similar situation retiring in 2028 would received £99 a week without the cuts but only £50 a week with the cuts. Average earnings for women being assumed to be £251 per week, this meant a reduction from 39.5 to 20 per cent of those earnings.

The youngest age group stand to lose most – and those in low-paid work will be the hardest hit, but even young people in well-paid employment would lose a great deal. At the highest band of earnings (£206 pension per week) a young man will lose £90 and a woman £67 per week. Men and women in mid-career, aged forty or more will lose up to a third of the pension they would have received. The UCSS concluded:

> It is clear, therefore, that the background against which the proposed cuts in SERPS must be judged is one of steady erosion of the basic pension as a proportion of earnings. The combined effect being to halve the pension expectations of low paid workers and to make pensioners even poorer, relative to the general level of incomes, than they are today.

These are the policies which are now in force. These are the pension prospects for people retiring after the end of the century. They represent a future cycle of poverty in work and in old age – a cycle which would have been broken by the original SERPS provisions, and by the commitment to earnings-related pensions. Poverty in old age had been seen as a problem; for this government it became the solution.

Picking on Widows

For women, the effects of the cuts in SERPS were set out by Age Concern in its comments on the bill: 'Both withdrawal of the 20 years rule and reduction of transferability to spouses will disadvantage women, and elderly women on their own are amongst the poorest in British Society.' They are among the poorest precisely because previous pension schemes failed to take account of their needs. In 1982, 1,288,000 women were on supplementary pension – 72 per cent of all pensioners claiming supplementary benefit. Low pay means low pensions; part time often means no occupational pensions. SERPS, therefore, was more beneficial to women than to men. The EOC said it provided 'the best opportunity the majority of women have ever had to acquire economic independence in their old age'. Evidence from the DHSS has shown that the twenty-years provision would ensure that, despite interrupted work histories, most women would qualify for SERPS. Abolition of SERPS would, therefore, be a 'serious setback' but, equally, the modification of the scheme, especially the abolition of the twenty-years rule, scrapped precisely those features most advantageous to women.

For widows the modified SERPS scheme proposed that, instead of gaining the whole of their husband's pension as the original scheme had allowed, they would in future be entitled to only half of it. This policy in halving women's benefits was complemented by another change in the benefits available to existing widows. It was another example of the government's obsession with 'targeting'. The Green Paper proposed that benefits for widows should be 'restructured' to concentrate help on those widows most in need and at the time they most needed it. Three changes were proposed: first, that at bereavement, instead of the widow's allowance paid for six months of widowhood, a lump sum of £1000 would be paid.

Second, widowed mother's allowance and widow's pension would be paid from the onset of widowhood and not after six months as at present. Third, to 'concentrate help on older widows' less likely to be working, the ages at which the various rates of widow's pension were payable would each be increased by five years. Thus, the lowest rate (£11.40) would not begin until forty-five instead of forty, the full rate at fifty-five rather than fifty. This would, said the government 'direct resources more effectively'.

In sum, while the changes have increased the amount of help available to widows with dependent children and older widows at the time of bereavement, there will be a substantial reduction in the overall amount of money going to widows. The Government Actuary estimated that while the initial changes would cost £24 million in 1988–9, savings by 1993 would amount to over £50 million, and £117 million by 2013. The widows who have lost most are those who are either widowed or who cease to be eligible for widowed mother's allowance (because their youngest child leaves school) between the ages of forty and fifty-five. Women ceasing to qualify for the widowed mother's allowance before the age of forty-five will lose all benefit and those who cease to qualify between the ages of forty-five and fifty-five will receive less benefit than previously. About 1500 women widowed between the ages of forty and forty-five will fail to qualify for a widow's pension, and about 3500 widowed between the ages of forty-five and fifty-four will qualify for a lower pension. In specific terms it means that a widow who is forty-one in 1988 and has a fourteen-year-old child who would have transferred on to an age-related widow's pension at the age of forty-three when the child reaches sixteen and leaves school will not now qualify for a pension when her widow's allowance ends. In addition, 11,000 widows widowed at age fifty or above will qualify for the lower age-related pension.

The impact on young widows was immediate, and the first appeals against the age limits to widow's pensions were being heard in January 1989. The case of Mrs Doreen Whitbread, widowed on 18 February 1988 when she was under forty-five and thus disqualified from receiving any pension when her six months' widow's allowance ran out on 22 August 1988, was taken as a test case by NACAB. Twenty thousand widows won benefit back when the DSS was found to be at fault in March 1989.

Pensioners and Housing Benefits: 'Is This What I Fought for?'

'The April changes are not cuts' . . . I wish he would tell that to the thousands of pensioners in my constituency.

(Andrew Bowden, Conservative MP for Brighton Kemptown, quoting from a letter received from the Minister for Social Security, House of Commons, 27 April 1988)

In Chapter 2 we set out the background to the changes in housing benefit and described how those changes had a devastating effect, on pensioners in particular. From the 'structural tables' it was clear that 26 per cent of pensioners would be better off and that 49 per cent would lose out. Despite this, Mrs Thatcher insisted – in a reply to Neil Kinnock in the House of Commons on 31 March 1988 – that '87 per cent of pensioners are getting more or less the same'. Essentially, 2.7 million pensioners lost all or some entitlement to housing benefit. Those who lost all housing benefit were those with capital over £6000 (later £8000), war pensioners and people with industrial disability pensions who no longer had their income discounted against housing benefit, and those 400,000 people whose housing benefit supplement was summarily abolished. Apart from those dramatic losses, in some cases over £20 a week, the most common losses were suffered by those who, for the first time, found themselves paying 20 per cent of their rates and all their water rates out of very small incomes, with a pension which did not match the rate increase, and those with small additional pensions who lost some rent and rate rebates because of the increase in the housing benefit taper. Many were both elderly and disabled; the majority were women, and many of those were widows.

The cases which poured in to MPs, the CABx, housing officers and the newspapers revealed some of the extent to which the elderly lived on the margins of poverty, with incomes barely sufficient, after their housing costs, to meet basic necessities. In particular, the costs of fuel, food and transport were major preoccupations. Often the key grievance was that the basic pension did not match the increase in rates, while at the same time the pensioner's cost of living was soaring. Many wrote of the service given during the war, of lives spent working in jobs which paid very little and which, at best, had brought a tiny occupational pension, of lives spent caring for parents and children. Many, with great dignity, spoke of the sense that they were better off than others – but nearly all betrayed a sense of personal grievance that, having been told there would be no losers and no cuts to people on benefit, they found themselves, suddenly and without warning, facing what in some cases were massive losses.

As rent levels rose and benefits were reduced, the confusion in local DHSS and housing offices, with rent arrears piling up, assessments challenged and the rules changed in Parliament, generated across the country a sense of total bewilderment. Some of the instances quoted below were collected by local housing officers; others from MPs' postbags or from cases cited in the House of Commons. For many people it was literally months before they heard from the special unit in Glasgow set up to unscramble the situation and provide compensation for those losing more than £2.50. During that time they were still liable for the levels of rents and rates first notified to them in April 1988.

Those who lost entitlement because of the new capital limit were among the most dramatic and at first attracted the most political attention, since those thrifty pensioners who had saved more than £3000 and who were credited with having £1 a week income for every £250 and those who lost all benefit because they had capital over £6000 were precisely the people of whom Mrs Thatcher would have approved. Thus, a widow living on a weekly income of £50, comprising a state pension plus a little interest on savings, with just over £8000 capital, wrote to complain of having lost all housing benefit: 'Mrs T. is resorting to an outright lie over our incomes by saying that every £250 is worth £1 a week to us. Do they think we're too senile to work out that that would need interest rates of 20 per cent and where can you get that in safe investment?'

Another widow with savings of over £6000 but with a weekly income of only £31 found her housing benefit cut by £28.70 leaving her, after paying rent, with an income of £2.30. She wrote:

The Government demands that I use my savings for gas, electricity, telephone, television, spectacles and all living expenses. That leads me to complain that the very qualities Mrs Thatcher extols – hard work, self-reliance, independence, thrift and honesty have led to this cruel sentence.

The anomalies and hardship created for such pensioners and the immense political embarrassment they caused swiftly brought changes. Other pensioners, on lower incomes and with no savings, found that they had to sustain losses without such assistance. In particular, the loss of the local authority discretion to discount industrial disablement as income caused anger and disbelief.

Writing on behalf of his parents, who were required to find an extra £17 a fortnight, one gentleman protested that the government had consistently ignored those who were 'worse off':

> When [my father] was 62 he suffered an Industrial Injury and was forced to retire prematurely. He was awarded an Industrial Injuries Pension as compensation for the effects of his injury and the loss of a full time income. This loss was a considerable blow but he was assured that his pension would be 'safe'. That he would always receive it. Not safe from the cruel policies of the Conservative Party which is to let those who have, have more, and those who have tried but did not succeed be penalised for their failure.

Another ex-serviceman, signing himself 'An Ex-Tobruk Desert Rat', wrote:

> My wife and I live in a two bedroomed council house (our pride and joy). We are both disabled (registered). Both are ex-service. Our shock came today. From our state pension we must find a further £8 a week to cover our new rent and rates – leaving us with £61.70. From this, due to our age and ill health we must find £10 a week for coal. When I phoned the council officers . . . I was coolly informed that the reason why our increase was so great was, quote, 'The disabled allowance no longer applies to those over 50 years of age.' My blood boiled.

Thomas McAvoy, MP for Glasgow Rutherglen, shocked the Houses of Commons with a constituency example of a couple, both aged seventy-three, 'the husband with a disability pension of

£33 a week', who had to find, immediately, an extra £90 a month in rent and rates. Perhaps, he added, 'that is the worst example I have encountered but there are many others where housing benefit cuts have resulted in a dramatic decrease in senior citizens' weekly income'.

Others, on even lower incomes, lost both rent and rates rebates. A widow from Grangemouth with a weekly income of £50, consisting of her widow's pension and a small occupational pension, described how her housing benefit had been cut by £13: 'Being a pensioner and a widow . . . I have now to find another £13. If I want a pair of shoes I will have to do without food for a month.'

Meanest of all and most significant, because the changes anticipated the poll tax, was the impact of having to pay 20 per cent of rates from the lowest incomes. One widow, on supplementary benefit, describing how she had lost her first husband and a son on active service, illustrated in her letter some of the many reasons why elderly women are poor:

> I took in washing to help me and my two children, later on I worked in a shop as all had to live on was 30/- a week. It was very hard for me often . . . I nursed my second husband until he died of cancer. I am now 81 years old and even though I have worked nearly all my life I still do not enjoy good health, so as you can appreciate . . . I was so hoping we should get a pension where I would not have to look at every penny. . . . We were sent forms in time for anyone who needed things to apply for help for a pair of shoes. I was turned down. . . . Since April I have had to pay £10.50 a month rates which until then was paid for me. Every week the shopping gets dearer . . .

Others described graphically what they would have to do without in order to meet their new rates bills:

> My wife and I are 73 year old pensioners, we receive a pittance on a supplementary pension. With the new changes in the supplementary pension rules . . . we will be £200 a year worse off in our weekly pittance. Today we had to have our telephone taken out of our house. This was our only means of keeping in touch with the outside world. It was an imperative life line for

our survival. We have also stopped using our gas central heating and converted to a paraffin heater.

I was mentioned in despatches during my service in SEAC in the last war. Is this what I fought for – a selfish, uncaring, unreasonable . . . society? . . . Where did it all go wrong?

Finally, as one lady put it:

Now that Mrs Thatcher is thinking of making different concessions on housing benefits with up to £10,000 savings couldn't something be done for the thousands like myself who have nothing and are now having to pay 20 per cent of the rates. We waited months for our rise and then found we had to pay this and some more for rates. I am a widow and my only income is my pension. Previous to April I received £43.38 per week including supplementary. After the budget I was due for £1.30 rise . . . but now I have to pay £1.68 rates which brings me a little worse off than before. When I get my pension I have to put £25 away for bills. Gas, electricity, life insurance, house insurance and contents, ground rent, water rates, telephone, TV licence. This leaves me £18 to live on, which isn't much fun. All my home is getting worn out like me and cannot be replaced. By the way I have got £400 in the bank but dare not break into it as it is for my funeral.

And pensioners knew that these new rate demands were just the prelude for the poll tax, which according to one pensioner would mean 'devastation for many many people: indeed, many, including myself, will be unable to meet it. What happens then? I think this Bill . . . is a truly evil one. It does not make any allowance whatsoever for a person's ability to pay. Many pensioners are going to be in deep trouble.'

Many pensioners *are* in deep trouble and, because of the cuts in SERPS, today's lowest-paid workers, part-time workers and a high proportion of women workers will be in even deeper trouble when they retire.

The erosion of the value of the basic pension and the virtual abolition of any commitment to earnings relation in the future give rise to real concern about the future living standards of pensioners.

High fuel and food costs, poor housing, under-funding of geriatric care in the health and community services and the fundamental changes threatened in the NHS offer a devastating prospect. At this rate, British pensioners will remain the poor relations of the rest of Europe. Those who have chosen to opt for the high risks of investment-based money-purchase pensions in a market which was seen in November 1987 to be totally unstable will now add this burden of anxiety to the others which accumulate in old age.

As all the evidence which brought the condition of our elderly people to public attention shows, millions of pensioners today live on the margins of a poverty so stringent that every price increase, whether in food, fuel or television licence becomes a source of real anxiety. Not for these pensioners the choice of a second holiday, private residential care or a few luxuries: no one would deny that for millions of pensioners Britain is another country. For high-earning couples, occupational pensions and mature private pensions make all the difference. The cycle of riches and poverty divides the nation in old age with even more force than it does for younger people – for there is no opportunity to close that gap and make up the ground. Ultimately, however, policies for retirement are not just about economics or demography. They also concern ethics and the shared responsibility which maintains a community not only within generations but between generations. Sir Douglas Wass, former Permanent Secretary to the Treasury, put it most succinctly, in August 1986 in the *Observer*:

> We are sometimes encouraged to look on the elderly as a rather tiresome burden on the wealth creators. But that is to ignore the moral claim that the elderly are entitled to make on those in work. They, after all, created the stock of physical assets, the factories, the roads, the houses, the schools and so on which their children use to generate their own incomes. The claim of the retired is the legitimate claim of those who have collectively saved out of past income not in any narrow financial sense, but by forgoing consumption when they were in work.

That moral claim must be revived and honoured if the next generation is to have the secure and dignified living standards which would have followed from the principles enshrined in the link with earnings, and with SERPS, which this government has discarded precisely so that the present generation of those in work can, in a very 'narrow financial sense', increase their consumption. Whether they know the price they are being required to pay is not clear.

7 'Policing the Workshy'

> We care that unemployed people should have proper
> help, but above all that they should be brought back
> into work.
>
> (Norman Fowler)

This statement to the Conservative Women's Conference in 1986
provides the rhetoric against which to test the reality of what the
Conservatives have done for the unemployed since 1979. In this
chapter we review the government's policies for providing 'proper
help' to the unemployed and see what the attempts to bring them
back into work have meant in practice. The government has
succeeded in removing roughly half a million names from the
unemployment register, largely by dint of well over twenty different alterations to the ways in which the register has been
counted, but that is not the same as putting those half million back
to work. We document the sustained attack on the living
standards of the unemployed and the attempt to drive them off the
register and into any kind of work, no matter how badly paid,
insecure or unfitted to the skills and aptitudes of the employee.

Families where the head of the household is unemployed are
among the poorest, with incomes around half those of families of
the employed. The Family Expenditure Survey of 1985 showed
that, even for those out of work for short periods, family income
was half that of families with working heads, and their position
deteriorated as the period of unemployment lengthened. Richard
Berthoud carried out research for the DHSS on all those on
supplementary benefits in the early 1980s; he summed up the
position of the unemployed with this comment: 'With the possible
exception of the down-and-out homeless, direct measures of

hardship show there is no poorer group of people than unemployed couples with children.' It is against this background that government policies for the unemployed should be viewed.

These policies have had a coherence about them which has made their overall intention unmistakable. Benefit levels have been systematically cut, resulting in a shift away from insurance benefits toward means-tested benefits; the qualifying conditions for unemployment benefit have been made harder; the period for which one may be disqualified from receiving benefit has increased fourfold; the administration of benefits has been considerably tightened; and special fraud squads have been imported into benefit offices. At the same time the rights of low-paid employees have been eroded in respect of both wages and job security. The cumulative effects of these changes have been to lower the living standards of almost all unemployed claimants, to deprive many others of benefits altogether, and to drive others into either very low-paid jobs or government 'training' schemes, which in turn help to reinforce a low-wage economy. Once in such work, employees are often obliged to remain there or risk being disqualified from benefit. Commenting on the Poor Law Amendment Act 1834, which also set out to drive the poor back to work by offering the workhouse as the only alternative, Sidney and Beatrice Webb, the Poor Law historians, said that it had 'put the whip of starvation into the hands of the employers'. In their own genteel way, that is precisely what Fowler and his successors have tried to do in the 1980s.

Benefits for the Unemployed: Twenty-five Cuts

> The Government's aim throughout is to provide a
> better, a more economic and a more efficient service to
> unemployed people who are claiming benefit.
>
> (*Payment of Benefits to Unemployed People*)

The seeds of government policies can be found in the report from which the quotation above is taken. Written in 1981 by Sir Derek Rayner, it reviewed the system of payments of benefits to the unemployed. The flavour of the report can be inferred from chapter headings such as 'Policing the Workshy' and from the refusal of the staff of the Department of Employment and of the DHSS to co-operate with the review. Rayner, brought in to apply the know-how of industry to the world of welfare, favoured the abolition of unemployment benefit altogether and its replacement by supplementary benefit, but fell short of recommending it because 'the idea of means testing every claimant might not be politically acceptable'! Nevertheless, the idea was attractive to government, which, instead of abolishing the benefit outright, has reduced its value by stealth.

In a comprehensive review of cuts in benefits from the unemployed from 1979 to 1988, entitled 'Turning the Screw', Professor Atkinson and J. Micklewright list twenty-seven separate cuts that have worsened the lot of the unemployed, in contrast to four changes which have benefited them and seven which had both positive and negative effects. They summarise the changes:

> Although many of the measures are limited in their individual impact, the majority have made the system less generous and have weakened the role of unemployment *insurance* as opposed to unemployment *assistance*. The total effect of the Conservative Government's actions is such that the structure of benefits for the unemployed in 1988 is quite different from that in 1979. It is a matter of concern that little by little the system has undergone major changes of principle without widespread public recognition. . . . Moreover, the extent of income support for the unemployed has become markedly less generous at a time when it is most needed.

Among the changes in unemployment benefit they note the abolition of the earnings-related supplement in 1982; the taxation of unemployment benefit in 1982; the reduction of unemployment benefit for those with occupational pensions of more than £35 per week in 1981 (though the £35 limit has never been increased, thus adversely affecting more people each year); the extension of the maximum period of disqualification from benefit from six to twenty-six weeks; the abolition from 1986 of the lower and intermediate rates of benefit for those without a full contribution record; and more stringent qualifying conditions for benefit coming into effect in 1988. All these changes have reduced either the amount of benefit paid or the numbers of people claiming unemployment benefit. Depending on their circumstances, many people will have been deprived of benefit altogether or pushed on to supplementary benefit/income support.

Once on supplementary benefit/income support they have of course been subject to all the cuts in those benefits. Many of those on unemployment benefit would have been affected by these cuts in any event since about two-thirds of those with unemployment benefit have to rely on supplementary benefit/income support as well. One of the more important cuts is the carry-over effect on supplementary benefit/income support of the extension of the disqualification period; if an unemployed person is disqualified from unemployment benefit any entitlement he or she may have to income support is automatically paid at a reduced rate, so any such extension has a double effect. Other cuts include the payment of only 50 per cent of mortgage interest for the first sixteen weeks of benefit, from 1987; the abolition of payments to sixteen- and seventeen-year-olds from 1988; and the replacement of single payments by the social fund.

Atkinson and Micklewright calculate that the combined net effect of all these changes in benefits has left the unemployed in 1988 £560 million worse off than if the system as at 1979 had been left unchanged. That is the 'proper help' given by Norman Fowler and his colleagues.

They also calculate the changes in the value of unemployment benefit between 1978 and 1988. Broadly speaking, although it fluctuated from year to year, the real value of the benefit remained the same in 1988 as it had been in 1978 in the sense that the single person's benefit increased in line with the rise in the retail price index. What it failed to do was keep up with the rise in average earnings of those in work; by 1988 the single person's benefit was worth 20 per cent less when judged as a proportion of average earnings. What this means is that although the unemployed could buy exactly the same things with their money in 1988 as they could in 1979, those in work had seen their standards of living rise sharply and could buy a good deal more. The unemployed have been deliberately left behind and have not shared in the general prosperity of the 1980s; the gap in living standards between those in and out of work has widened as a result of government policy.

The government is fond of referring back to Beveridge as a

benchmark and using his arguments to support its policies. In fact Beveridge recommended that unemployment benefit should be paid as an insurance benefit, without test of means, for as long as the period of unemployment lasted, *without time limit*. The conclusion that Atkinson and Micklewright reach is that the government has moved in the opposite direction: 'There has been a major change in emphasis, amounting to the covert abandonment of the insurance principle as far as the unemployed are concerned.' They also point out that this has happened without any public discussion of the changes, and this despite the government having had every opportunity to announce its intentions at the time of the much publicised Fowler reviews.

Abandoning the Insurance Principle

The drift away from the insurance principle has been achieved piecemeal. Four insurance benefits – the earnings-related supplement, the two lower rates of unemployment benefit and unemployment benefit for students during short vacations – were simply abolished. In addition, the qualifying conditions which bring claimants into the insurance scheme have been made harder to meet; the period of disqualification from benefit has quadrupled; and the government has taken powers to reduce the period of benefit for some of the unemployed from twelve months to six.

The Social Security Act 1988 introduced complicated rules which have the effect of making it harder to qualify for sickness or unemployment benefit. In effect they require the unemployed person to have worked for longer periods in *one* of the two tax years preceding the claim for benefit, and in addition require him or her to have either paid or been credited with more contributions in *each* of those two years, instead of just one. The effects of these changes will be to remove about 350,000 from unemployment benefit, and it will particularly hit young people and married women returning to work, since neither group will have had the chance to build up a contribution record.

Quadrupling the period of disqualification, which is discussed in the next section, has the effect of removing over 400,000 unemployed from benefit every year. In 1986 the government also took the power to include the period of disqualification, now six months, *within* the one year for which unemployment benefit is paid. At present the year of benefit payment begins *after* the period of disqualification stops; when the new power is used it will have the effect of halving the length of time unemployment benefit is paid to all those disqualified.

The taxation of unemployment benefit since 1982 has had the effect not of reducing the weekly amount of benefit but of treating it as taxable income, so that when the claimant becomes unemployed the amount of tax rebate he or she receives is considerably reduced.

The effect of the erosion of the insurance principle depends on the personal circumstances of the unemployed. For those with capital over £3000, or from April 1988 £6000, or for those with a working partner, it would probably mean they would receive nothing at all. For the remainder it could mean reliance on means-tested supplementary benefit or income support, with all the well-known problems associated with that benefit. One of the most unjust features of the old supplementary benefit scheme was the way in which it particularly discriminated against the unemployed. There were two rates of benefit, one for those on benefit for less than a year and a considerably higher rate for pensioners and those on benefit for more than a year, because it was recognised that the short-term rate was not sufficient to meet long-term needs. By 1988 the gap between these two rates was as much as £18.50 per week for a couple and £8.25 for a single person. The only group of claimants who were never allowed to proceed to the long-term rate were the unemployed. This gross injustice was deplored repeatedly, both by the old Supplementary Benefits Commission and by the SSAC, but to no avail.

As if to underline the decline of the insurance principle, in April 1988, for the first time since the Second World War, the government set the rates of unemployment benefit *below* that of the single person's rate of income support. Unemployment benefit is now paid at a rate below that which is supposed to be the minimum one can be expected to live on.

The Disqualification Rules: 'Penal, Harsh and Unreasonable'

The above judgement on the changes to the rules governing the disqualification from unemployment was given by the opposition spokesman Michael Meacher during the debate which saw the length of the maximum period of disqualification more than doubled. These rules are one of the principal devices used by the government to force people back into work and, more important, to keep them there however bad the pay or working conditions. What was originally a sensible safeguard in the insurance scheme, which attracted all-party support over three-quarters of a century, was transformed in the space of eighteen months into a vicious penalty against the so-called 'voluntary' unemployed.

Disqualification dates back to 1911, when its purpose was to protect the contributors to the insurance fund from having to pay out benefits to those who had brought their unemployment on themselves. If someone left a job for no good reason, or was dismissed for misconduct, he or she could be disqualified from receiving unemployment benefit for a maximum of six weeks in order to safeguard against the abuse of the insurance fund. If after that period the unemployed person had not found other employment, he or she qualified for the benefits for which, after all, he or she had paid contributions. This six-week maximum period remained in force for seventy-five years until October 1986, when the government more than doubled it to thirteen weeks. In April 1988 it redoubled the period to twenty-six weeks, making a fourfold increase in the space of eighteen months.

Over 400,000 claimants are affected each year; those unable to claim income support will have no benefits at all for six months, a loss of anything up to £1400. They will also lose credits toward their contributions, which may make it harder for them to qualify for benefit in subsequent years. Even those who can claim income support, by definition among the very poorest, also suffer from the effects of the disqualification, which carries over into income support; they will find their benefits cut by 40 per cent of the single person's basic rate, which could cost them up to £450 over the six months. As an added bonus for the government, all those disqualified who are not eligible for income support will have no reason to sign on, and will conveniently disappear from the register, thereby 'reducing' the number of unemployed.

The extension of the period to thirteen weeks prompted a joint investigation into the operation of the disqualification by the Low Pay Unit and NACAB. The results, published in a report entitled *Disqualified From Benefit*, are a damning indictment of the way in which the disqualification is administered and of the government's flimsy reasons for introducing the change.

If the government had believed that only feckless, work-shy young men were being penalised, it could no longer hold such beliefs after the report was published. It gives many examples of people being disqualified even though the jobs they had left were positively harmful to their health, or where the pay and conditions of work were appalling and even illegal. The following examples, taken from the report, could be repeated many times over by CABx:

A woman was advised by her doctor to give up her job, which involved heavy lifting, following the threat of a miscarriage. When she did so she was disqualified from benefit.

A man injured his hand whilst engaged on a short-term job erecting marquees. His doctor advised him that he would not be fit to do this work for about a month. He left in order to find other work that he could do. Disqualified for the maximum period.

A man gave up his Community Programme job because the sawdust in the factory made his asthmatic condition worse. Disqualified for the maximum.

A 17 year old left a job where he was expected to work over 12 hours a day, including week-ends. Disqualified for four weeks, *even though it is an offence under the Factories Act to allow a young person to work such long hours*.

One of the more common reasons for disqualification is when a woman leaves her job in one area to follow her partner to another part of the country. As so often with the government's measures to remove people from benefit, it is women who are most affected.

153

Similar instances of the harsh use of the penalty were found in cases where workers had been dismissed for alleged 'misconduct' – often nothing more than rows with employers where blame could be evenly apportioned. Sometimes, as in the following example, the imposition of the penalty defies all sense of justice.

After fourteen years with the same employer a London man had a bundle of work thrown at him by his employer. He went home early to allow his boss to calm down. When he arrived for work the next day he was told by his employer that he (the employee) had resigned. He was disqualified from benefit for the maximum period and only got his benefit back by going to an appeal tribunal after an industrial tribunal found that he had been unfairly dismissed.

A man was employed as a bar manager for a probationary period of six months. The wage – £1.80 an hour for 39 hours a week – was almost certainly below the legal minimum wages council rate. After six months the contract came to an end and was not renewed. The employer claimed the man had been dismissed. Maximum disqualification.

CABx expressed great concern at the operation of the rules. The following quotation from an organiser of a Cheshire CAB catches the general mood of the many who responded to the survey, and explains some of the effects of the disqualification.

In our area a thirteen week [then the maximum] suspension of unemployment benefit automatically applies in all cases other than those of redundancy. This is causing hardship for our clients and is quite unfair in particular circumstances.

The clients who give up work to look after a spouse or relative who becomes ill and clients who experience relationship breakdown and can no longer work because of having to care for children are worst hit. They are faced with reduced income and all the problems that this brings as well as having to cope with the new emotional and logistic demands being made of them. In addition to the above there are of course those who are forced to leave their employment by intolerable working conditions or bad behaviour by their employer. We feel that this regulation causes unnecessary hardship and hits people hard at a time when they are most in need. The situation has deteriorated since suspension was increased from six to thirteen weeks.

The Department of Employment adjudication officers who take the decisions are required to follow the *Adjudication Officers' Guide*, which contains hundreds of paragraphs of guidance on, for example, what constitutes 'misconduct' or 'just cause' for leaving one's job. Evidence from CABx all over Britain showed that many disqualifications are imposed *in clear contravention of these guidelines*.

Disqualifications are nearly always given for the *maximum* period despite clear guidance, not only from within the Department but also from Social Security Commissioners, that the proper course is to decide an appropriate period of disqualification on the merits of each case. What was intended as a maximum period of six months is now likely to become the norm.

The report from the Low Pay Unit was compiled before the further extension to twenty-six weeks, and was sent to ministers before they decided to redouble the period. Among the points it made were:

(1) Claimants are frequently disqualified in clear contravention of the Department's own rules and of the guidance of the Social Security Commissioners.

(2) The maximum period is imposed as the norm, with no regard to individual circumstances, in direct contravention of Commissioners' decisions.

(3) Disqualification is implemented automatically before any evidence is gathered to support the decision, and if it is eventually withdrawn the claimant will have been without benefit for many months.

(4) Even where the rules are followed properly this often results in harsh decisions.

(5) Many disqualifications, as many as 43 per cent in one three-month period in 1987, are overturned on appeal, showing the poor nature of the original decision.

Despite this evidence, and despite a strongly worded appeal from the director of NACAB, the government pressed ahead with the extension to twenty-six weeks, thus ensuring that all the faults in the system would affect claimants doubly. With stunning disregard for the evidence, Michael Portillo, the responsible minister, argued that the 'adjudicating authorities base their decisions on the regulations governing the benefit and any relevant case law. They also take into account the particular circumstances of an individual case.' Certainly that is what they are *supposed* to do; the fact is that they do so very imperfectly at great cost to claimants. Given the appalling pressure that many adjudication officers are under, especially in inner cities, and given that they are expected to reach decisions on these often very complex cases in an average of sixteen minutes each, it is scarcely surprising that so many poor decisions are made. Portillo's refusal to acknowledge this betrays both the contempt in which he and his colleagues hold the unemployed and their intention to force them back into the labour market at all costs. This is what Norman Fowler meant by bringing them back into work.

Why did the government break with the seventy-five-year consensus and extend the period in the first place? The reasons were so weak that it felt unable to explain them during the committee stage of the bill, Tony Newton contenting himself with vague statements like 'we came to the conclusion that there was a case for extending the length of the period involved' but declining to say on what evidence this conclusion was based. Moreover, the amendment enabling the extension was slipped in to the 1986 Social Security Bill at the last minute, thus avoiding not only any public debate but also scrutiny by the SSAC. There had been no mention of any intention to change the disqualification period at any time during the two years of the Fowler reviews which preceded the bill, and no such clause in the original bill itself. Such figures as were produced in committee and since show that the numbers disqualified in any year are far more closely related to employment prospects generally than to any changes in the disqualification period, and thus gave no grounds for the extension.

Disqualifications will increase now that sixteen- and seventeen-year-olds have been forced off income support and on to YTS. In section 27 of the Employment Act 1988 the government has reserved the right to make refusal to attend the new adult ET scheme grounds for disqualification, and given its record in this field so far (it originally claimed that YTS would be voluntary) it can be only a matter of time before the government does so, despite Norman Fowler's denials that this is the intention. Brian Wolfson, Fowler's appointee as chairman of the Training Commission, told the press that it might be necessary to 'make it compulsory', and the Prime Minister was prepared to say only that it was voluntary 'for the moment'. The effect of disqualifying this group of claim-ants will be that they will be forced not just to take any low-paid job, however unsuitable, but also to take a place on training schemes where wages are likely to be even lower. It will, in effect, signal the full introduction of 'workfare', where claimants will be required to work for their benefits.

The new disqualification rules penalise hundreds of thousands who, far from having made themselves 'voluntarily' unemployed, have usually left their jobs reluctantly, either for compelling personal reasons or because of oppressive employment conditions. All the evidence points to the need for a full inquiry into the way the disqualification is currently being applied, an easing of some of the harsher regulations, stronger departmental guidance about the need to set reasonable periods rather than impose automatic six-month maxima, and more staff to ensure that enough time is given to each case. Instead, the government chose to deprive the unemployed of millions of pounds a year in the name of weaning them off dependency and back into the enterprise culture.

Availability for Work: Guilty until Proved Innocent

Alongside the changes in unemployment policies the government tightened up considerably on the administration of benefits. The government continually claimed that in doing so it was merely strengthening procedures intended to ensure that benefits went only to those legally entitled to them. It had long been the case that unemployment benefit was intended only for those who were available for work; ministers claimed that all they were doing was making sure that this availability was properly tested. While this was hard to disagree with in principle, the practice of availability testing revealed a very different intention behind the govern-ment's new-found zeal for the minutiae of administration. Taken by itself it would have given rise to questions about the government's motivation; taken in conjunction with all its other measures against the unemployed its motives must stand condemned. Indeed, the repeated air of injured innocence affected by ministers whenever challenged about their attempts to dress up as mere prudent housekeeping this additional persecution of those with the misfortune to lose their jobs calls to mind Eliot's scathing lines: 'The last temptation is the greatest treason; / To do the right deed for the wrong reason.'

Availability testing came out of Sir Derek Rayner's review of the operation of unemployment benefits in 1981. Until 1982 claimants had been tested simply by asking them if they were available for work whenever they made a new claim for benefit. If they said they were that was generally accepted; if subsequently that availability was called into doubt, either because they refused to take reasonable job offers or were suspected of being involved in activities incompatible with employment, e.g. child-minding or taking a course of study, it was always open to the Department's staff to call the claimant in for interview and, where appropriate, to stop payment.

This procedure, relying as it did upon the truthfulness of claimants, was considered too lax and a tougher test was instituted in 1982, which was made even tougher in 1986 and tougher still in 1987. As with the extension of the disqualification period, this was despite all the evidence showing that very few claimants were 'failing' the test. The obvious interpretation of the lack of success of the tests in removing claimants from benefit is that almost all claimants are in fact genuinely seeking work; the interpretation the government chose was that the test was not stringent enough to identify the 'work-shy'. It therefore issued revised rules and instructions to staff in benefit offices, the main results of which were to cause additional unjustified hardship to thousands of people already suffering the loss of their jobs.

The 'availability for work' tests were transferred from Job Centre staff, who had administered the test prior to 1982, to staff in unemployment benefit offices. Every new claimant for unemployment benefit, with very few exceptions, was then required when making a new claim for benefit to fill in two forms: the ordinary claim for benefit, and a special questionnaire designed specifically to probe the claimant's availability for work. This questionnaire later underwent two further revisions designed to make the test even harder to pass, and staff were issued with detailed instructions on how to administer it. By February 1988 the questionnaire comprised eighteen separate questions, and one 'wrong' answer could and usually did result in the claimant's benefit being immediately suspended. Once benefit was suspended further action would be taken within the Department which would result either in the claimant being deemed to be unavailable for work and therefore ineligible for unemployment benefit, or in a decision in the claimant's favour, in which case benefit would be restored and backdated, though often not until weeks or months later. In the meantime no benefit would have been paid, often causing considerable hardship and distress. Since payment of benefit would resume only when it had been established that the claimant was in fact available for work, the delay in payment would have been for no good reason; a clear case of the claimant being considered guilty until proved innocent.

The questions on the form reveal clearly the intention to try to force claimants off the register or, failing that, to force them to take the lowest-paid jobs available and then to keep them trapped at that level. In December 1987 the Department of Employment issued a circular to all benefit managers setting out in detail the steps to be taken when administering the form. It begins with a declaration of the policy:

> A claimant must be able to accept at once (or at 24 hours' notice in certain specified circumstances) any opportunity of suitable employment. This also means not just being ready to take a job, but taking active steps to draw attention to their availability for work.
>
> A claimant must not place restrictions on the nature and conditions (such as pay, hours of work, locality, etc.) they are prepared to accept which would prevent them from having reasonable prospects of getting work.

These general principles are followed through in detail. For example, claimants must demonstrate that they have been taking specific active steps to find work; staff are instructed that an answer such as 'looking for work' is not good enough. It must be

159

remembered that many claimants will only just have lost their previous job, so it will be quite unrealistic to expect them to be able to bring proof of active job-searching activities. Nevertheless, failure to do so could result in the suspension of benefit.

Not placing restrictions on the nature and conditions of work is another way of saying that the claimants must be prepared to work for rock-bottom wages, and at considerable distances from their homes. On pay the form is specific; claimants are asked to state the last three jobs they have had and then asked: 'What is the minimum weekly wage or salary you are willing to take?' If the answer is more than their recent earnings, and the rate being asked is more than the prevailing rate for the job sought in the area, or if the claimant's answer is deemed to be 'not sufficient', benefit officers are instructed to suspend payment, and benefit could then be disallowed. Thus, not only are claimants forced to take the lowest wages, but having once done so they cannot again seek work at a higher wage without putting their benefit in jeopardy.

Claimants may not seek temporary work unless there is a good reason for doing so, they must be prepared to take alternative jobs to the one they would like, they must not look for part-time work or place any restrictions on the hours they will work, and they must be prepared to travel some distance to find work; failure in any of these tests will result in the suspension and possible complete disallowance of benefit. Moreover, managers of benefit officers are under instructions to ensure that these policies are followed to the letter; they are told to monitor the 'availability awareness' of their staff and to see that the procedures are being properly applied, and to make *daily* quality control checks on all decisions where benefit has *not* been suspended. These administrative procedures are part of a concerted plan to squeeze claimants off the register, bring down the monthly unemployment statistics (while at the same time leaving the number of people unemployed unchanged) and underpin a low-wage economy.

Availability testing does not apply only to new claimants. Under the euphemism 'Restart', in 1986 the same test was also introduced for the long-term unemployed. Anyone who had been drawing benefit for a year, later reduced to six months, was called in for interview to have his or her availability for work questioned.

160

These tests place more or less unlimited discretion in the hands of the adjudication officers, who, in the first instance, are the arbiters of whether claimants are being 'unreasonable' in the restrictions they place on their availability. With managers under instruction to see that the tests are strictly applied local officers will be under pressure to make sure that at least some claimants are refused benefit. What this means in practice can be judged by the cases which began to come to the notice of MPs in their surgeries. During a debate on the tests in July 1987, Gwynneth Dunwoody gave the following examples:

A woman with a three year old child said she was available for work from 9.00 a.m. to 5.00 p.m., as these were the only hours for which she could arrange child-minders. Suspended from benefit.

Another woman with two children under four years of age said she was prepared to work from 9.00 a.m. to 5.00 p.m., Monday to Saturday, and that she was ready to start at 24 hours' notice. Because of the children she was unwilling to take night work; she was therefore suspended from benefit.

A woman who was trained as a flat-bed machinist was in receipt of unemployment benefit. Because she could not find full-time work she took part-time work. Despite there being no full-time jobs for flat-bed machinists, and despite the fact that she continued to go to the Job Centre to seek work, she was suspended from benefit for the part of the week when not working on the grounds that as she had part-time work she was not available for full-time work.

Other examples can be found in the cases that come to CABx for help; for example the following cases were all suspended during 1987: a man who had been unemployed for three years who refused to take a job which paid less than his supplementary benefit and which would not have covered his weekly expenditure; a man who had recently had a heart attack and was prepared to work only from 10.00 a.m. to 4.00 p.m.; three young mothers who, while being prepared to work from 8.30 a.m. to 5.00 p.m. were not prepared to travel more than ten miles to work; a pregnant woman who said she would need time off to attend antenatal clinic.

The test was applied particularly harshly to students in the summer of 1988. The value of the student grant has fallen by at least 20 per cent since 1979, forcing many students to work not only during the vacations but also in term time; even then most students end their academic careers in considerable debt to credit card companies, bank managers and anyone else who will lend them money. Having abolished unemployment benefit and supplementary benefit for students in the short vacations, it looks as though the government has now decided to try to prevent students obtaining any unemployment benefit and, more important, income support during the long summer vacation by a strict application of the availability test. Students who signed on in Brighton, which was being used as a pilot area, were faced with offers of jobs, many of them very low paid, and in effect told to apply for them or lose benefit.

The effect of introducing the tests originally was to reduce the number of people claiming benefit by between 5 and 7 per cent. In 1986, when the revised tests were used in twelve pilot benefit offices, between 3 and 4 per cent of claimants did not pursue their claims when faced with the questionnaire, and a further 2 to 3 per cent had their benefit disallowed. This 'success' led the government to introduce the test nationwide, phasing it in region by region to avoid any concerted show of resistance. However, for every claimant disallowed benefit there are many more who are temporarily suspended while their claim is investigated further, but whose claims are subsequently judged to be in order. For example, in the last two months of 1986 nearly 30,000 claimants were suspended from benefit after 'Restart' interviews because their availability was thought to be in doubt; of these only 10,000 were disallowed. In Crewe, during three months in the summer of 1986, of 138 claimants suspended only twenty were subsequently disallowed. In Newton Abbot, an area with a strong tradition of claimant support groups, of the ninety people suspended in a drive at the end of 1986 to remove the over-fifties from the register only one was eventually disallowed. All those claimants who were suspended but who were not subsequently disallowed benefit had to go without any benefit until their cases were decided; suspension from unemployment benefit automatically suspends supplementary benefit or income support also. The only benefit open to these claimants would be, up to April 1988, an urgent needs payment, which, for those with the necessary determination and knowledge to secure one, would be fixed below normal supplementary benefit requirements. After April 1988 even that possibility was removed, to be replaced by a crisis loan from the social fund. Faced with the evidence that the new tests were causing thousands of claimants considerable hardship, far from relaxing the measures in any way, the government reversed its usual trend of cutting civil servants and took on an extra 1400 staff specifically for availability testing.

The harassment of the unemployed finally came out of the administrative closet and into the domain of official policy with the introduction in the winter of 1988 of a new social security bill which extended the requirement that claimants should be actively seeking work to all the unemployed. Henceforth it will be government policy that claimants must demonstrate each week that they have actively taken steps to find work, and failure to do so will make them liable to lose both unemployment benefit and income support. Given all the evidence of how these rules have so far been applied it is inevitable that thousands of claimants will be subjected to wrong decisions which, for the majority who appeal against them, will take months to rectify. In the meantime they will suffer hardship, or be forced to take whatever job is on offer, however badly paid and however poor the working conditions. The bill also contains measures to force those with skills and qualifications to take any job after being unemployed for three months, again on penalty of losing all entitlement to benefit, and measures to make it harder for those previously in part-time work to obtain benefit, which will particularly affect married women. The introduction of this bill, the second reading of which took place in January 1989, shows that the relentless drive to reduce the unemployment figures by worsening the conditions of benefit, at no matter what cost to the unemployed and their families, is still very much at the forefront of the government's agenda.

Fraud Control: 'It's Scum like You that Ruin this Society'

Every government must take steps to control abuses of the social security system and to prevent and detect fraud; that is not in dispute. But, as with the procedures for tightening the checks on claimants' availability for work, it is not so much the policies that betray the government's ulterior motives in the control of fraud as their implementation and the relative emphasis given to them. Since 1980 there have been a number of initiatives, all with the effect of highlighting the issue of fraud control, which have produced some extremely nasty practices. One consequence of such practices has been to support the myth that many claimants are 'on the fiddle' and to add to the general stigmatising of welfare, which cannot be unintended by a government hell-bent on discrediting the 'dependency culture'.

While one cannot condone social security fraud it is not difficult to understand that the temptation to maximise one's very meagre income on benefit must at times be overwhelming. The more that benefits are cut, the harder it is made to claim, the easier it is to be disallowed or disqualified from benefit, the more grants are replaced by loans – while at the same time billions of pounds are given away in tax hand-outs to the rich and the pursuit of money is elevated to the level of high moral principle – the easier it becomes to appreciate the temptation facing those on benefit to do a few hours' work here and there and not declare it. In that sense there is no doubt that the actions of this government have significantly increased the likelihood that people will be tempted to defraud the system; the wonder is that there is so little fraud, not that there is so much.

To see the distorted emphasis given to the control of social security fraud one has only to consider two related matters. Estimates of fraud are difficult to make with any accuracy, but it is not difficult to make estimates about the orders of magnitude involved. Figures given by the DHSS for the early 1980s show that staff engaged on fraud control were estimated to have saved the Department about £200 million a year. At the same time the chairman of the Inland Revenue Board estimated that tax fraud was costing the country £3.5 *billion* a year. For every fraud officer deployed in the DHSS about £50,000 was 'saved' in fraud detection; the equivalent figure in the Inland Revenue was £138,000. Similarly, while estimates about the amount of benefit not taken up by claimants through ignorance or unwillingness to claim are difficult to judge accurately, it is believed that, in the early 1980s, the amount of money lost to claimants on supplementary benefit alone was likely to be well over £1 billion.

Faced with these facts, in 1980 the government chose to employ an extra 1050 staff, at a time when it was otherwise cutting back on civil servants, not to ensure that claimants received the money to which they were legally entitled, not to pursue tax dodgers, but solely for the purpose of fraud control in the DHSS. As Geoffrey Beltram, a former under-secretary in the DHSS pointed out: 'A policy shift in that direction was likely to be taken as a signal to get tough by those staff who were disposed to interpret it thus.'

Such staff would have been equally encouraged by other measures taken by the government. Throughout the 1980s several specialist groups were set up to track down fraud; in 1981 the notorious specialist claims control teams were deployed nationally within the DHSS; in 1983 the Department of Employment set up regional benefit investigation teams; and in 1985 the same department established regional fraud teams. With the introduction of such specialist hit teams the nature of fraud investigation changed dramatically; chief among the critics of the new techniques were the staff unions in the two departments, who were alarmed at the changing nature of the benefit services and who feared that their already shaky relationship with the public would suffer.

During the course of his investigation into the DHSS, Beltram noted:

> Allegations were heard of oppressive methods and unjustified harassment, not only from claimants' representatives but also from a number of DHSS staff, including a few fraud officers. The DHSS trade unions have joined with groups representing claimants in a campaign against the Specialist Claims Control teams; in certain offices staff have refused to co-operate with the teams.

This non-cooperation also applied to the Department of Employment's regional fraud squads. In the summer of 1986 the

165

Hove unemployment benefit office was so incensed at the tactics used by the fraud investigators, who, because they were in the office for only a few weeks, had little regard for the damage their activities did to local staff–claimant relationships, that the staff came out on strike on three separate occasions. Despite denials, it became apparent that the fraud squad was working to a target of removing 5 per cent from the register, and they were prepared to use some very unpleasant tactics to achieve this. They were very well equipped, with two-way radios and concealable mini-recorders for recording interviews, and were not above using such dubious tactics as conspicuously trailing claimants, questioning neighbours and delivering cards accusing claimants of working and asking them to sign off. There was evidence to suggest that the members of the squad were working in concert with the police, and were using the national police computer to trace the number plates of their 'suspects'. As one of the regular staff wrote: 'If only half the criticisms of the public were true, we were witnessing a wholesale shift of the Department of Employment away from its traditional bungling bureaucratic role as the provider of benefit to unemployed people and towards some sort of community policing role.'

By its nature, investigation into fraud is secretive and usually takes place behind closed doors. An insight into the style of interviewing used by the fraud squad at Hove is provided in a written statement given to the staff of the benefit office by a woman subjected to investigation:

On Wednesday July 9th I was visited by three people who wouldn't give their names. . . . One of the blokes spoke first. His first words were 'You've been working, haven't you?' I said 'No, of course not. I haven't been well.' He said 'Why did you give up your last job?' I told him. He said again, 'You've been working.' Then he said 'It's scum like you that ruin this society. There are a lot of people who go out to work to pay for scroungers like you.' Then the man with the dark hair said 'You haven't really been ill, have you? That's just a put on.' I said 'Look, you can have the certificates from me, saying what jobs I can and can't do.' He said 'We think your doctor was lying about your operation, and what's more he is a Jewish socialist

166

who reads the *Guardian*.' Then he kept saying, 'You've been working, we know you've been working. You've been working in cafes and hotels, haven't you?' They said I shouldn't be entitled to any money. They said 'You shouldn't be signing on because we believe you shouldn't get any money because you are working.' The girl said 'You've been working, haven't you?' Then I said I didn't have any more comments to make. The interview was nearly over, except for a few more digs. As they went they said 'And if you say anything we'll deny it.'

Of course, such methods would not be given official approval, and would no doubt be viewed with as much horror by the higher officials of the Department as by most other reasonable people. The fact remains that, with the emphasis given by ministers to hounding those suspected of fraud, staff using such methods had every reason to believe they were doing their masters' bidding just as surely as those who murdered Thomas à Beckett. That such practices occurred has been well documented long before 1986. Roger Smith, CPAG's lawyer, had already written about the trail of destruction left behind the specialist claims control teams in 1981:

> Claimants so often described being locked into interviewing rooms that there must have been some substance to this complaint. Similarly, allegations that SCC officers tore up benefit books in front of claimants were repeated too often to be regarded as just hysterical or untrue. Claimants also consistently reported that they had undergone bullying and humiliating interviews.

He also reported that claimants frequently complained that their benefit had simply been stopped in the hope that they would not reclaim, and even that the DHSS unions claimed that one SCC tactic was to stop batches of the forms authorising payment to unemployed claimants from being sent out, again presumably in the hope that those stopped would simply not reclaim.

On 11 August 1988 the *Guardian* carried a report that the crackdown of fraud was to be intensified. Offices were told by the DHSS to increase their savings from fraud detection by 'at least 22 per cent', with the London South area being expected to produce an increase of 47 per cent! Cash targets were to be set for each local office, (though the Department denied that the cash figures set were 'targets', coyly preferring the term 'indicators'). This prompted the civil service unions to suggest that staff would come under unfair pressure to meet their targets 'and could be tempted to act without sensitivity'. With pressure for fraud detection being given such a boost the likelihood of more interviews like the one reported above is bound to increase.

As well as the continuing drive against fraud by the use of specialist hit squads, in 1982 there was the more spectacular one-off media event Operation Major. The DHSS and Thames Valley Police masterminded a mass arrest of 286 claimants suspected of claiming benefits from an address at which they were not in fact resident. Such a high-profile event inevitably attracted huge media coverage. One-third of those arrested were completely innocent, and no evidence was obtained against the landlord who was at the centre of the fraud. But Roger Smith points to the very sinister implications of the fact that the DHSS had been in a position to prevent the fraud but chose not to, preferring to wait until it had taken place and then to exploit it for its media value. The DHSS knew that the building was registered to take a maximum of ninety people, yet as the numbers supposedly living there rose from ninety in May 1982 to 290 by the following September it took no action. Indeed, the DHSS actually stopped making its usual visits there in early June. As CHAR commented:

> The police figures, Rossi's (the responsible Minister) House of Commons statement [that the DHSS spotted a sudden rise of claimants in early July] and Minchell's (the local office manager) evidence in court about DHSS visits point strongly to a deliberate policy of stepping back from the scene and allowing numbers to rise in order to 'catch' a maximum number of claimants.

According to Roger Smith this was a 'deliberately manufactured demonstration of "strong-arm" tactics against a vulnerable group of claimants'.

It is not only claimants under suspicion of fraud who may be investigated; the fraud teams sometimes select claimants at random for this type of humiliating treatment. How effective such tactics are is difficult to measure; Beltram claims that about half of those seen by the specialist claims control groups had benefit reduced or withdrawn, though whether as a result of fear and intimidation rather than because they were actually not entitled to benefit is not clear. What is clear is that the government has deliberately set out to give the control of social security fraud a very high profile, supposedly in the name of saving public money, even though it knows that the same staff deployed on fraud detection in the Inland Revenue would probably have saved the taxpayer nearly three times as much. The government chose not to do so because discrediting welfare claimants, and especially the unemployed, is all part of maintaining the stigma associated with welfare aimed at discouraging people from claiming. To achieve this objective it is prepared tacitly to condone the harassment, humiliation and bullying of claimants by specialist teams who are so disliked that colleagues in benefit offices often refuse to work with them. Ministers may publicly wring their hands and deplore the worst excesses of the fraud squads they have created; those working in them know that they are expected by these same ministers to remove their quota from the register and they will not be thanked if they fail. And the same ministers who would publicly deplore such excesses know that a standing ovation at the 1988 Tory Party Conference was theirs for the asking when they pandered to the party faithful by promising yet bigger and better crackdowns on the dole cheats.

The Enterprise Culture: 'Oh Enterprise, What Crimes are Committed in thy Name!'

One of the main aims of these attacks on the living standards of the unemployed is to drive them off benefit and into work. But what sort of work? In answer to a parliamentary question in July 1987 the Employment Minister, John Lee, revealed that the numbers of full-time adult employees earning less than two-thirds of average earnings, the so-called 'decency threshold', rose from 3.5 million in 1979 to 4 million in 1980. Independent analysts would claim that these figures are unrealistically low; for example, in 1986 the Low Pay Unit estimated the number to be nearer 9 million. Even so, the government's own figures show that the number of workers in very low-paid jobs increased during the 1980s. The New

Earnings Survey shows similarly that between 1983 and 1987 the gap between the highest- and lowest-paid workers widened considerably; while some workers in the City were making their fortunes the low paid were falling further behind those on average wages. Increasing the pool of badly paid jobs has been a deliberate government strategy; all the measures against the unemployed have been taken to ensure that these badly paid jobs will be filled.

The many steps taken to bring wages down have included the following:

(1) In 1982 the Fair Wages Resolution was scrapped, which meant that firms tendering for the privatised public services could no longer be required to include fair wages clauses in their contracts of employment; this inevitably led to the reduction of wages and conditions for many people already in poorly paid jobs such as cleaning and catering.

(2) In 1986 the Wages Act drastically curtailed the effectiveness of the Wages Councils which had regulated wage rates for almost three million low-paid workers. All those under twenty-one, about half a million people, were removed from their protection altogether while other workers had their protection reduced. Wages Councils had already had their effectiveness seriously eroded by administrative action; in 1979 there were 158 wages inspectors charged with seeing that the Council's rates were properly enforced; by 1987 there were only seventy-nine with further reductions planned. Employers who pay below the set rates are committing a criminal offence; in 1986 the total amount of underpayment uncovered by the inspectors was £2.3 million, but, in contrast to numbers of fraudulent claimants who are pursued, only three employers were prosecuted. Some idea of the levels of wages set can be seen from the rates set for the retail and catering trades, which between them account for over two-thirds of all workers covered: in August 1987 these were between £72 and £86 for a thirty-nine-hour week for those over twenty-one.

(3) The many training schemes, such as YTS for young

people or the JTS for those over twenty-five, and now the new ET scheme, with training allowances pitched at more or less the same level as benefits, have all contributed to maintaining a pool of very low-paid trainees who depress wage rates. The ET scheme allowances are paid under social security regulations, which means that employers cannot top them up in any way without the trainee losing the equivalent amount of benefit, thus ensuring that the rates stay at benefit levels. The government has even paid subsidies to employers to employ young people on the Young Workers' Scheme and New Workers' Scheme *on condition* that they hold wages down below £65 per week. The same principle of offering inducements to employers to pay low wages has been extended to the long-term unemployed throughout Jobstart. Bringing down wages is a deliberate government objective in pursuit of which it is prepared to spend public money.

The jobs which make up the real experience of the 'enterprise culture' for the low paid have not just had wages protection removed. Other employment rights have been eroded, in particular employees' protection against unfair dismissal. In 1985 the rules were changed so that full-time employees had to have been in the same employment for two years and part-time workers for five years before establishing rights against unfair dismissal, with similar reductions in the right to written reasons for dismissals. Alongside this erosion has gone the very substantial weakening of trade unions and all that that has meant for their ability to safeguard the working conditions of their members.

In a much publicised speech to a Conservative Political Centre Conference in September 1987, emphasising the government's determination to move away from a dependency culture, John Moore extolled the virtues of enterprise: 'We believe the well being of individuals is best protected and promoted when they are helped to be independent, to use their talents to take care of themselves and their families, and to achieve things on their own, which is one of the greatest satisfactions life can offer.' These lyrical words and uplifting thoughts are the driving force behind cutting unemployment benefit, disqualifying and disallowing more and more people for longer periods, making people wait months for benefits to which they are entitled, tacitly condoning bully-boy fraud investigations, cutting the wages of those already in the lowest-paid jobs, and weakening their employment rights. Whether such policies lead to 'the greatest satisfactions life can offer' readers must judge for themselves.

Part 2

The Poor Laws in the 1980s

Introduction

In Part 1 we have shown the development of Conservative policies for the poor. Part 2 continues the story with particular reference to supplementary benefit, the major benefit affecting nearly five million claimants plus nearly four million of their dependants, nearly one in six of the population of Great Britain. Because this benefit constitutes the safety net below which no one should be allowed to fall it brings into sharp focus all the issues about social policy and social values. How exactly should we expect people to live in Britain in the 1980s when they depend for their livelihood on the state? Should we aim to provide a reasonable standard of living, since almost all claimants are so by necessity rather than choice? Should we aim to provide the barest of existences in order to wean claimants from the dependency culture to self-sufficiency? Should we treat claimants with respect and in ways which enhance or at least do not detract from their dignity, or should we deliberately set out to stigmatise and humiliate them, *pour encourager les autres*? How we frame our laws, rules and regulations about supplementary benefits gives the answers to these questions, and shows exactly how we expect, indeed how we have forced, the poor to live.

In Part 2 we first show what life is like for those on benefit in the 1980s by examining the standard of living provided for claimants and their families. This provides the context against which to set the debate about gainers and losers; it was from people whose standard of living was already at intolerably low levels that money was taken.

In subsequent chapters we focus on one aspect of the supplementary benefit system which more than any other has provided a detailed insight into how we as a society treat our poor; the provision of single payments for sudden emergencies. Here more than anywhere the government has had to make very detailed statements about precisely what the poor can expect to have provided for them and what they must do without; every one of the many regulations governing this part of the benefit system reveals the social values which lie at the heart of our Poor Laws. The story of what has happened to these rules under a decade of Tory government is more than just a history of the arcane mysteries of social security; it is the story of the impoverishment and pauperisation of the weakest and most vulnerable members of our society, who have been systematically deprived not only of much-needed money but also of their legal entitlements. In brief, it is the story of their gradual decline from the status of 'claimants' with rights to that of 'applicants' with none. It is the story of the 'other' Britain created as the inevitable result of the pursuit of private profit at the expense of collective provision.

In Chapter 12 we draw attention to a different but integral part of the process of pauperisation; the near-breakdown of the system of administration of benefits. This also reveals the value placed upon the poor, since we expect them to tolerate a level of service which is often unacceptable and which further stigmatises those in receipt of it. In the final chapter we draw some conclusions about the nature of the social security system that a decade of Thatcherism has created and relate this to the wider social values in which such a system is embedded.

8   Life on Benefit:
How Much is Enough?

To keep out of poverty, [claimants] must have an income which enables them to participate in the life of the community. They must be able, for example, to keep themselves reasonably well fed, and well enough dressed to maintain their self-respect and to attend interviews for jobs with confidence. Their homes must be reasonably warm; their children should not feel ashamed by the quality of their clothing; the family must be able to visit relatives, and give them something on their birthdays and at Christmas time; they must be able to read newspapers, and retain their television sets and their membership of trade unions and churches. And they must be able to live in a way which ensures, so far as possible, that public officials, doctors, teachers, landlords and others treat them with the courtesy due to every member of the community.

This modest prescription for how any civilised nation ought to treat its citizens who depend upon it for their support appeared in the annual report of the Supplementary Benefits Commission for 1978. The hand of the chairman, David Donnison, is clearly visible, and this humane and by no means extravagant statement of intent has been much quoted since, notably by the SSAC in its 1984 report, when it allied itself publicly to these aims in its evidence to the Fowler reviews. The paragraph deliberately invites comparison with another much quoted paragraph which appeared in 1901, in Seebohm Rowntree's classic study of poverty in York. Rowntree devised a poverty line to enable him to count the numbers falling below it. The line was drawn at a level of income which would provide 'mere physical efficiency', by which he meant the barest of subsistence. Describing life at this level his paragraph begins:

> A family living upon the scale allowed for must never spend a penny on railway fare or omnibus. They must never go into the country unless they walk. They must never purchase a half-penny newspaper or spend a penny to buy a ticket for a popular concert. They must write no letters to absent children, for they cannot afford to pay the postage. They must never contribute anything to their church or chapel, or give any help to a neighbour which costs them money. They cannot save nor can they join a sick club or trade union, because they cannot pay the necessary subscriptions. The children must have no pocket money for dolls, marbles or sweets. The father must smoke no tobacco and drink no beer. The mother must never buy any pretty clothes for herself or her children . . .

The grim catalogue continues until the point where death has of necessity to be followed by a pauper's funeral.

The echoes are not without significance, for it was Rowntree who helped Beveridge to devise the poverty line which forms the basis of our present social security system. In 1942 Beveridge proposed a set of scales which he believed would provide minimum subsistence, and in doing so he was much influenced by Rowntree's methods. He decided that such scales would need to provide food, clothing, fuel, light and 'household sundries', and he costed these as best he could by reference to data on the spending patterns of average households, suitably reduced to make them apply to households living at subsistence level. He added a very small amount for any other spending not included, and these, amended to take inflation into account, became the rates for benefit levels in 1946 and 1948 when the post-war social security system began. And that was the last time any British government has attempted to devise social security rates which have any empirical basis.

The decision about how much to pay in weekly benefit, especially for those who have no other form of income and who are therefore totally dependent on what we choose to give them, is the most fundamental question in social security. If we pay too little, not only will claimants and their families suffer hardship but all the problems associated with the payments of 'extras' like the additional requirements and single payments will be aggravated; if these extras are abolished to make the system simpler, without sufficient compensation being built into the basic rates, claimants will suffer hardship. Many of the organisations which gave evidence to Fowler made this point emphatically. No review of social security, least of all one claiming to be the most fundamental since Beveridge, could afford to ignore the central question: are social security rates now adequate to meet those aims set over a decade ago by the Supplementary Benefits Commission which are quoted at the beginning of this section?

There are many difficulties associated with determining whether the weekly benefit rates are adequate – the most obvious can be posed simply: adequate for what? Are we, for example, to take Rowntree's standard of 'mere physical efficiency', or Donnison's idea, much championed by Professor Townsend, that those on benefit should be able to 'participate in the life of the community'? If we opt for the latter, what does it mean in practice? Inevitably we shall find that whatever notion of adequacy we choose we shall be forced to make many assumptions and value judgements about what is an appropriate standard of life for claimants. Other problems arise when considering the needs of different claimants: are the needs of a pensioner couple the same as those of working age? Should teenagers living at home be given as much as teenagers living away from home? How much should be allowed for children of different ages? Are the needs of those who have just come on to benefit less or more than those who have been on benefit for many years? All these kinds of issues must be addressed when trying to answer whether benefit rates are adequate, and whether they are more adequate for some claimants than for others. Nevertheless, complex as it is, there are some pointers which can provide at least some answers to our question.

First, we can see what has happened to benefit rates since Beveridge. From the evidence given in the background papers to the Fowler reviews we can see that, between 1948 and 1984, the real value of benefits, taking into account inflation, more than doubled. Using 1983 prices as the base, the weekly amount of supplementary benefit for a single person rose from just over £12 a week in 1948 to just over £26 in 1984, while that for a married couple rose from just over £20 to £43. Taking just the last decade, Professor David Piachaud has calculated that the real level of supplementary benefits rose by about 5 per cent between 1978 and 1987. What this means is that claimants now are better off in absolute terms than claimants in 1948, in the sense that they can now buy twice as much as they could in 1948; and claimants can now buy about 5 per cent more than they could ten years ago.

But because there has been a huge increase in the general standard of living since 1948, this is not very revealing. For a fuller picture we need to compare the rise in benefits with the general rise in affluence, and this is usually done by comparing benefits with movements in average earnings. In 1948 a married couple with two children received in benefits an amount equal to 50 per cent of net average earnings; by 1984 this had risen to 67 per cent and there have been similar improvements for single claimants and couples without children. This means that claimants have improved their position relative to those on average earnings, and in that sense are also better off than their 1948 counterparts. However, this trend has been put into reverse in the last decade. Professor Piachaud has shown that while in 1978 a couple on the ordinary rate of supplementary benefit had an income equivalent to 61 per cent of the personal disposable income per capita, it had fallen to 53 per cent by 1987. His conclusion is that those on supplementary benefit have fallen behind the incomes of those in work and are relatively worse off than in 1978. This means that they have not shared in the general increase in living standards of the Thatcher years to the same extent as everyone else.

However, knowing what has happened to the general drift of benefit levels since Beveridge does not answer the question about adequacy. Benefit levels may not have been adequate in the first place, so that any improvements may still leave claimants unable to live decently, and even if they were adequate in 1948 they would almost certainly now be considered inadequate in the light of rising standards. Whether the absolute and relative improvements since 1948 have been enough to compensate for the general rise in expectations has still to be answered. There are several ways of attempting an answer; we can make our own judgements about the likely adequacy in the light of relevant data; we can see what the actual amounts of benefit can provide in the way of goods and services; and we can see what empirical research has shown about the actual living standards of claimants.

Adequate? Could You Live on This?

The weekly rates of supplementary benefit are meant to provide for all normal living expenses. According to the relevant regulations they are supposed to include:

> food, household fuel, the purchase, cleaning, repair and replacement of clothing and footwear, normal travel costs, weekly laundry costs, miscellaneous household expenses such as toilet articles, cleaning materials, window-cleaning and the replacement of small household goods (for example crockery, cutlery, cooking utensils, light bulbs) and leisure and amenity items such as television licence and rental, newspapers, confectionary and tobacco.

In April 1988, before the change to income support, the amount allowed for an unemployed couple with two small children for all these necessities was £70.15, *including* child benefit. (This sum did not have to cover rent or rates, as these were paid separately for claimants by the DHSS. However, owner-occupiers did have to pay half their mortgage interest out of this amount for the first four months on benefit.) As a first approximation of whether this amount is adequate, readers can imagine how they would manage to live, week in, week out, on that amount. By way of comparison, in 1985 the average weekly expenditure, excluding housing costs, for all couples with two small children was £166.60; by 1988 this figure would have risen still further. The change to the new system in April 1988 was specifically designed to improve the position of families with children, and our hypothetical family now has an income of £79.10 (though at the same time they lost the right to have one-off single payments to help them meet sudden extra expenses).

Adequate? What Does It Buy?

Professor Jonathan Bradshaw, the director of the Social Policy Research Unit at York University, and Jane Morgan, a home

economist, have calculated what such an income enables claimants to buy. Using data from the government's Family Finances
Survey, which included information on the spending patterns of
seventy-six families with two small children living on benefit, they
were able to calculate how, if they followed the average spending
habits of this group of claimants, such a family could have spent
the total weekly amount of benefit across the range of necessities it
is supposed to buy. Their calculations relate to 1986, and the total
weekly amount they used was £74.88, which was in fact 10 per cent
above the basic benefit rates, on the grounds that families often
have some slight extra income apart from benefit.

The results give a general idea of how much of what sort of
commodity families on benefit can buy. For example, the family
had £30.50 to spend on food for the whole family for a week. This
compared with the average weekly expenditure of all families with
two small children of £45.20. The claimant family had £11.46 to
spend on fuel, as compared with the average family's £12.26. On
most of the other items the gap between what the claimant family
could spend and the average family was vast; whereas the claimant family had only £3.55 for clothes and footwear the average
family spent £16.64; on durable household goods the respective
figures were £3.13 and £19.56; on transport, £4.40 as against
£30.46; and on services £4.78 as against £25.04.

To make £30.50 cover all food for the week it was necessary to
buy the very cheapest line in a supermarket. This resulted in a
week's diet which was judged to be nutritionally deficient by about
6500 calories.

The family had only £3.55 to spend on the purchase, repair and
replacement of clothes and footwear for all the family, which was
about a quarter of what Bradshaw and Morgan estimated would
be sufficient to maintain a *minimum* wardrobe for each family
member. Spending at the rate of £3.55 a week meant that clothes
would have to be made to last incredible lengths of time if the
family was not to fall below this minimum standard. For example,
the mother would be able to buy one coat, which would then have
to last her fifteen years, one bra every two and a half years, one pair
of shoes every eighteen months; the father would be able to buy his
one coat, but he would have to make it last twenty-five years, as he
would his one pair of pyjamas; he would fare better with his

trousers, as the two pairs he would be able to buy would have to last him only ten years. The children would be allowed three T-shirts between them every two years; the boy could have one sweater every three years, and the girl one sweater every two. Obviously, as the authors acknowledge, these periods of time are absurd, and are the product of the application of their method of allocating the tiny amount of money available to families on benefit in the particular way they have. Nevertheless, the point is that these absurdities show just how little is available to families on benefit and how few clothes can be bought, and how long they must be made to last, unless money is taken from some other part of the week's budget, from which there will be precious little to spare. Families on benefit would have found it hard to recognise the brave new world being described by John Moore in his speech to a Conservative Political Centre Conference in 1987 when he informed them that 'the average man owns seven pairs of trousers and twenty-five shirts'.

Similar details are made available on all the other parts of the weekly budget. On what might be termed the luxuries of life, the amount of money available meant that the family could never go to the cinema, could not afford to rent a colour television and pay the licence fee, or a telephone, or holiday. They were able to afford one day-trip to a nearby seaside town, and the mother could afford one haircut and blow dry *a year*. The authors call the standard of living of those on benefit 'harsh', and the lifestyle it allows 'bleak'. On the evidence they give, few could disagree.

From this analysis one would expect life on benefit to fall some way short of Donnison's aspirations. What of the evidence from claimants themselves?

Adequate? Life on Benefit

I never have enough money to pay for all the things I have to each week and continually struggle to stretch the money. There is very rarely any money to spare for extras for the children and I can't very often afford to buy them things like fresh fruit as regularly as I would like.

The last time I had a good meal was when I was in hospital.

These quotations show how two of the mothers living on supplementary benefit described what it meant for them in a survey carried out in 1980 by the Family Service Units and CPAG. The survey report was called *Living From Hand to Mouth*, which gives an indication of the findings. It is full of such quotations, all bearing witness to the drudgery and shame of life on benefit, and in particular to the guilt and humiliation felt by parents who could seldom provide the ordinary treats for their children, and sometimes had to see them go without necessities. Chronic debt, going without meals, being unable to keep warm in winter, not having ordinary things like cleaning materials, crockery, etc., being short of clothes and shoes, rarely being able to buy new clothes, seldom going on outings, let alone holidays, feeling too ashamed to invite friends round – all these consequences of poverty were commonplace among the sixty-five families in the survey.

After listing the problems the families experienced in buying the ordinary necessities of life, the report concluded:

> The problems the families faced were made worse by the sheer drudgery and monotony of such restricted standards of living, they were compounded by the misery of being hungry, of being cold, of continually worrying about stretching the money through the week and about the health and wellbeing of their children. More than anything else, it was for their children that the parents were anxious. The strain and worry was itself a cause of ill health and guilt, and such burdens were intensified by the much felt disapproval of the rest of the community; the feeling of humiliation at having to claim supplementary benefit; of being labelled and made to feel like a scrounger.

For these families, life on benefit was a very long way from living up to Donnison's modest ideals.

In 1984 the Policy Studies Institute published a report of research into, among other things, the income and expenditure of people living on supplementary benefit. This was based on a very large sample of claimants, nearly 1800, and confirmed the bleak picture of life on benefits. Given the size of the sample the report must be accepted as authoritative. It was certainly known to the government, which quoted from other parts of the report in the

Green Paper. The following gives the general picture of its findings:

> It is hardly surprising, then, that the various indicators of money shortages all suggested considerable financial hardship – especially among couples with children. More than a third of all adults in the survey (including both members of married couples) were missing items from a standard set of clothing, usually a warm coat or a change of shoes. For parents (and also for their children . . .) the proportion was three out of five. Well over a quarter of all claimants said that they had been 'really anxious' about some expense or problem over the previous few months; nearly a quarter were in debt at the time they were interviewed (not counting credit arrangements they were up to date with) and a fifth of all claimants said that it was *most weeks* that they 'ran out of money too soon, before their next pay day, so that they were in trouble to last out the week'.

This research showed that families with children were particularly hard-pressed. While the overall proportions of claimants in difficulties were as given in the quoted extract, the comparable figures for families with children were much higher. Fifty per cent ran out of money most weeks, 63 per cent had recently had a period of real anxiety about money, 60 per cent lacked a complete standard set of clothing, based on the DHSS standard of adequacy, and 52 per cent were in debt when interviewed.

A crucial point made in the report was that these difficulties were mainly due to the insufficiency of the weekly income, and not to the fact that the claimants had particularly unusual or exceptional needs. As the report put it:

> It turns out that both debts, and occasions of 'real anxiety', were mainly caused by routine needs – rent and fuel bills in the former case, clothing and fuel bills in the latter. *It can be inferred that these problems about routine expenses are a normal consequence of living on a supplementary benefit budget, not caused by unusual events, nor affecting unusual people.*

From this report, sponsored by the DHSS itself, it is clear that

benefit rates are not adequate to prevent many, and in the case of
families with children most, claimants from experiencing real and
continuing financial difficulties, not because they are bad
managers but simply because they do not have enough money to
manage on.

Also in 1984, the year before the Green Paper, Geoffrey Beltram
published his book on his own researches into aspects of the
supplementary benefit system. He had just retired as under-
secretary at the DHSS, where he had been very much involved in
bringing the post-1980 reformed system into being. He therefore
had impeccable credentials as one who knew the issues. At the end
of his chapter on the adequacy of benefits, befitting the circum-
spection born of a lifetime in the Civil Service, he cautiously
concludes:

> To sum up, while there is no way of arriving at an objective
> measure of adequacy of SB levels, the balance of opinion and
> research evidence suggests that the basic scale rates (at least)
> represent bleak poverty for those with no other resources to fall
> back on, unless they are exceptionally gifted at budgeting on a
> low income.

Finally, in 1983 London Weekend Television broadcast four
programmes on 'Breadline Britain', vividly depicting the plight of
Britain's poor. In 1984 these were followed by Mack's and
Lansley's *Poor Britain*, a book which was important not simply for
its wealth of information about life at the poverty level but because
the authors set out to demonstrate that it is possible to arrive at
some socially agreed set of minimum standards below which our
citizens ought not to be allowed to fall. In other words, they were
attempting to turn Donnison's vision into a practical set of
proposals. Their findings on the standard of life for those on
benefit confirmed and amplified the findings of previous researchers. Of all those living in poverty, those dependent on supplementary benefits were demonstrably the worst off. Having constructed
a list of twenty-two items which, by general agreement, could be
said to be necessities (for example sufficient heating, two pairs of
all-weather shoes, new rather than second-hand clothes, the
ability to afford presents once a year), families on benefit consistently lacked more of these than other poor families. Having

established this point they conclude about all poor families in general:

> It was not just that they could not afford to go on holiday or that they could not afford a refrigerator – though these would be deprivations by the standards of today – but that their whole way of life was affected. Many could not afford modest items of food, such as a roast joint of meat, many could not afford to clothe themselves according to the minimum standards of today, lacking, for example, a warm water-proof coat; virtually all could not afford the kinds of leisure activities that make life more than just a matter of existing. The personal consequences are a life that is often depressing and nearly always full of worry. This is the reality of 'relative' poverty in Britain in the 1980s.

Adequacy: The Government's Response

In the face of the consistency of this evidence, nearly all of which came out in the run up to 'the most fundamental examination of our social security system since the Second World War', what attention was paid in the Green Paper to the crucial issue whether benefit levels were adequate? Given that benefit levels were nothing more than the regularly updated levels set by Beveridge over forty years earlier, and given that Fowler was out to make his mark as a second Beveridge, now was surely the time for a fundamental review of the standard of living provided by benefit levels. But no. The Green Paper disposed of the problem in just two sentences: 'There have been many attempts to establish what would be a fair rate of benefit for claimants. But it is doubtful whether an attempt to establish an objective standard of adequacy would be fruitful.' With these intellectually and morally empty words Fowler condemned the next generation of claimants and their families to remain unable to 'participate in the life of the community'. From then on, the Green Paper has nothing more to say about the question of adequacy, and attention is turned instead to the relative degrees of poverty suffered by different claimant groups.

The reason for this refusal to address the most important issue of all is self-evident: the government was primarily interested in saving money. Since it was clear that any research into the adequacy or otherwise of benefit rates would be bound to conclude that they were not adequate, the outcome would have been pressure to increase the budget, not reduce it. And the claim that it would not have been 'fruitful' to attempt to establish an objective standard of adequacy is simply not true. It would have been difficult, but no more so than when Beveridge did just that in 1942. Mack and Lansley had shown that it is possible to achieve some kind of consensus across a wide range of people about what constitute the necessities of life, and there are other possible methods for reaching reasonably objective criteria, such as the use of hypothetical budgets of what people need to live on from week to week. Had the government wished to address the problem there were ways in which it could have been done, if not perfectly then at least to leave claimants better placed than they are now. For claimants it would have been the most 'fruitful' part of the reviews. In its absence, all they were left with were proposals which shuffled little bits of money around between claimants, taking it away from pensioners and young people and giving it to families with children, robbing the poor to pay the very poor. If small amounts of money were to be found to ease the position of those most in need they had to come not from the community at large, and certainly not from the wealthiest in the community, but from other claimants, depressing still further their already meagre standard of living. That was the promise and vision of Norman Fowler and his cabinet colleagues.

9 Single Payments: How We Expect the Poor To Live

The change to a regulated system of supplementary benefits in 1980 meant that for the first time ever Parliament had to state openly what it believed to be the appropriate standard of living for claimants. Previously Parliament had been responsible for setting the level of the scale rates but had left the details of the scheme to the Supplementary Benefits Commission (SBC) and its various predecessors. Between them, these had developed a highly complex set of rules and guidelines, the A Code, which determined all departmental policies such as the conditions under which benefit should be paid, extra weekly payments might be made to cover special expenses or benefit might be withheld or reduced. In fact every decision involving any discretionary judgement was meant to be covered in the A Code, which itself had grown up over many years and embodied the conventional practice of the SBC.

Under pressure from the poverty lobby, and from CPAG in particular, and with the active co-operation and encouragement of David Donnison, the SBC chairman, the DHSS published a very much simplified version of the A Code in the form of a handbook. This set out departmental policy in terms which the layman might be expected to understand, but the policies being made public were the SBC's, not Parliament's; not until the Social Security Act 1980 did Parliament assume responsibility for the detailed workings of the scheme. As a result of that Act supplementary benefits were taken out of the hands of the SBC, which was abolished, and administered through a mass of very detailed regulations requiring Parliament's formal approval. Of course, many of these regulations were the old departmental policies served up in more legalistic language, but the crucial point remains that at that time, in approving the regulations and all the many subsequent amendments, Parliament made clear its wishes and intentions about how

189

the poor should live. The Poor Laws had to be openly stated; they were no longer internal departmental staff directives but the will of the majority party in the House.

With the regulations governing single payments we reach the fine tuning of the Poor Laws, the point at which Parliament had to be precise about what exactly it regarded as reasonable for the poor to be able to buy from public funds, how much it was reasonable for them to spend on each item and under what conditions it was reasonable to approve or withhold expenditure. Every regulation was an explicit statement of the values the government has about the poor and their dependants. It is this attention to detail which makes the regulations so rewarding to study since they are a precise guide to the values implicit in the Poor Laws which governed our system of poor relief from 1980 until their abolition in April 1988. The history of single payments under the Conservatives provides a clear statement of government attitudes to Britain's poor in the 1980s. It is a history which begins with cuts in the living standards of the poorest people, is followed by more cuts, and ends with the outright abolition of entitlement to almost all single payments and their replacement by the social fund.

This account of the history of single payments under the Conservatives begins with an explanation of the difficulties and obstacles facing claimants wishing to make a claim. This will make clear that such payments were by no means easy to come by, and often involved claimants in humiliating experiences at the hands of the DHSS. It will show also the lengths to which the DHSS was prepared to go to limit the numbers of such payments, and the absurd arguments it was forced to use to do so. This will be followed by an account of the major cuts which the government made in the single payments budget, which both depressed still further the living standards of the poor and paved the way for the much bigger cuts to follow with the advent of the social fund. Above all, this history of single payments reveals vividly the government's considered view of how the poor of Britain should live.

Before embarking on the story it is necessary to explain briefly how the system works. In the first instance, a claimant would make a claim to the local office of the DHSS. This would be considered by an adjudication officer who would either allow the claim or not, depending on whether the claim was permitted by the single payment regulations. If the claim was refused the claimant had a right of appeal to a local appeal tribunal, which was entirely independent of the DHSS. The tribunal would be equally bound by the regulations but would not necessarily interpret them in the same way as the adjudication officer. Once the appeal tribunal had given its decision it was then open to either the claimant or the DHSS to appeal to a social security commissioner. The commissioners were the highest authority, and once they had pronounced on the meaning of a particular regulation their judgement had the binding force of precedent, and had then to be followed in all subsequent cases by both the DHSS and appeal tribunals. Their function was rather like that of judges in the judicial system, whose interpretation of the law itself becomes the law.

The General Conditions of Entitlement to a Single Payment

What the poor must do without

A single payment for an exceptional or emergency need, which was not covered by the normal weekly benefit, could be given only if it was expressly allowed for in the very detailed set of thirty regulations. These regulations, while potentially conferring entitlement to benefits, could equally well be framed so as to preclude entitlement. One such listed items for which it was impossible ever to be awarded a payment. The proscription of the listed items was absolute, so that payment could not be made even under the reserve discretionary powers included in the regulations to cover cases of special hardship. There were thirteen separate headings under which single payments were expressly forbidden. Some were items which it was assumed would be supplied by other authorities, and some were quite simply items which it was assumed claimants should not have at public expense.

The first category comprised the following: an educational or training need; distinctive school uniform or sports clothes or equipment; travelling expenses to or from school; school meals and meals taken during school holidays by children entitled to free school meals; mobility needs; removal charges where a claimant was permanently rehoused following a compulsory purchase order; domestic assistance provided by a local authority; a medical, surgical, optical, aural or dental need. The absolute prohibition of these items is an example of simplification through abolition, and while such items may often have been provided by other authorities that was by no means always the case, with the result that claimants were left stranded in the middle of departmental demarcation disputes. Compared to the pre-1980 scheme these prohibitions represented a net loss for claimants, as some may have succeeded with claims for certain of these items under the earlier, more discretionary scheme.

Of more immediate interest for the purposes of this section are those items excluded simply because Parliament decided that the poor should not receive them out of the public purse: the garaging parking, purchase and running costs of any motor vehicle; installation, rental or call charges for a telephone; a television or radio or licence, aerial or rental charges for either; holidays; expenses arising from an appearance in a court such as travelling expenses legal fees, court fees, fines, costs, damages or subsistence.

Supplementary benefits thus made no provision at all for claimants to possess a car or motor cycle, a telephone, a television or even a radio, and claimants should not expect ever to take a holiday. So much for all the stories which have haunted the DHSS for years about the ease with which claimants can acquire televisions or take holidays in Spain at the taxpayer's expense. They can, of course, but only if they use their savings or pay out of the amount allowed each week for their daily living expenses. Officially, paupers should not expect to be able to afford to repair or replace even a radio unless they do so at the expense of their other normal requirements, which in practice means food or warmth.

As for the ban on costs arising from court appearances, note that this applied also in cases where the claimant was acquitted. In such cases no fines or costs should arise, but travelling expenses and legal fees certainly might, but with no possibility of recovery Paupers therefore must take care not to be wrongfully arrested.

The prohibition on the payment of damages led to an absurdity which evoked colourful language from one of the commissioners

A claimant had requested a single payment to meet the hire-purchase debt on her cooker and gas fire, which in the ordinary way she would probably have been granted. Prior to her claim she had defaulted on her payments and the Gas Board had obtained a county court judgement which had the effect of terminating the agreement and substituting an award of damages in its place. In considering the case on appeal the commissioner reluctantly agreed with the judgement of the adjudication officer that no single payment was possible because of the regulation expressly forbidding the payment of damages arising from court cases. He expressed his reluctance at being forced into so arbitrary a distinction in the following terms: 'The implications and consequences of the findings to which I have been driven are a little short of ludicrous.'

The obstacle race

To qualify for any of the remaining items for which single payments could be made the claimant had to meet certain qualifying conditions. These were often spoken of as the 'hurdles' which he or she had to overcome simply to reach the point at which another set of hurdles, specific to the particular type of payment being sought, must be cleared. These general conditions were deceptively simple and in themselves appear to be quite reasonable; their application in practice, however, often transformed hurdles into insurmountable obstacles. The qualifying conditions gave much scope for the exercise of interpretative judgement on the part of the adjudication officer and once again revealed very clearly the underlying assumptions about how the poor should live.

What were these hurdles? First, claimants had to show that the item for which they required a payment was allowed within the regulations. As we have already seen, some items were specifically proscribed, but it did not follow that payments could be made for all non-proscribed items – only for items specified in the regulations. Claimants then had to show that they had a need for the item in question, that they did not already possess the item, that they did not have available a suitable alternative and that they had not unreasonably either disposed of or failed to avail themselves of such an item, and that they had not failed to exercise reasonable care to preserve or protect such an item. Having thus established a genuine need for the item, they must then establish that they had not already had a single payment for it unless the circumstances surrounding the payment had since changed. Finally, neither they nor their partner must be involved in a trade dispute; paupers must not be strikers.

However reasonable it may seem that a claimant must first establish a need for an item it was sometimes no easy matter to do so. What is a 'need', what does 'suitable alternative' mean, what constitutes 'unreasonably' disposing of or 'failing to avail oneself of', and how much care is it 'reasonable' to use to preserve one's possessions? The claimant had to traverse these linguistic minefields as well as jump hurdles. If we turn to the commissioners' decisions we can see how they have resolved some of the difficulties which such necessarily imprecise language poses, and we can also see how adjudication officers, presumably with the agreement of their departmental managers, had chosen to exercise their judgement on these issues.

The first hurdle was to establish that the item was one for which a single payment was permitted. We have already seen that the claimant mentioned above, who might have been eligible for a payment to discharge her hire-purchase debts, was unable to claim for damages representing the same debts. The lesson is clear: do not assume that some notion of general equivalence runs through the regulations and that if they allow one thing they will usually allow something similar. The regulations meant exactly what they said and unless they specified that equivalents might be substituted, they could not be. For a particularly absurd example, while it was permissible to make single payments in respect of settling hire-purchase debts it was not permitted to settle debts incurred on goods bought under a credit sale agreement. Relying on common sense to interpret the regulations was not to be recommended.

A more common way in which claimants fell at this first hurdle was when they may have known that a single payment was allowable for a particular item and, in anticipation of a payment, they bought it with borrowed money. For example, a claimant found that his water tank had suddenly burst, so not unreasonably he immediately called a plumber and paid him with money borrowed from his neighbour. He then applied for a single payment for the cost of the repairs, which was allowable under the regulations. The adjudication officer refused on the grounds that he was not in need of a payment to cover the cost of the repairs, since they had already been paid for; the claim was actually for money to repay the debt to the neighbour. There is, however, no provision in the regulations for the repayment of debt, so his claim was disallowed. The claimant appealed to the commissioners, who had to agree that the adjudication officer had acted correctly. While such distinctions may also seem 'little short of ludicrous', they were commonplace in the bizarre logic of the regulations. Quite what Parliament expected the man to do on discovering that his tank had burst is a mystery.

At the time the commissioners considered this claim, in 1983, there was an additional reason why it would have failed even if the claimant had paid the plumber with his own money rather than borrowing it. This takes us on to the question whether 'there is a need for the item in question'. Had the claimant paid the plumber and then applied for a single payment he would undoubtedly have been refused because, at the time of the claim, there would not still be a need for the item because he had already paid for it. He may be short of money as a result, but that is not the same as still having a need for repairs to his tank. Common sense, remember, is no guide in what one commissioner has called 'this legislative labyrinth'. The discomfort of the commissioners in being forced to reach this decision is plain from their comments:

> the consequences of this removal of a discretion is that hard cases may, and will, arise through oversights in the relevant legislation. We consider that, where emergencies arise rendering it impractical for a claim to be made before a claimant is required himself to make payment for 'the need in question', some suitable relieving provision should be incorporated in the regulations.

In fact 'some suitable relieving provision' was subsequently introduced when, in August 1984, it became possible to make a claim up to five working days after the date on which the need first arose, though even this relaxation was subject to the conditions that the need had to be met immediately and that it was not practical for the claim to have been made before the need had to be met. (This particular claimant would, however, still have fallen foul of the lack of any provision for the repayment of debt, so the amendment was of no use to him.) Until this belated amendment it was very common for claims for single payments to fail simply because claimants had unwittingly been foolish enough to buy what they needed before making their claim, thus being unable to establish a 'need' for the item.

We have seen that borrowing money to pay for items excluded claimants from the possibility of obtaining a single payment. What if the claimant borrowed the item itself? Does he or she then 'possess' it and so no longer have a need for it? Or does this constitute having a 'suitable alternative item', which would then preclude a single payment? Consider the following cases: a woman borrows a set of clothes from her sister to attend a job interview; a pregnant woman borrows an overcoat from a relative; a child borrows a pair of shoes; a young mother borrows a bed for her son, and an electric fire, a wardrobe and a three-piece suite. Do they still have a need for the items they have borrowed? In each of these cases adjudication officers have taken the view that they do not and have refused to grant single payments, and in each case the commissioners have had to decide whether borrowing is an acceptable way to meet need. The DHSS fought very hard to establish the principle that borrowed items were good enough for claimants.

A woman claimed a single payment for a raincoat, dress and shoes in order to 'look decent' at job interviews. She had been attending interviews in clothes borrowed from her sister. The adjudication officer refused, and on appeal two of the three tribunal members allowed her appeal, the third dissenting. When it came before the commissioner the adjudication officer mounted a strong defence of his original decision, arguing that the items did not constitute an 'exceptional need', that even if they did she had a 'suitable alternative' available to her, and in any event the need, if it could be proved to exist, had arisen from 'normal wear and tear', which as we shall see later precluded payments for clothes.

Faced with this spirited defence, the commissioner addressed the question of borrowing in these terms:

I do not consider that if a person temporarily borrows clothes that he or she 'possesses' these clothes. Though possession is not the same as ownership, nevertheless the word 'possess' does, in my view, mean something more than having a transitory right to wear clothes conferred by a temporary loan from some other person. . . . I do not consider that it can normally be said that borrowed clothes are a 'suitable alternative item' for a man or woman wanting to attend job interviews for responsible jobs.

He went on to consider the question whether the need had arisen through 'normal wear and tear' and decided that it had not, and he therefore allowed the claimant's appeal.

Fearing that the DHSS might appear to be a 'soft touch' in the light of this liberal view that borrowed clothes are not necessarily suitable even for paupers, the Chief Supplementary Benefit Officer appealed to the High Court. They in turn held that the commissioner had been wrong in deciding that the need had arisen other than by 'normal wear and tear'. However, on the issue of borrowing they remained silent. Thus in this one case no less than nine different people were directly involved in reaching a decision about the merits of the claim, three of whom thought she was entitled to her coat, dress and shoes, six of whom thought not. That it should have been taken to the High Court is a clear indication of the reluctance of the DHSS to concede any principles which might have extended the scope of single payments.

If the clothes were needed during pregnancy, should the same considerations about borrowing still apply? A pregnant woman asked for a single payment for an overcoat as her own was too small; meanwhile she was borrowing one from a relative. The adjudication officer refused, and this decision was upheld by the appeal tribunal. When it came before the commissioner he concluded that the appeal tribunal was correct:

It was entirely open to the tribunal to decide (as they did) that since the claimant had the use of a borrowed overcoat she did not have a need for new or replacement clothing on account of pregnancy. There may be cases where a borrowed item does not satisfy a need. But where the situation giving rise to the need is pregnancy, which is obviously a temporary condition, a borrowed item may well be capable of satisfying the temporary need.

He added that in reaching a decision about the appropriateness of borrowed items the 'terms of the borrowing' should be borne in mind – for example how soon the owner wanted it back. Nevertheless, the effect of this decision would be to require adjudication officers not to give single payments for maternity coats if they could be borrowed.

The terms of the borrowing were given more explicit meaning in the judgement relating to the borrowed bed, wardrobe, electric fire and three-piece suite. A single mother applied for a single payment for these items for herself and her eighteen-month-old son. The adjudication officer refused on the grounds that she was already borrowing them, and the appeal tribunal agreed. When it came before the commissioner he held that the crucial fact in this case was 'the length of time for which the borrowed items were likely to be available to the claimant'. Since this was not clear in this case he referred it back for further deliberation, but the principle was established that borrowing was acceptable provided the items could be borrowed for long enough. Adjudication officers should thereafter always have asked claimants to borrow, since payments should be made only if the claimant had no suitable alternative. It gives new meaning to the idea of claimants being 'scroungers'; under these regulations that is exactly what they were encouraged to be, but from friends and relatives rather than from the state.

The question whether the claimant has a 'suitable alternative item' available raised issues other than simply whether such an item could be borrowed. Who should decide what is a suitable alternative? Are boots and wellingtons a suitable alternative to shoes? Are plastic tiles, PVC floor coverings, linoleum and carpets each a suitable alternative for the others? Is a coal fire the equivalent of a gas or electric fire? These questions have all been answered at one time or another so as to prevent the award of single payments and have been appealed to the commissioners. This in turn has led to the pronouncement of some general principles about the suitability of alternatives.

Single Payments: How We Expect the Poor To Live

Who should decide what is suitable? Should the adjudication officer or the claimant have the right to decide whether one item is the equivalent of another? This matter was addressed in the case of an elderly lady who claimed for a gas fire because she found dealing with coal fires too much trouble. The commissioner decided that coal fires were not to be regarded as suitable alternatives to a gas fire (the adjudication officer had refused her claim for a gas fire on just that ground). He made the general point about where the decision lay in this way:

> The supplementary benefit legislation is directed to satisfying the requirements of claimants, and the approach must broadly be subjective rather than objective, although, of course, it cannot be pursued to such absurd lengths that personal idiosyncrasies are catered for to the exclusion of all objective criteria based on reasonableness.

This may or may not have clarified matters; it illustrates the difficulty of attempting to legislate in the field of human wishes. Probably all the judgement did was to substitute the difficulty of distinguishing 'personal idiosyncrasies' from 'reasonable objective criteria' for the difficulty of deciding what constitutes a suitable alternative; one might consider this a small gain if any gain at all. At any rate this principle did not unduly influence the adjudication officer when deciding that a claimant was not entitled to a single payment for floor covering for her hall which was already laid with thermal plastic tiles that she herself considered unsuitable. The DHSS again went to great lengths not to concede an inch of principle, this time that carpets, however cheap, were too good for claimants; cheap plastic tiles or linoleum were as much floor covering as they could expect.

A woman claimed for a payment to clear her hire-purchase debt on a carpet, the adjudication officer refused but the appeal tribunal allowed the claim. The DHSS considered this a matter of such grave import that it appealed to the commissioners. The DHSS solicitor solemnly advanced three grounds for saying that the differences between PVC floor covering and cheap carpets were such that it was impossible to regard one as the equivalent of the other, and therefore the words 'PVC floor covering or equivalent' in the regulations excluded carpet. He argued (a) PVC has a smooth surface whereas carpet has a pile; (b) PVC is cleaned and maintained in one way, carpet in another; (c) carpet is more readily damaged by the activities of children and does not wear so well. The commissioner, in the customary polite language of lawyers, commented: 'I must confess that the materiality of (a) and (b) . . . escapes me. There is, however, some force in (c).' Not enough force for him to agree with the learned arguments put forward by the Department, however, whose appeal he dismissed. In the course of his judgement he observed: 'After much reflection, the only ground of which I can think for excluding cheap carpeting from the scope of the regulation is that carpeting is "above the station" of those who are in receipt of supplementary benefit. I cannot imagine that such an outmoded notion would find favour today.' Nevertheless, since the DHSS solicitor had readily agreed that there was no difference in the price of PVC and the claimant's carpet, it is hard to see why the Department should go to such extraordinary lengths to establish the exclusion of cheap carpeting from the regulations unless it was precisely because such luxuries were considered to be above the expected lifestyle of paupers.

As to whether boots and wellingtons are the equivalent of shoes, the answer is more simple: the commissioner decided they were not. That is, they are not equivalent in the ordinary way, though they become a suitable alternative when considered under the reserve fall-back regulation, as we shall see later. When dealing with these regulations one should not suppose that what counts as a suitable alternative item under one regulation will necessarily be a suitable alternative under another.

Having established a need for an item and that no suitable alternative was available, the final hurdle claimants had to jump was a double fence designed to test that it was reasonable that they should be in need of the item. To do this they had to show that they had not unreasonably disposed of such an item, or failed to avail themselves of such an item.

A woman had left her flat empty for nine months while she went to look after her sick mother. On her return she claimed a single payment for furniture because her flat had been vandalised during her absence. The adjudication officer refused on the grounds that by leaving the flat unoccupied she had given an 'open invitation to

vandals' and had therefore unreasonably disposed of her possessions. The appeal tribunal agreed with this judgement and refused
her appeal. When it came before the commissioner the DHSS had
had second thoughts and conceded that this was perhaps a harsh
interpetation, which the commissioner readily confirmed.

In a different case, a very clear principle was established that,
lest there be any lingering doubt about it, the supplementary
benefits scheme 'is not there so that [claimants] can give expensive
presents to their friends and relations'. While this may come as
something of a surprise to tabloid journalists, it is unlikely to be
news to claimants. In the case which gave rise to this truism a
couple had three children, the eldest of whom was aged seventeen
and in full-time work. This placed him out of the reach of the
supplementary benefits scheme, leaving only the needs of the
parents and the two younger children to be considered. The father
had already had a single payment for a bed to enable his two eldest
boys to have a bed each rather than share. This bed was used by
the second child. A few months later the eldest boy's bed collapsed, whereupon the father gave him the second child's bed and
claimed a single payment for another bed for the second child.
Should he be allowed one? The question which fell to be answered
was whether the father had acted unreasonably in disposing of the
first bed. In considering this, the commissioner said he had, giving
the opinion already quoted. Pauper parents have no business
giving presents to their seventeen-year-old children.

By now it should be plain that merely to reach the point at
which a specific claim can be entertained the claimant must not
merely jump a formidable flight of hurdles, but that, because the
conditions to be met were so open to differing interpretations, it
was as though the hurdles were of indeterminate and constantly
changing heights. We have seen how every one of the qualifying
conditions could be interpreted very differently by adjudication
officers, appeal tribunals and commissioners. Claimants had to
cross each and every hurdle in turn; to fall at any one of them was
to lose the payment. If they failed, only those very few who went on
to appeal stood any chance of having the judgement reversed. The
vast majority who did not appeal may have fallen foul of the
correct application of the regulation or of the 'personal idiosyncrasies' of the adjudication officer.

A little bit of flexibility?

It will be readily conceded that the likelihood of claimants having a working knowledge of the single payments regulations was remote. This meant that they were very likely to fail to meet one of the conditions which would entitle them to advance a claim and, since ignorance of the law is decidedly no defence in the case of supplementary benefits, whether claimants succeeded in their claims was very often a matter of chance. In recognition of this unsatisfactory state of affairs the regulations contained a provision which allowed for the possibility of reimbursement of benefit if it had been spent on items for which a claim made for a single payment might have been allowed. That at any rate was its intention but its wording and interpretation afforded the usual scope for differing judgements to be made as to its exact meaning, with the usual result that chance played a conspicuous part in the outcome.

In essence, the regulation stipulated that money set aside for normal weekly living expenses must have been spent on some item for which a single payment might have been possible, and as a consequence the claimant was unable to afford to buy an essential item of normal daily living. The problems arise in determining whether the money was 'set aside' for normal living expenses; whether it was spent on an item for which a single payment might have been made; whether, if it was, that had the direct consequence of leaving the claimant short of money for normal living expenses; and whether the items which the claimant was then unable to buy were 'essential'. (The complexities do not end there, since the regulation also allowed for the possibility that in the past the claimant did not receive benefit to which he or she was entitled, and that the inability to buy essential items was a consequence of that non-payment. However, for the purposes of showing the arbitrary results of the application of this regulation we can leave that on one side.)

A man claimed a payment in respect of his boots, which he said were 'falling to bits and are a definite danger to my feet'. The adjudication officer refused on the grounds that the boots had worn out through 'normal wear and tear', one of the conditions which precludes a payment. The man appealed, and the appeal tribunal decided to deal with the claim under the regulation which allows reimbursement. (This immediately points up one of the arbitrary applications of this regulation; why had the adjudication officer not considered using it but the appeal tribunal did?) The claimant was asked if he had spent money set aside for clothing and footwear, which count as items of 'normal' expenditure, on any other items. The answer to this question was critical, since it would establish whether he had spent his money on an item for which he might have received a single payment. Had he been familiar with regulations he could have claimed that he had spent it on repairs to his cooker, or on some essential item of furniture, or on any one of the many items for which he might have claimed a single payment. Better still he could actually have spent the money on such an item before making his claim for the boots. In short, he could easily have either acted, or even merely claimed that he had acted, in a way that would probably have won him his case. However, truthful man that he was, he merely stated that he had spent money on clothes for his four children, for which he would not have been entitled to a single payment, so his claim failed. That it did perhaps owed rather more to chance than justice.

In a later case a man claimed a single payment as reimbursement for bedclothes bought for his wife who was suddenly admitted to hospital. The adjudication officer refused the claim, as did the appeal tribunal. The reason given by the tribunal was itself very interesting; the members deemed themselves to be unable to grant a payment for such a request when it was in fact one of the few categories of clothing expressly allowed for in the regulations. The appeal tribunal appears to have completely misunderstood this, and had not the claimant appealed to the commissioners that would have been the unjust end of the matter.

In considering the case the commissioner set out precisely the steps that would need to be taken for a claim under the reimbursement regulation to succeed. First, the claimant would have to show that all the usual rules about establishing a need for the item had been met, including all the riders about no suitable alternatives and so on which have been discussed above. The claimant must then show that he or she had 'set aside' money from normal requirements, though here the commissioner allowed that the idea of setting money aside should be liberally construed even to the point of having been only 'mentally set aside'. The claimant would then have to show that as a consequence of using the money set aside he or she could not meet the cost of the item for which the money had been set aside, and furthermore that the item he or she could now no longer afford was 'essential'. Finally, the commissioner concluded by closing the circle and stating that if the item could be shown to be 'essential' the claimant would still have to show a 'need' for it. To underline the point that this regulation should not be used merely to get round the usual governing regulations he added by way of emphasis:

> In particular it is not sufficient simply for it to be shown that the claimant used his weekly supplementary benefit to make a payment which could have been the subject of a single payment if claimed before the money was spent. It must be shown in addition that the claimant would otherwise have spent the money on an item or items of 'normal, additional or housing requirements' for which the money was 'set aside' and that it was 'essential' that the claimant should meet the cost of that item or these items.

Whether this interpretation of the regulation meant that claimants were more or less likely to obtain judgements in their favour is anybody's guess. The same regulation was subsequently considered by a tribunal of commissioners, who extended still further the liberal interpretation of the meaning of 'set aside'. In this case, as in the previous one, neither the adjudication officer nor the subsequent appeal tribunal considered invoking the 'reimbursement' regulation when the claimant, a widow, claimed in respect of decorating materials which she had already bought. When the commissioners did so the DHSS solicitor defended the original decision not to consider it in a tortuously argued series of submissions, the essence of which was that claimants ought to know the workings of the regulations and make their claims accordingly. The commissioners had no hesitation in rejecting this submission. They went on to say that the adjudication officer should have considered the possibility of a claim for reimbursement, and set out their view of the proper way to interpret it;

> Persons in receipt of supplementary benefit very commonly have nothing but the money set aside for their normal, addi-

tional and housing requirements with which to pay for anything. Very commonly, accordingly, if they do divert such money to other purposes, they have to forgo some item of normal or additional requirements or fall into arrears in respect of the commitments represented by their housing requirements. Accordingly, it is in general right that, in cases where the claim is not made until after the item has been acquired or paid for, the adjudication officer and the appeal tribunal should consider the possibility that there may be entitlement under reg. 28 [the reimbursement regulation].

Such a generous interpretation of the regulation, so clearly at odds with the prevailing DHSS orthodoxy, was not to the government's liking. This decision was reported in 1985; in 1986 all the problems surrounding the regulation disappeared when it was simply abolished. Nothing similar was put in its place; the tiny bit of flexibility it had afforded was gone.

Regulation 30: the 'significant safety net'

The infamous regulation 30 shows at its starkest the standard of living we expect of claimants. This regulation provided the fall-back power intended to help claimants in extreme circumstances if they had needs that could not be met in the ordinary way. It was recognised from the outset of the new scheme that the attempt to cater for all human needs through regulation would not succeed and that there would inevitably be some hard cases, so the system which came into being in 1980 included this regulation designed to relieve undue hardship. However, the determination to eliminate as much discretion from the scheme as possible led to the regulation being very tightly drawn, and it was expected to apply only to very few claims, as indeed proved to be the case. Being the one explicitly discretionary area left it acted as a focus for enterprising welfare rights workers trying to prise open the door to benefits – which was equally stoutly defended by the custodians of the public purse, the DHSS. Needless to say, it gave rise to problems of judgement and interpretation, some of which yet again show the extraordinary lengths to which the Department went to keep the use of this potential loophole to a minimum.

The first problem, more one of semantics than substance, is whether the regulation could be said to allow the exercise of discretion at all. Regulation 30 forms a separate section of the regulations, headed 'Discretionary payments', but whether it allowed the exercise of discretion soon became a matter for dispute. Before looking at that issue, let us first see what exactly the regulation allows. The essence of it is that 'a single payment to meet [an] exceptional need shall be made . . . if, in the opinion of an adjudication officer, such a payment is the only means by which serious damage or serious risk to the health or safety of any member of the assessment unit may be prevented'. There are some exceptions even to this stringent rule, since no payment can be made for any of the long list of exclusions mentioned earlier, and from 1986 payments for items of miscellaneous household furniture and equipment were excluded.

In one of the earliest considerations of the regulation a commissioner, while recognising that it was 'designed to introduce flexibility into the provisions . . . in a deserving case', gave his opinion that

> it is not an absolute discretion and must be applied judicially with proper regard to its limitations. . . . Whether or not such a payment is the only means by which serious damage or serious risk to the health or safety of any member of the assessment unit may be prevented is essentially a question of fact and degree for the opinion of the tribunal.

Five months later the same commissioner made the same point even more strongly. He began his discussion by saying that he thought the heading 'Discretionary payments' was misleading, and went on:

> In my opinion, entitlement under regulation 30 does not depend upon the exercise of a discretion in the legal sense of the word. Either a person satisfies the provisions, in which case a claimant is entitled to a single payment, or, if the provisions are not satisfied, there is not nevertheless an innate discretion to award a payment.

The anguished quest for legalistic certainty in the face of the stubborn refusal of claimants' needs and circumstances to fit into predetermined categories could scarcely be better stated. Lawyers love facts; as long as an issue can be said to be a matter of fact, it can be readily decided. The problem with this regulation, as stated in the first of the two quotations from this commissioner, is that whether a claimant 'satisfies the provisions' is a 'question of fact and degree for the opinion of the tribunal'. While not being as clearly expressed as it might have been, it is clear that what is meant here is that, once the facts have been established, it is for the adjudication officer to interpret the significance of those facts. Much as the commissioner might wish to think that a person either 'satisfies the provisions' or does not, it was seldom that clear cut.

Two requirements of the regulation gave rise to problems of deciding whether or not claimants satisfy the provisions: that the damage or risk to health be *serious*, and, if it is, that the award of a payment must be *the only means* by which it could be prevented. A moment's consideration would lead one to think that these conditions are very likely to be open to differing interpretations and so it proved. The obvious question in relation to the first condition is how serious is serious? Are shoes that leak a serious risk to health? One commissioner clearly thought they may be: 'Shoes that let in water seem to me to present an obvious risk to health. . . . Damp is an insidious cause of ill health. It is not necessary for a tribunal to spell out in terms of their decision in every case a precise damage or a serious risk to health.' In two subsequent, similar cases a different commissioner held a contrary view. When a claimant sought a payment for shoes that were split the commissioner, while not disputing that the shoes were split, decided that:

> The tribunal have failed to reach any findings of fact indicating why the defective shoes constitute a serious health risk. . . . Moreover, even if the tribunal had made a finding of fact that the defective shoes did constitute a serious risk to health . . . such a conclusion would, in my judgement, have been perverse, in that there is no evidence to suggest that the claimant's health was *seriously* endangered by reason of his admittedly defective shoes.

So it was conceded that leaking shoes might be a health risk, but not necessarily a *serious* health risk. Was it all right to have leaking shoes in summer but not in winter? Was it all right to wear wellingtons that do not leak in place of shoes that do? And of course clothing was not the only source of such questions. Was it damaging to health to be without the means of cooking warm food, and if so, was it seriously damaging? Was being racially harassed seriously damaging to one's health, such that one might qualify for a removal grant under this regulation? Such grotesque wranglings as these were the stuff of everyday decisions in the arcane inner workings of the Poor Laws. To the lawyers and laymen of appeal tribunals such questions offered interesting intellectual puzzles; meanwhile claimants were left baffled, angry or upset that there could be any doubt at all that being without a cooker or shoes for one's child could ever be anything other than a cause of hardship.

Even if the claimant managed to show that the item needed would prevent serious danger to health he or she had then to show that a single payment was the only means of acquiring it. The only means? It is immediately apparent that this will be problematic; should the claimant be expected to steal it? Clearly not, but what other limitations should be put on this apparently draconian requirement? The DHSS internal guidance manual ruled out the use of jumble sales, sending claimants to social services departments for payments under the Children and Young Persons Act, and recourse to charities or voluntary organisations, including the WRVS for clothing needs. (As we shall see, in doing so the DHSS was a good deal more enlightened than the government, which brought all these possible sources back into use with the social fund.)

One obvious source of potential 'other means' was credit. Again, until the advent of the social fund it might have seemed strange to suggest that those on supplementary benefit should be encouraged to get themselves into debt, yet this is precisely the force of this regulation. Attempts were made to set some limits on the requirement that claimants should seek credit, which made it easier for a claim to succeed, but at the expense of once more blurring the meaning of 'the only means'. In the words of a commissioner:

In my opinion, other available means must be proved on a balance of probabilities, and not simply suggested as possible.

208

For instance, in the case of clothing or footwear, it might be shown that an applicant is a member of a clothing club. Evidence as to borrowing or credit would have to be compelling before it should be determined that such means are available to a person entitled to a supplementary pension or allowance.

This limitation was further restricted in a later decision when it was held that it was not enough to assume that, because a claimant was a member of a clothing club, credit would automatically be a proper alternative means of finance. That case involved a woman who had previously bought clothing for her son from a catalogue but had been unable to keep up the payments. In this situation the commissioner decided that: 'Whether or not the claimant had actually been refused further clothing, it was for consideration whether, if she had already incurred indebtedness that she could not discharge, it would be proper for her to incur further indebtedness that would increase her financial embarrassment.'

These exclusions have nevertheless left plenty of room for imaginative adjudication officers to exercise their ingenuity in deciding how claimants might meet their needs other than by way of a single payment. To return to the matter of the boots and wellingtons, a commissioner decided that, while it was correct to regard these as not a suitable alternative for shoes in the ordinary way, in the context of regulation 30 they could reasonably be considered as an alternative means of preventing a health risk. Adjudication officers have seriously suggested that claimants have no need for bedding since they can always keep the heating on all night or sleep in their clothes or even ask to share the bedding of other members of the household.

Two examples will illustrate the ludicrous lengths to which some adjudication officers and tribunal members were prepared to go to avoid making payments. In the first case, a claimant asked for a payment for safety clothing on starting work. It was conceded that the claimant needed safety clothes to protect himself at his newly acquired part-time job. He had been out of work for a considerable period, so it can be imagined how important this first step back into employment must have been for him. The claim was refused, and on appeal to the tribunal it was again refused, the tribunal solemnly recording their opinion that:

Appellant does not come within the terms of regulation 30 . . . because, although there is a serious risk to his health and safety by working without the necessary protective clothing, a single payment is not the *only* means by which that risk can be prevented, since he has the option of leaving the employment in question.

This absurd judgement brought the wrath of the commissioner down on the heads of the tribunal, who regarded it as 'so unreasonable as to be unsupportable in law' – even, it should be added, social security law. He was moved to say that:

A totally literal reading of the expression 'the only means' as implying the absence of any other means whatsoever cannot have been intended by the legislature. It cannot have been in contemplation for instance that the possibility of criminal means, such as theft by shoplifting, was to be taken into consideration.

We must be grateful for this display of common sense, but the important point to note is that this reasonable interpretation was starkly at odds with the interpretation made by the original adjudication officer, with the backing of his department, and by the appeal tribunal, all of whom would have been happy to see this young man give up his job and remain on benefit, at a cost to the taxpayer much greater than the trivial payment for his safety clothes. This apparent absurdity can be understood only by recognising the determination of the DHSS, and of this particular tribunal, not to concede any principles which might open the way to more payments.

The second example shows the DHSS once more going to extraordinary lengths to make the words 'no other means' mean exactly what they say. A single parent with two small children, the younger aged two, claimed for a payment to replace a broken fence through which the younger child could have had access to a street and to a fast-flowing stream approximately a hundred yards away. The claim was dismissed on the grounds that there were 'other means', namely that 'parental control and supervision would eliminate the risk'. This argument was amplified at the appeal tribunal, where the Department's representative stated that there were two courses open to the mother to prevent risk to the child:

(1)   The child should be kept indoors at all times when she [the mother] was.
(2)   The child should be supervised every second he was at play in the back garden. He further suggested that she bring him indoors each time she needed to deal with a caller at the front door, answer the telephone or attend to food being cooked or indeed if she went to the toilet.

The appeal tribunal, not surprisingly, rejected these arguments, allowed the claim, and gave the Department's representative a well-deserved piece of its mind. That the adjudication officer should have thought that such arguments were remotely reasonable is another chilling insight into the world of social security.

While blame can sometimes be laid at the door of over-zealous adjudication officers it would be a grave error to think that they were the main culprits in driving down the living standards of claimants. They had no choice but to apply the regulations, which often led to claimants being deprived of the most basic items because that was the will of Parliament, as in the following example of a young couple who sought advice from a CAB in the North-East. They applied for a payment under regulation 30 on the grounds of hardship, only to fall foul of the principle that they may have had other means of meeting their needs:

> She is six months pregnant. When they got married they moved into a council house, she from a bedsitter, he from his mother's. They have no furniture at all and are sleeping on the floor in a sleeping bag. They have to have all their meals out in cafes as they have no cooker. This also costs in bus fares. Her doctor has written saying this is dangerous to her health, but the DHSS refused payment and said they should obtain credit.

And, according to the regulations, so they should. The individual benefit officer was not to blame; this case could quite properly be refused within the regulations existing in 1987.

Examples such as these could be readily provided by any welfare rights officer or advice bureau. DHSS adjudication officers, following the interpretation of the commissioner that the risk

211

to health must be demonstrably *serious*, refused thousands of claims, leaving claimants in the most appalling circumstances. It was commonplace for claimants with next to nothing in the way of clothing to be refused payments because being without all but the barest minimum of clothes was not regarded as a serious risk to health. A CPAG survey of the working of the regulations in 1987 gave the following frightening applications of regulation 30, which, it will be remembered, was *designed* to *minimise hardship*:

> DHSS officers refuse to provide cookers for families, even where there are young children. DHSS officers have frequently stated that they consider there is no risk, let alone serious risk, attached to the lack of cooking facilities and hot food, even for children as young as three and four. Claimants have been told that cup-a-soups, sandwiches and fish and chips are sufficient. In one instance a family were told that they could go to friends to get hot food, a view which was sadly supported by an appeal tribunal and recorded in its decision.
>
> Bedding was refused for a family because they had central heating 'which could be left on at night'.
>
> A young child was refused shoes because she had three pairs of socks which, when worn together, the DHSS officer considered to be a suitable alternative to shoes.
>
> One local authority provided case studies of several claimants including single parents, families with large numbers of children and people suffering serious respiratory complaints. All of them had managed without cookers, beds and bedding through one of the coldest winters on record.

These examples may be extraordinary, but only in the sense that it is almost beyond belief that Parliament legislated for such Dickensian poverty. They are by no means extraordinary in the sense of being unusual or infrequent applications of the rule.

Finally, even this regulation, offering the slenderest of escape routes through the labyrinth of the single payment regulations, was available only to the absolutely destitute. Anyone with savings of over £500 was deemed to be too well off to need it and was explicitly barred from its meagre protection. We can see clearly from this regulation that the government was quite content to allow the very poorest families to go without clothes, beds, bedding and cookers in all but the most extreme circumstances, and even then it expected claimants, however poor, to borrow to meet their needs. When justifying the huge cuts in single payments in August 1986, which are the subject of the next chapter, the government sought to counter the fears expressed by the SSAC by reminding it that regulation 30 would remain as 'a significant safety net'. Quite apart from the fact that, as part of the package of those cuts, the government abolished its use in respect of all items of miscellaneous furniture, the examples given above show just how valueless that safety net was. They showed also that the government, which knew full well how useless it was, was not above misleading Parliament by making such claims in an official report prepared for the debate on the August 1986 cuts.

10   Single Payments Under the Tories: Cuts and More Cuts

I applied for winter coats and shoes for my twins. My twins are four and growing very fast. I am on social receiving £32.05 per week. I am supposed to buy food, pay bills plus buy clothes which is not possible on the small amount I receive. When I applied I was refused. In the end I had to buy their coats which they badly needed out of my money, costing £20 each, and almost starving for the next two weeks.

Clothing Grants

This letter to the CPAG from a London mother expresses vividly the choices facing those on benefits. This woman, and millions like her, were in this position because of deliberate policies made by the government about how the poor should live. Cuts in single payments for clothing grants were the first and most extensive of all the cuts introduced by the Conservatives when in 1980 they took over responsibility for the new supplementary benefit scheme.

The extent of the cuts can be seen very easily: in 1979 there were 360,000 single payments for clothing grants; in 1981 there were only 57,000. How and why did this reduction come about?

Under the supplementary benefit system in existence until 1980 there was no legal definition of what the weekly amount of benefit was supposed to cover. In the absence of any such definition the SBC had made up its own rules and decided that, among other items, it was supposed to pay for the normal repair and replacement of clothing. However, in recognition of the impossibility of buying clothes out of the weekly amount of benefit, the practice had grown of making awards of single payments to meet some

214

clothing and footwear needs; these became such a large proportion of all single payments that they usually totalled more than all other types together. The rapid growth in the number of claims, from 270,000 in 1975 to 360,000 in 1979, coupled with the enormous work they created for the DHSS, since each claim had to be individually assessed, made them an obvious target for reform. They were assessed by benefit officers, who had a wide discretion whether to make or withhold awards, so that they were also justifiably open to the charge of being unfair and arbitrary, since identical claims might be and often were decided differently in different DHSS offices.

The problem was that thousands of families had come to rely on them to supplement their inadequate weekly benefit. This was acknowledged by the DHSS's review team who, in the late 1970s, were charged with carrying out the review of the supplementary benefits system. They referred to research which showed that over half of all claimants with children had less clothing than the list of items regarded by the SBC as minimum requirements, and that over half of all claimants with children had to borrow money to buy items supposedly covered by their weekly benefit. They added: 'Most claimants said that they had had to cut down on expenditure when they came on to benefit, and many said they had "unmet" needs, often for clothing and shoes.'

Faced with this evidence the review team were forced to conclude that it would not be possible to discontinue single payments for clothing 'without causing considerable hardship for some claimants', and particularly singled out all families with children. The government had no such qualms; in 1980 it drew up such stringent regulations for paying clothing grants that at a stroke it reduced the number of awards by 84 per cent. This was done by legislating that the basic weekly benefit was deemed to cover the normal repair and replacement of clothing and by allowing single payments only in the most exceptional circumstances. These specifically excluded the most common reason that people might need help with clothing or shoes – normal wear and tear – leaving only cases where the need had arisen other than in the normal course of events. Specifically, this meant where the need had arisen through pregnancy, the birth of a child, rapid weight gain or loss, exceptional wear and tear resulting from physical or mental disability, the need to go into hospital or because of accidental loss, damage or theft.

The result of these changes was immediate and drastic. Hundreds of thousands of claimants in effect suffered a cut in their living standards as they were now forced to budget for all clothes and shoes out of their weekly income. Some of the effects were documented in a CPAG report published in 1984, from which the letter at the beginning of this chapter is taken. CPAG reported many claimants being forced to turn to social services departments, whose expenditure on clothes and footwear shot up by over 20 per cent in the year after these cuts, and to charities, which reported huge increases in demand. The CPAG commented that 'Many claimants reported to us that they met the minimal clothing needs of their children by going without something else. It is clear that, to keep going, many claimants juggled fuel, food, clothing and rent payments.' So much for the government's oft-repeated aim of giving families more power to choose how to run their own lives. For many families on supplementary benefit it meant the power to choose which particular essential items to do without in any one week.

More evidence of the effects of the cuts is provided by Geoffrey Beltram in the study quoted earlier as to how the post-1980 supplementary benefit system was working. He refers to a study of the families of unemployed men in Swansea in 1982 which disclosed 'extensive deprivation, particularly in large families':

> Even those without children lacked, on average, over half the basic clothing requirements on the list formerly used by Supplementary Benefits Commission officers in considering claims for single payments. Most claimants found that, despite economising on food, juggling debts, and cutting out small pleasures, they could not stretch their money to meet basic needs. Many tried unsuccessfully to get grants for essential clothing, the lack of provision for which bore especially heavily upon the long-term unemployed.

As the grants officer for the Family Welfare Association put it in the CPAG report referred to above: 'The past few months seem to have wiped out the last 50 years. Young people are having problems now that my parents knew about but that I have never seen.'

What did all this mean for claimants and their families? It meant that no matter how few clothes they had, or in what condition they may have been, they could not expect a single payment to help them provide clothes or footwear for themselves or their children unless they met the very tight conditions of the regulations. Claimants frequently applied for help because their children had outgrown their clothes or shoes only to be told that there was no longer any provision for them. Women who were forced to leave the matrimonial home with whatever they could take with them could not qualify for a payment even if they had only the clothes they stood up in. The DHSS internal code of guidance set out a list of clothes to be regarded as essential items. It was very basic, providing for example for one cardigan, pull-over or sweater, two pairs of shoes, two shirts or two dresses, three pairs of underpants and so on in similarly meagre quantities. But even if claimants had less than the clothes on this minimal list they could not be given a single payment except in the circumstances set out above. They were simply expected to buy what they needed from their weekly benefit. The only other way they could qualify for a payment was under the fall-back regulation, regulation 30, and we have already seen what little relief that afforded.

After 1980, in order to obtain a clothing grant it was necessary to come within one of the categories provided for in the regulations. As usual, these were by no means straightforward and gave rise to problems of interpretation. For example, while normal wear and tear was excluded, it was possible to obtain a grant if the clothes were needed following rapid weight gain. Where did this leave adolescents? Is the adolescent growth spurt normal, or an example of rapid weight gain? Clearly the answer is critical since the clothing costs of adolescents will form a substantial charge on the very small sums of money at the disposal of claimants. Needless to say, the DHSS code of guidance interpreted the regulation so as to exclude any weight gains due to the normal process of growing up, thereby specifically excluding all claims brought for these reasons. When invited to comment on the meaning of this regulation a commissioner gave his support to this restricted interpretation with these words: 'I do not think that it would be right to award a payment for clothing in these circumstances unless the rate of growth has been of a different order from the normal.'

This judgement arose from a case involving a claim on behalf of a thirteen-year-old boy who had suddenly shot up six inches in less than a year but who had been refused a grant for clothes. On appeal the boy won his case, and in giving its decision the tribunal stated that the embarrassment and ridicule the boy suffered as a result of not having clothes that fitted constituted a 'serious risk to the child's mental health'. This boy was fortunate; but many thousands of adolescents do have to suffer such daily indignities as the price of being on benefit.

For some claimants, such indignities amount to nothing less than humiliation. One case before a commissioner involved a man's claim for clothing for himself and his wife. At the appeal tribunal it emerged that the wife was incontinent and 'often had a mishap'. They awarded a single payment for the underwear and clothing which she was claiming on the grounds that the need had arisen other than in the normal course of events. There the matter might have ended, at the cost to the state of the grand sum of £17.20, if the DHSS had not seen the decision as the thin end of the wedge and taken the appeal to the commissioner on the grounds that, while it was reasonable to say that the underwear might have worn out other than through normal wear and tear, that did not apply to the rest of the clothes, two bras and a jumper. The commissioner duly weighed this grave matter at some length and concluded that he was prepared to allow the claim of £3.60 in respect of the two pairs of pants for the claimant's wife, and then directed that the claim for the other items should be resubmitted to a differently constituted appeal tribunal.

To get her £3.60 this woman had been obliged to disclose the facts about her incontinence to the benefit officer, an appeal tribunal, the commissioner and, finally, to another and different appeal tribunal. We can only guess what that must have cost her. There were thousands more elderly and disabled claimants in similar circumstances who would have had either to bear the costs of their incontinence in silence or go through such humiliating disclosures in order to secure even this minimal help with their clothing needs. That is the inevitable effect of depending on single payments to top up otherwise inadequate benefit rates.

What if the claimant wished to join the enterprise culture and lift herself off benefit by getting a job, but has nothing suitable to wear for job interviews? Should this qualify her for a clothing grant? Is this a need which has arisen other than through normal wear and tear? Such questions make lawyers happy, and it took the Court of Appeal to reach the final decision that the need was one which had arisen through normal wear and tear and therefore the claimant was ineligible for a grant – but not until the benefit officer, appeal tribunal and a social security commissioner were involved. Even then another social security commissioner was subsequently able to rule that in some cases a claim might be justifiable, if the claimant had not possessed any suitable clothes in the first place.

This latter claim was able to succeed because the regulation admitted the possibility of a need which had arisen other than in the normal course of events. In 1986, soon after this last judgement, alarmed at the flexibility which this tiny loophole gave to claimants, the government acted swiftly to close it by tightening the regulations still further. It was no longer possible to claim merely that the need for clothes had arisen other than in the normal way; from then on the need had to be one that was specifically itemised in the regulation. As a result, claimants wishing to better themselves would in future find it even harder. Not content with this, at the same time the government removed the possibility of payments in cases where the need arose through damage, loss or theft of clothes. From August 1986, if claimants or their children had their clothes stolen or accidentally damaged there was no provision to help them.

All these cuts in clothing grants were carried out knowingly and deliberately by the same government that continually claims to have targeted help particularly on families with children.

Furniture and Household Expenses: Before August 1986

Once the bulk of clothing grants had been abolished the largest and most expensive categories of claims were those to do with housing needs. The majority of these claims were for furniture, household goods of various kinds and removal expenses. Once the government decided to reduce still further the use of single payments it was inevitable that these regulations would be tightened. The major changes came in August 1986, and by comparing the rules before and after then we can see a number of trends. The most obvious is the continuation of the tendency to cut the cost of single payments and reduce their scope, which was effected in a number of ways. While this was the main purpose of the changes, an important secondary effect was to continue the squeeze on discretion by the removal of some of the more problematic conditions and by the introduction of set amounts of awards rather than leaving the amounts to adjudication officers to determine. A third effect of the changes was to provide a revised version of the government's beliefs about the appropriate standard of living which claimants should expect after 1986. The revision was downwards.

Weekly benefit is designed to cover normal living expenses. It is clear that the amounts allowed could not be expected to cover the occasional large expense of moving or setting up home, or replacing or repairing essential items such as beds, cookers, tables and so on. The question then arises, what is it reasonable for the state to provide to those who depend upon it for their sole source of income? Given that there must be some limitations on what is allowed, how much is it reasonable for claimants to spend on household goods and furniture and how often should they be allowed to claim? It is issues such as these that the regulations governing these categories of single payments attempt to resolve. The answers to these questions tell us a great deal about the standard of living we impose upon the poor. Single payments are paid in full only to those with savings of less than £500, so we are dealing here with the very poorest claimants.

The following comment by a commissioner sets out the daunting task facing anyone trying to pick their way through the complexities of the single payment regulations:

The regulations cannot be adequately applied without the most careful scrutiny. Each phrase, indeed each word, must be carefully considered before any given regulation, paragraph or sub-paragraph is applied to the facts of a particular case. This is especially true of regulation 9 [essential furniture and house-hold equipment]. Paragraph (4) sets out a long list of items of furniture and other household equipment. No payment can be awarded in respect of any of these items, however, unless the claimant can satisfy:

(a) the general provisions set out in regulations 3 to 6;
(b) the particular provisions set out in paragraphs (1), (2) and (3) of regulation 9; and
(c) in respect of certain items listed under paragraph (4) . . . special provisions peculiar to these items.

It is a legislative labyrinth through which the appeal tribunal must pick its path with consummate care.

We may rightly deduce from this preamble that obtaining a furniture grant was no simple matter; having cleared all the general obstacles set out in the preceding chapter the claimant wanting a furniture grant then had a whole new obstacle course to overcome. The reason these particular regulations were so complex is that they dealt with three different interrelating elements: first, the kinds of items for which it was reasonable to allow claimants to have payments; second, the specific conditions under which some claimants but not others were allowed to claim for them; and, third, the amounts of money to be allowed for each item. To understand fully the effects of the cuts we must take each of these in turn.

Removal costs

It will be simplest to begin with the regulations governing the award of removal costs because some of the other items refer back to these. Should we place any limitations on the frequency with which claimants can move and expect to have their removal costs met from public funds? If so, what limitations? Until 1986 the answers to such questions were laid down in regulation 13 of the single payments regulations. This set out the conditions which might either give or preclude entitlement to a payment. The conditions which conferred entitlement were the *only* conditions under which a claim could be allowed, so that they in turn, by implication, also revealed the conditions under which claims

221

could not be allowed. The fact that any limitations were placed upon claimants answers the first of our questions; unlike other people they could not simply move because they wanted to, they had to have a legitimate reason if they wanted the costs met from public funds. Once this is accepted the actual conditions imposed seem reasonable, but they left some curious gaps which are difficult to explain away.

Broadly speaking, the claimant was required to show good cause for his or her wish to move, which had to be because the existing home was 'structurally deficient or insanitary'; or 'unsuitable either in size or structure or because it is too far removed from close relatives'; or as a consequence of the ending of a marriage or relationship as a result of death, divorce or any other breakdown; or because the claimant's job prospects would be 'significantly improved'; or that he or she would be enabled to take in a close relative who was in need of care; or if as a result of the move some specific housing costs of the claimant would be reduced.

The first point to note about the requirements is the now familiar one that most of them are open to widely differing interpretations. What do expressions like 'deficient', 'insanitary', 'unsuitable', 'too far removed', 'significantly improved' mean in practice? The imprecision of such concepts was bound to lead to discretion once more creeping in by the back door, and claimants had their claims allowed or not according to the interpretation of their particular adjudication officer.

The second point is that, while they may all be good and sensible reasons for making a payment, they were the *only* acceptable reasons. What about those having to move because their tenancy agreement came to an end through no fault of theirs? Since the government has encouraged the growth of tenancies that are unprotected by the Rent Acts it is by no means uncommon for a tenant to have to leave simply because he or she has no protection and the landlord wishes to repossess; why should these claimants not be able to claim their removal expenses? Or what if a tenant has been unlawfully evicted by an unscrupulous landlord? The regulations made no provision for such claimants, or for many others whose move may have been forced upon them in circumstances beyond their control. As John Mesher, the officially recognised annotator of the regulations, succinctly put it, 'The list far from exhausts all the circumstances in which a move of home and assistance with expenses would be reasonable.'

Mesher makes a further point which reveals still more arbitrariness. A commissioner held that for a claim to succeed it is necessary to show only that one of the requirements of the regulation is *satisfied*, not that it is the *reason* for the move. Thus, for example, in the case of a tenant evicted through no fault of his or her own, whether or not a payment was awarded would depend upon the tenant being able to show that one of the permitted conditions applied, regardless of whether that had anything to do with the reason for the move. Chance, once again, was a crucial determinant in the success or otherwise of many claims.

When the great axe fell in August 1986 the regulation governing removal expenses remained unchanged. While matters were not made any worse for claimants, neither was the opportunity taken to amend the insupportable anomalies whereby some reasons for moving were deemed to be acceptable and others, quite beyond the power of the claimant to alter, were not. The government, it must be assumed, approved of withholding grants for removal expenses from claimants who had to leave their tenancies through no fault of their own.

Furniture grants

Furniture grants were payable to two different sets of people. One group consisted of those moving into their own homes and setting up house, whether for the first time or as a result of matrimonial breakdown, who will often have nothing or very little in the way of furniture and household equipment and will in effect need to be kitted out by the DHSS. The other consisted of those already living in their own homes but who need to add to, repair or replace certain items, either because there has been an addition to the household or because something has broken or worn out. Which items is it reasonable to provide and which items is it reasonable to help claimants to repair or replace?

The list of items considered 'essential' was very important in that it constituted a precise statement of what Parliament considered to be the appropriate standard of living for those on benefit. For those claimants moving into their own accommodation who met

the qualifying conditions for a single payment the pre-1986 list
was as follows:

(a) sufficient beds and mattresses and dining and easy chairs
     for all the members of the assessment unit;
(b) a dining table;
(c) sufficient storage units for clothing, food and household
     goods;
(d) a cooker;
(e) heating appliances;
(f) fire-guards;
(g) curtaining and fittings;
(h) PVC floor covering or equivalent;
(i) an iron;
(j) light fittings;
(k) towels;
(l) a pushchair;
(m) a high chair;
(n) a hot water cylinder jacket;
(o) safety gates;
(p) minor items such as cleaning implements, cooking uten-
     sils, crockery and cutlery;
(q) garden implements where necessary.

Other items were also available subject to the claimant meeting
further health conditions:

(r) a covered hot-water bottle was available to an elderly or
     infirm claimant;
(s) a washing machine, but only where no adult in the
     household was fit enough to do the washing, or where
     there were no suitable washing or drying facilities in the
     home and there was no suitable laundry or launderette
     that could be used;
(t) a vacuum cleaner, but only where a member of the
     assessment unit was allergic to house dust; and
(u) a refrigerator, but only where a member of the assess-
     ment unit required, for medical reasons, a special diet for
     which it was necessary to keep foodstuffs at refrigerated
     temperatures.

In addition to the above it would also be possible to claim a payment for bedding where a need existed.

This list defines the standard of living laid down for those setting up home. Readers can judge the adequacy or otherwise for themselves. We would only point out that for the vast majority of claimants, while it provided a basic minimum it did not allow for such common items as a vacuum cleaner, washing machine or refrigerator, and provided for no means of heating water other than a stove.

The position was only slightly different for those claimants who were already in their own homes. Here the issue was what it was reasonable to allow them to buy or, more commonly, to repair or replace. Before August 1986 such claimants could always have their cooker or heater repaired or replaced and, subject to further conditions, all the items on the same list other than the miscellaneous 'minor' items.

Should all claimants be allowed to buy these items, or should we place limitations on who could have which ones and how often they could have them? Under what conditions should claimants be awarded payments for the items? Following the path mapped out by the commissioner, quoted above, they would first have to demonstrate an exceptional need for each item, which was by no means unproblematic. They would then be required to use any savings they had in excess of £500. Then they would have to meet all the specific conditions described in what follows.

Before the 1986 changes there were two sets of qualifying conditions depending on whether the claimant had recently become a tenant or owner or not. In the case of claimants who had recently moved, which was taken to be within the previous three months, the move had to be into an unfurnished or partly furnished home. Once this was established, the claimant had to meet one of the conditions described in the next section for the claim to succeed.

People setting up home

The first condition was that one or more of the conditions that would have entitled the claimant to a removal grant applied. Thus any anomalies in those conditions were carried over into the award of an essential furniture grant, thereby increasing their significance. In particular this could and very often did exclude young people who were moving from their parental home to set up home for themselves since this was not one of the permitted reasons. It might make sense to preclude such people from obtaining any removal expenses on the assumption that they would probably have little in the way of furniture to move when they first left home, but for that same reason it made very little sense to exclude them from the possibility of a grant for furniture once they had moved. Nevertheless, that was the effect of making furniture grants conditional on the reason for the move.

Second, the claim could succeed if any member of the claimant's immediate family was a dependent child, over pensionable age, pregnant, chronically sick or mentally or physically disabled; in other words, if there was a potentially vulnerable person in the household.

Third, the claim could succeed if the claimant had been on benefit for at least six months and had 'no immediate prospects of employment'.

Fourth, the claim could succeed if the claimant had moved to the new home from one of a number of specified institutions, such as prison, hospital, resettlement unit or the like, provided he or she had been in the institution for more than a year.

In the case of the last two groups of claimants one further condition had to be satisifed: that there was 'no suitable alternative furnished accommodation available in the area'. Readers of the story so far will need no prompting to see at once the difficulties raised by that condition. Each word in it was open to problems of interpretation, and indeed every single word was subjected to detailed analysis by a commissioner in an attempt at clarification. For many claimants it proved to be the fatal stumbling block.

The problems caused by this one condition were such that the Social Security Policy Inspectorate was asked by the DHSS to look into the operation of the regulation. Its report, published in 1985, contained some interesting revelations, both about the way the condition was being used and about the standard of life of those on benefit.

It is clear from the report that the condition was being interpreted in widely differing ways by the eighteen offices examined in the study, so much so that half of them had abandoned the use of it entirely while the other half were struggling on with it. Offices had abandoned it because so many of their decisions that suitable alternative accommodation was available in the area were regularly overturned by appeal tribunals. As is usual with any detailed study of decision-making in the DHSS, the Inspectorate found that many of the decisions had been wrongly made. Of the eighty-nine cases refused a furniture grant eighteen (20 per cent) should not have been as the claimant had qualified on grounds which made the application of the 'alternative accommodation' rule unnecessary. Of the sixty-four cases which had gone to appeal exactly 50 per cent were successful, casting doubt on the quality of the original decision. In other words it was clear from the report that thousands of claimants were being denied furniture grants either in contravention of the regulations or as a result of judgements about the availability of alternative accommodation that did not bear closer scrutiny.

Of even greater interest was the Inspectorate's findings about the claimants themselves. It had confined the study to single people or childless couples, most of whom were youngsters wanting to leave their parental home and start life in a place of their own. When the inspectors examined the files on the 270 claimants in the study they found that 'few of our sample seemed to have had any essential items at all'. These destitute and unemployed young people turned to the DHSS for help. In view of the widespread myth that there is a good deal of fraudulent use of such payments it is very important to note that those who were given a single payment used the money sensibly for the purpose for which it was given. The inspectors found that of the 142 claimants who had received a payment the money had been 'properly spent' in all but two cases. Only seven had abandoned or sold the furniture they had bought, and even in these few cases there was no suggestion that the furniture had been sought fraudently; rather that the experiment in living alone had not worked out. Of the remainder the inspectors commented: 'we gained the firm impression that all had a serious intent to remain, even where they were not too happy with the accommodation or surroundings'. For these people the payments had helped considerably in setting them out on the path of independent living.

Of the eighty-nine refused cases, six gave up the tenancy and so lost their chance of independence. The rest struggled on and made do as best they could, borrowing from relatives, friends or neighbours. Only two had reapplied to the DHSS for help after they had been tenants for some time, though many of them could probably have made successful claims under the rules governing existing tenants, which would have applied once they had been in their accommodation for three months. Whether they had been told of this possibility when their initial claims were refused is not clear. The results of the refusals were described in the detached and passionless prose to which civil servants are accustomed:

> The refusal to make an award may have caused discomfort and inconvenience but we did not come across any claimant whose health appeared to have been affected. Most claimants have few, if any, of the essential items when they claim. Some who have been there as long as a year were still lacking items such as floor coverings and wardrobes. However, most claimants had obtained the basic necessities such as a bed and cooker reasonably quickly and most had been awarded a single payment for bedding as an immediate separate award. . . . Most claimants were also able to borrow as a stop-gap.

The reference to the award for bedding has its own quaint interest. Bedding was not governed by the general regulation covering furniture but by a separate regulation with less stringent qualifying conditions. The inspectors noted that claimants who were refused a grant for a bed were often 'puzzled and confused' to be awarded a grant for bedding! As well they might be. No doubt greater experience with the mysterious ways of the DHSS would soon have made this lunacy seem perfectly normal.

Before leaving this study it is worth giving the example of one claimant in particular, offered by the Inspectorate as being 'typical of the claimants refused and making slow progress':

> a young girl of nineteen had been given a single bed by her grandmother and had bought a bedroom carpet for £10, a dressing table for £3, and a cooker in good working order for £20. This had taken her three months. She had been promised some other furniture from relatives and had £10 saved towards a three-piece suite. From adverts in the paper she expected to

228

obtain one in good condition for £30. . . . [She] had a small but sufficient stock of kitchen utensils and some curtains.

This typical young girl was learning the hard way what it means to be a claimant in Thatcher's Britain in the mid-1980s. The poor-quality goods she was forced to beg, borrow or buy will start her off on a life of low expectations, and when they subsequently break or wear out she is unlikely to receive very much help, for reasons that will become apparent when we consider the ways in which the regulations subsequently changed. She will therefore continue to have to rely on begging and borrowing and continue to live surrounded by poor quality goods while she is on benefit – not quite the picture of the life of luxury with which claimants are often credited by some newspapers. Incidentally, she could almost certainly have claimed successfully for the essential items she needed by the time the inspectors saw her; let us hope they told her so. In that sense she is also typical of the very many claimants who do not receive many of the benefits to which they are entitled.

People already in their own homes

If the claimant had not recently become a tenant or owner the conditions were slightly different; 'recently' here was taken to mean within the previous three months. The claim could succeed if, as above, there was a vulnerable member in the family or if the claimant had been on benefit for at least six months and had no immediate prospects of work. (It was this rule that would have allowed those claimants refused an initial furniture grant to reapply with good hope of success once they had been in their homes for three months.) Finally, irrespective of the length of time the claimant had been on benefit or who was in the household, the claim could succeed if it was for either a cooker or a heater, because these items were deemed to be absolutely essential.

August 1986: The Axe Falls

Despite all the obstacles to obtaining furniture grants the number of successful claims grew considerably, rising from 146,000 in 1980 to 947,000 in 1984. Alarmed that people were actually claiming their benefits, and particularly because they were being encouraged to do so by welfare rights pressure groups, the government decided to put a stop to it. In August 1986 amendments to the regulations were passed which simultaneously reduced the list of items considered to be essential, standardised the amounts payable for these and all non-essential items, and tightened up the qualifying conditions in ways that drastically curtailed the possibility of gaining entitlement to a payment.

As we have seen, the list of essential items contained seventeen items plus four more which could be obtained in exceptional circumstances if the health of the claimant warranted it. This standard of living was regarded by the government as too profligate for the destitute in Britain in the mid-1980s. It was therefore pruned down to eight. The items no longer considered essential were tables, chairs, storage units, curtains and fittings, floor coverings, irons, light fittings, towels, cleaning implements, cooking utensils, crockery and cutlery, and gardening implements. Not for paupers the luxury of eating at a table and sitting on chairs, and such crumbs as might fall from their plates would have to fall on to bare boards, visible to any passing neighbour through the uncurtained windows.

All the items removed from the list were grouped together into a separate list called 'miscellaneous' items. It was still possible to secure a grant for them, subject to the qualifying conditions, but whereas before the claimant may have been given a grant to meet the cost of either new or second-hand goods, depending on the particular items, after the August changes he or she would receive one lump-sum payment of £75, plus £50 for each dependant, *regardless* of what was being claimed. This may or may not have been enough to meet the cost of tables, chairs, carpets, curtains, etc.; but whether it was or was not there was no possibility of any more. Moreover, it was not possible ever to obtain a further payment, for any other 'miscellaneous' item, under any circumstances. If any item not on the reduced list of essential goods broke, became worn out, or was damaged or stolen that was just too bad; no replacement was possible.

The qualifying conditions for both essential and miscellaneous items were tightened up in several ways, each of which made it harder for claimants to qualify. Even with regard to essential items, such as beds, cookers and heaters, claimants had to have been on benefit for a year before they could get a payment, and they could not then have another for the same item for a further three years. The only major exception was where the item was needed for someone who was over pensionable age, chronically sick or disabled. Even families with children had to wait the qualifying year and were debarred from repeat claims for three years. Given the restrictions this imposed on claimants it is not surprising that the government felt able to drop the contentious requirement that 'no suitable alternative accommodation' must be available, which was removed at the same time.

The savagery of these changes can best be illustrated in the case of cookers and heaters, two items which by any criteria must be considered essential to a reasonable standard of life. Before August 1986 cookers and heaters were the only two items which it was possible to obtain without any difficulty; after that date these, together with beds, became the items on the essential list for which it was the most difficult to qualify. The reasons for this startling demotion of such essential items can be only dimly guessed at. What it meant to claimants was that a family, even if they had small children, who came on benefit in March and whose cooker needed repair in October, would have to wait till the following March before they could have a payment towards its repair. If they had it repaired and it went wrong again within the next three years they would have to wait till the three years were up before once again becoming eligible for a payment. This, it must be remembered, was the intention behind considered changes which were deliberately introduced in 1986; they are not the incidental and unanticipated consequences of hasty drafting such as might have been the case with some of the curiosities introduced in 1980. Warmth, warm food and beds were no longer considered the right of those on benefit.

The change to paying standardised amounts rather than paying for the reasonable cost of items, as had been the case before, generally left those claimants who did qualify for payments receiving less than they would previously have been given. In respect of the essential items, for example, those fortunate enough to qualify for a cooker now had to find one for £150 or make up the difference out of their weekly benefit. Similarly, the few claimants qualifying for a washing machine, and remember these would be largely the elderly or handicapped living alone and unable to do their washing in any other way, had to find one for £100. The small lump sum for all 'miscellaneous' items probably meant that claimants could afford only some of items needed, and then of the poorest quality. If they were forced to buy shoddy goods it increased the likelihood of future breakages, and, as we have seen, no payment would be awarded to cover repairs either within three years in the case of cookers, heaters and beds, or ever, in the case of all other non-essential items like tables, chairs, carpets and curtains. Just for good measure, the government also decided to make it impossible to claim for any item of miscellaneous furniture under the fall-back regulation, regulation 30, which existed specifically to provide the possibility of obtaining a payment in the extreme case where the health or safety of the claimant might be at risk.

The Effects of the Cuts

The effects of the cuts were devastating. The amount spent on single payments fell by 45 per cent in the first six months of 1987 compared with the same period in 1986. The CPAG published a report detailing the effects on claimants and their families, drawing on evidence from various sources including NACAB, local authorities and an organisation representing welfare rights workers. Some of the consequences for claimants could be gauged by the types of cases presenting themselves to advice agencies for help, though it would have needed a Dickens to bring out the full extent of the humiliations. Claimants, many of them elderly, were condemned to live with bare floors and no curtains, poignantly illustrated by the case of one seventy-six-year-old Liverpudlian woman who was forced to choose between curtains for privacy and a carpet to cover her cold, damp, asphalt floors, as the £75 she received could not pay for both. The CAB reporting this case also mentioned that 'parents are bringing children along, showing our workers bandaged feet as a result of splinters from the bare boards'.

One particular source of concern, as was to be expected, was the effect on claimants' ability to buy or repair cookers. In one survey of over two hundred cases of applications for single payments coming to forty-four different agencies broken cookers were one of the most common problems. A single parent in south London was refused payment because she had been given £60 towards the cost of a cooker eighteen months before. Not surprisingly, it had become faulty and unsafe, but she had no prospect of any further payments until she had served her three-year qualifying period, which would not be for another eighteen months; meanwhile she and her children would have to go without any means of heating food. Another claimant was refused on the grounds that she had received a payment two years earlier, despite the fact that the gas board had sealed off her cooker as potentially dangerous. A third case involved a claimant whose cooker leaked gas so that the control knobs caught fire when it was on; there was a real danger of its exploding. Despite the presence of three school-age children in the house the claim was refused. According to the regulations, all these refusals were quite correct; in other words, there is no reason to doubt that thousands of other claimnts will also have been denied payments to repair faulty, even dangerous cookers. The presence of children provided no indemnity against this deprivation.

After cookers, beds were the item most frequently required. Here again, the August 1986 changes prevented many claimants receiving payments, and cases were known of claimants having to sleep on the floor. There were cases of parents with new babies having to sleep on the floor because their beds had broken and the regulations precluded payment for repairs.

One local authority, presumably echoing the experience of many others, reported: 'We see despair in many clients to a degree never before experienced. They feel shame at their inability to provide.'

Maternity grants

This shame must have begun very early in the lives of many parents due to the effects of the cuts in maternity grants. These were not strictly speaking part of the August 1986 cuts as they did not come into effect until April 1987, but such legalistic niceties would not have interested the young mothers who were caught by the virtual disappearance of single payments for maternity needs.

The April 1987 changes were the first instalment of the social fund, heralding the next wave of cuts which were to erode claimants' rights still further.

Before April 1987 destitute mothers could claim a single payment to meet the needs of having a new baby, up to a possible maximum of £187. This was to cover the necessary extra expenses such as baby clothes, bath, cot and bedding and pram or carry cot. Whether this amount was sufficient is another matter; the CPAG pointed out that the magazine *Mother and Baby* stated that £275 was a 'rock-bottom' estimate, while other knowledgeable sources recommended much more. However, even £187 was considered too much by the government, which, in April 1987 cut it back to £80. This could be claimed only by the very poorest mothers, since anyone with savings over £580 would not be eligible. Under certain strict conditions it may have been possible to secure a payment for a pushchair and highchair as well; otherwise it had to suffice for all the expenses associated with a new baby.

In a similar CPAG survey evidence was given of the effects of the changes on mothers. Since, as it points out, the cheapest Mothercare carry cot cost £75, it is not surprising that the survey revealed that the £80 grant was nowhere near enough, even for those mothers eligible for it. Evidence from CABx referred to the amount as grossly inadequate, and one commented that, 'when coupled with the difficulty of obtaining furniture grants the situation can be very bleak for young unsupported mothers and their babies'.

According to the survey, not one of the mothers in the sample of 231 claimants was able to purchase 'anywhere near' everything she needed with the grant. Borrowing, debt, relying on the generosity of others and using second-hand clothes and equipment were the only alternatives. It makes no sense at all to talk of weaning these mothers from the 'dependency culture' and launching them into an alternative 'enterprise culture'. They have nothing and they have no means of getting anything, and if the state refuses to provide, as this one does, they must beg, borrow or steal and live with the shame and guilt of not providing for their new babies. Since they continue to be deprived of adequate resources to live on, this soon develops into the shame and guilt at not being able to provide for their children.

Twisting the knife

One other change in August 1986 twisted the knife still further by introducing one more qualifying condition for any single payment and by removing one of the very few grounds on which it had been possible to claim for clothing or footwear. The new condition, which applied to all claims, was that the claimant should not have 'failed to exercise reasonable care to preserve or protect' any item for which a replacement was being requested, thus placing still more obstacles in the path of claimants; obstacles, moreover, that were capable of capricious interpretation. One example of this was when a claimant visited her doctor's surgery and followed the instructions in the waiting room to 'leave pushchairs outside'. The pushchair was stolen, but the claim for a single payment to replace it was refused on the grounds that she had not 'exercised reasonable care' to protect it.

Until August 1986 it had been possible to obtain a single payment for clothing or footwear where a replacement was sought due to 'the accidental loss of, damage to or destruction of an essential item of clothing or footwear'. This possibility was removed in the August cuts.

The combined effect of these changes was revealed in the CPAG survey. One case brought to a CAB illustrates the point exactly: 'The client's pushchair and child's coat were stolen. DHSS refused replacements as the claimant did not take reasonable care of the pushchair and the coat does not need replacing for one of the reasons specified in the new regulations' – that is to say, the coat having been stolen did not constitute a specified reason for replacing it.

In its conclusions to the report the CPAG wrote:

Time and again the same picture emerges. It is a picture of profound hardship, of claimants' health and safety put at risk. Individuals and families are having to go without bare essentials, commodities which most of us take for granted – beds and bedding, cookers, floor-covering, heaters and basic furniture such as chairs, tables and cupboards – have been put out of reach of many supplementary benefit claimants. Parents taking children with splinters in their feet only to be told that floor-coverings are no longer necessary household items; elderly and

235

chronically sick people enduring one of the coldest winters on record without adequate heating facilities, sufficient clothing or bedding; parents with a new-born baby sleeping on the floor; young families trapped in lodgings or overcrowded accommodation offered by friends or relatives because they cannot furnish a home of their own; families with young children told that a cooker is unnecessary as they can live off cup-a-soup, sandwiches and fish and chips or that three pairs of socks are an adequate substitute for a pair of shoes; claimants forced to make do with dangerous second-hand cookers; these are the kind of situations which are becoming increasingly commonplace and which we are willing to countenance in the midst of our affluent society.

That was written in 1988. It is crucial to understand that the reappearance of such shameful conditions was the result of policies deliberately and knowingly introduced by the government. They were not the unfortunate by-products of the system, they were exactly the effects that Norman Fowler and his successor, John Moore, and all the other ministers involved desired to achieve. This is what is meant by weaning people from a dependency culture and into the new enterprise culture. When they condemned our old people, families and children to live in such degradation and poverty they knew what they were doing.

Unfortunate By-product . . . or Deliberate Design?

There can be no doubt that the government knew very well what the effects of the August 1986 cuts would be because it was warned by its own Social Security Advisory Committee. The brief of this body, whose members are appointed by the government, is to vet and comment on all social security legislation before it goes before Parliament for approval. It exists to offer impartial and expert advice and is independent of all political parties or pressure groups. The 1986 changes were sent to the SSAC for comment before they were laid before the House for approval and its comments gave accurate warnings of the likely effects.

The SSAC commented first that it had received representations about the proposed changes from 159 organisations, 'almost all of which were extremely critical of the government's proposals'. It then gave a qualified welcome to the proposal to give fixed amounts for items rather than have detailed estimates, with the important proviso that the amounts should be realistic and frequently reviewed. Thereafter, in the genteel language of such eminent committees, it proceeded to tear the proposals apart one by one.

The SSAC deplored the removal of carpets and curtains from the list of essential items, items which in its view 'would be universally regarded as essential', and recommended that these, together with tables and chairs and towels should continue to be available. It proposed adding to the list of items available for new mothers, using the list prepared by the Health Visitors Association as the yardstick. As we have seen, far from adding to the list the government cut it still further. It condemned the restrictions on bedding which meant that it would now be available only for the elderly, sick or disabled and said that the decision to remove single payments for bedding from all other claimants was 'unjustifiable'. It considered all the new restrictions on eligibility for payments and condemned each in turn, pointing out that some of the changes would cause 'widespread hardship'.

The government had set great store by the argument that expenditure on single payments was becoming out of hand and that the prime reason for the cuts was to bring it under control. To this the SSAC replied that the increase in claims for single payments may have reflected 'the existence of a reservoir of unmet need' and ended its comments in unequivocal language:

> This response, because it seeks to attack the symptoms (increased public expenditure) without fully understanding the causes, must necessarily run the risk of causing widespread hardship amongst claimants who are already living at what is generally recognised as the poverty level. The collective impact of the representations made to us is that many claimants would face severe difficulties if the proposed changes were made, difficulties which we believe cannot be justified by the savings to be achieved.

The government cannot claim it was not warned. The splinters in the children's feet, the elderly ladies choosing between curtains

237

for privacy or carpets for warmth, the families going withou
cookers and the mothers borrowing their babies' clothes are all th
products of deliberate government policy.

But bad as these cuts were, worse was to follow.

11   The Social Fund: Let Them Have Charity

The Problems of Single Payments

Given that the basic level of benefit is not enough to enable claimants to meet every emergency it remains necessary to have a means of making one-off single payments. This has proved one of the most difficult parts of the benefit system to get right.

The team of civil servants whose review of the supplementary benefit system led to the 1980 reforms came up with recommendations for improvements. They wanted to reduce the role of single payments as far as possible and recommended that they should not be given for things which the scale rates were supposed to cover. (This suggestion was quickly taken up by the government, as we have seen, when it stopped payments for clothing and footwear.) The review team recognised that if this recommendation were followed extra help would still be needed for families with children. Alternatively they recommended that some or even all claimants could be given a periodic lump-sum payment instead of individual payments to meet particular needs. By way of illustration they suggested a possible six-monthly payment of £26. While this would have been fairer, because every claimant would have received the payment instead of only those with the initiative to make a claim for it, it would clearly have been of very little use to those families suddenly faced with the need to find hundreds of pounds. In effect what they were proposing was a general if very modest increase in the weekly benefit rates; it would have left untouched the problem of meeting the sudden and unforeseen need for extra money which single payments were designed to meet. However, it did mark a clear preference for an averaged-out system of rough justice, rather than attempting to meet individual needs, which was the approach later taken up by the Fowler.

239

The 1978 review team made two further recommendations which at the time were not taken up. One was to limit the role of appeals in respect of single payments, though they were not prepared to go so far as to eliminate them altogether. (They wanted appeals to be permissible only by leave of the tribunal chairman, and then only where an important point of principle was involved.) This was not accepted in 1980, but an important seed had been sown which was later to bear fruit.

The other was that the whole supplementary benefit scheme should be based in part on detailed and legally binding regulations but also in part on a code of practice:

> We find great attraction in the idea of a Code of Practice, which would ensure that decisions in particular cases were more clearly based on publicly-known rules which would influence – though not bind – the appeal authorities and would avoid the proliferation of regulations and amending regulations needed if the more detailed features of the scheme were embodied in statutory form. Such an approach also seems likely to permit the drafting of the rules in a language more accessible to claimants and their advisers, and we think this is an important consideration for a social assistance scheme.

This sensible recommendation was not followed, and all the problems foreseen in the passage quoted above bedevilled the 1980 scheme from its beginning to its end in 1988. In the absence of a code of practice, detailed regulations, which had to try to encompass every conceivable situation and eventuality, did indeed proliferate. The 1980 scheme had undergone no less than twenty-nine sets of amending regulations by 1988, many of them seeking to put right former errors, close loopholes or legislate for new eventualities. Furthermore, the language of the regulations rapidly achieved legendary status for its impenetrable incomprehensibility. Claimants had very little chance of understanding what they meant, and their opaque meanings were often beyond the wit not only of welfare rights experts but of many DHSS officers too. Once again, however, the germ of the idea of a code of practice, ignored in 1980, was due for a come-back under Fowler.

The issues surrounding single payments came to the fore in the mid-1970s, when their potential for scraping a little more money out of the system for impoverished claimants began to be used more effectively by welfare rights workers and claimants. Under the pre-1980 scheme there was too much discretion, inconsistency and secrecy; after 1980 the move to a wholly regulated system gave more entitlement, a little more consistency, and did away with secrecy; but these improvements were dearly bought. The regulations were so complex that few claimants could hope to understand them, and the government was able to amend them repeatedly so as to remove entitlements, leaving many claimants worse off than they would have been under the former system. For the DHSS, a crucial and growing problem was the disproportionate amount of staff time taken up by investigating, calculating and administering such payments, often in respect of relatively small sums of money. To these undoubtedly real problems in trying to achieve a fair and workable single payment system the Fowler reviews came up with a novel 'solution' – the social fund.

The Social Fund

The principles of the social fund were set out in the government's Green Paper. They were to replace the existing system of single payments, which the Green Paper described as 'unacceptably cumbersome and expensive'. The fund has four elements covering maternity and funeral needs, community care needs, budgeting loans and crisis loans, with each element subject to different rules. Maternity and funeral grants continued to be regulated on similar lines to the old single payments and claimants had rights of appeal. Very heavy cuts were made in the maternity grants, as we have seen, but no change of principles. The real changes, all to the claimant's disadvantage, came in respect of the other elements.

First, the goverment adopted a simple solution to the problem of the ever-increasing cost of single payments: it made the social fund subject to a predetermined budget. No longer were single payments to be made according to the need for them; under the social fund the budget determines the amount of need that can be met.

Second, entitlement, and with it the need for precise regulations, was abolished. The social fund is a discretionary scheme run by DSS social fund officers, who are bound by certain rules laid down by the Secretary of State – principally setting out the conditions limiting or prohibiting payments – but who also have discretion to decide whether to make or withhold payments. They are guided by the Social Fund Manual, which is in effect a code of practice, but unlike the suggestion put forward by the 1978 review team the manual is not an adjunct to a set of rules which themselves confer legal entitlement – it *replaces* legal entitlement. The loss of entitlement is an essential part of the government's plan to cut the cost of the scheme; it would not be possible to give claimants an entitlement and at the same time operate within a predetermined budget, since there would be no way of knowing in advance how many claimants would be entitled to payments. Claimants have lost an important legal right and are back in the position of not knowing what they may claim for or being able to predict whether they will or will not receive a payment. This is recognised explicitly in the language of the manual, which refers not to 'claimants' but to 'applicants'.

Third, as the scheme is discretionary the government was faced with the possibility that appeal tribunals might have interpreted the guidance in the Social Fund Manual differently from the social fund officers so that applicants may have been able to make successful appeals, as had increasingly been the case under the old discretionary scheme before 1980. The government's solution to this problem was simple: it abolished the right of appeal to an independent tribunal. The only redress open to applicants who feel they have been unfairly treated is to ask for a review of the decision by the same department that refused them in the first place. Again, the abolition of appeals was essential if the government was to succeed in its overriding objective of cutting costs.

Fourth, the bulk of the money in the fund was to be given out not as grants but as *recoverable loans*. Payments to meet what were now grandly called 'community care' needs, which in reality were little more than the old single payments for furniture, were still to be given as grants, but all other payments were to be loans, recoverable from the applicant's weekly benefit. In other words, most single payments were effectively to be abolished; whereas previously claimants were not expected to pay for unforeseen and exceptional emergencies out of their weekly benefit, under the social fund they were now expected to do just that. The fund would merely give them an advance of their own money, which in effect was to give them nothing. The price of such loans for applicants is a reduced rate of weekly benefit until the loan is repaid. The cost to the Exchequer is only the cost of administering the fund, since the money going into it comes from the applicants themselves.

The Social Fund: The Details

The Green Paper's social fund proposals received a totally hostile reception from almost all those who responded to them. The CPAG published an analysis of the responses of sixty major organisations including representative organisations from the professions, the churches, pressure groups representing families, women and children, groups from industry representing employers and business interests as well as trade unions, local authority associations and national consumer organisations, all the main political parties and groups representing a wide range of voluntary organisations with special interest in potential claimants. It was a very broad spectrum of informed, knowledgeable and experienced opinion. Of the fifty-two organisations which commented on the social fund only the Monday Club was in favour, and only three other groups, while still being critical overall, could find anything to support in it; the remaining forty-eight groups opposed the proposals. The principal objections were to the abolition of entitlement and reliance once more on discretion, the use of repayable loans instead of grants and to the cash limits. At this very early stage in the consultation process the government could have been under no illusions about the overwhelming opposition of informed opinion to the general principles of the social fund.

Over the next three years, as more information emerged about the scheme and the general principles began to harden into concrete proposals, this hostility increased. Initially ministers responded to their critics by saying that their objections were based on speculation since no details of the operation of the scheme were yet known. In March 1987 the government published the draft manual containing the detailed guidance on the operation of the fund. If it hoped that this would quieten the critics it was badly mistaken. As the details became clear, and with them the government's intention to make cutting expenditure the prime objective, opposition intensified to the point where highly responsible and well-respected organisations were forced to take very unusual steps to make their objections plain.

The Social Fund Manual was published in draft form and sent to a few selected organisations for their comments. It left no doubt that control of the budget was to be the overriding principle, taking precedence over all other considerations regardless of cost to claimants. This principle was established very early in the draft manual: 'The overriding principle upon which the budgeting system is based is that *the total cost of payments made by any local office must not exceed its budget for the financial year*' (emphasis in the original). Thereafter the social fund officer is constantly reminded that, with the exception of funeral grants and maternity grants, no payment of any kind may be made without first ascertaining whether there is sufficient money in the budget. There are no exceptions to this principle, so that even families who have been subject to disasters such as fire or flood could find that they were denied help simply because there was no money left in the kitty that month.

Details about the loan arrangements also gave cause for alarm. If the applicant was considered to be unable to repay the loan, no loan was to be offered, thereby ruling out the very claimants who were likely to be most in need. These applicants would therefore have no way of meeting the costs of any emergency such as a broken cooker. For those who were offered loans, repayment rates were normally to be set at 15 per cent of weekly benefit, which for a family with two small children could mean almost £12 a week would be deducted from their £79 weekly income. Furthermore, debts were recoverable not only from claimants' partners, but even from any new partners they may acquire in the event of the breakdown of relationships.

What the manual also revealed was the impossibility of reaching fair and consistent decisions in a cash-limited scheme. Social fund officers are expected to sort applicants into groups of varying degrees of priority (for example, the elderly, the physically disabled, drug abusers and so on) and at least ten such categories are identified in the manual. They are also expected to rank the items claimed for into high, medium or low priority (so that, for example, a cooker would be high priority while rent in advance is considered low priority); and, finally but crucially, they are obliged to see how much money is left in the budget. From this mix of ingredients they are expected to decide who should be helped and who refused. Moreover, they are told that they must meet the highest priority applications first, but at the same time they are told they must *not* keep a waiting list, which would be the only way of having even a slim hope of deciding priorities. Social fund officers are therefore in the unenviable position of deciding between low priority applications from high priority applicants, high priority applications from low priority applicants, and medium priority applications from low, medium and high priority applicants, and all with due regard to the state of the monthly budget. Ruth Lister, then director of CPAG, has rightly dubbed this the decision-making of the 'fruit-machine'. To add one final obstacle, the government also decided that no application to the fund could be repeated for the same item within six months, regardless of the reason for the refusal. So if an application was refused simply because it was late in the month and there was no money left in the office budget, when it may well have succeeded if it had been made earlier in the month, the applicant is not allowed to ask for it to be held over and reconsidered.

Many of the other detailed provisions in the manual also served to confirm the critics' worst fears. Many items were excluded from the possibility of even being considered for a loan or grant. Two of the most important of these were help with heating costs, always one of the main items with which claimants had difficulty due to the high cost of fuel and because these were just the sort of costs which arose periodically in the shape of a demand for a large lump-sum payment, and, except in very rare cases, deposits on rented accommodation, which will make it very difficult for claimants to secure places to live, especially as rent in advance is also accorded low priority.

Apart from concerns about the loss of money and clear legal rights, considerable fears were also expressed about the general treatment of applicants implied in the manual. Of major concern were the references in the draft manual to the intention to direct some applicants away from the social security system altogether and toward other and more humiliating forms of help. In deciding whether to make any loan or grant the social fund officer is required to have regard to 'the possibility that some other person may wholly or partly meet the need', thereby opening the way for zealous officers, at their discretion, to redirect the applicant to any other source of help, and as we have seen from the way in which the previous fall-back regulation was interpreted this is no fanciful suggestion. Even more explicit was the guidance about deciding on crisis loans, which are the loans given to people who have absolutely no other source of income and have no money immediately available to them. Having already made it clear that the applicant will be expected to use all his or her own resources and any available credit facilities the guidance went on to say:

> SFOs should ... have regard to any help which might be available from any other source to meet or partly meet the need provided that there is a realistic expectation that help would be available, and available in time, if the applicant were to seek it *Possible sources of help might be employers, relatives, close friends, and charities and benevolent funds which are known to be likely to provide the required assistance* [emphasis added].

Critics were quick to see this as yet another return to Thatcher's vision of Victorian values, with the poor being told to beg from their relatives, friends or charities, and if they were too proud to do so they always had the freedom to go without. Even after the deluge of opposition the final version of this paragraph, watered down very slightly, still reflected the government's intention further to stigmatise and degrade those who depended on it for their incomes. The final version of the last part of this paragraph in the manual now reads:

> Possible sources of help might be charities and benevolent funds which are known to be likely to provide the required assistance. SFOs should not routinely refer applicants to employers, relatives or friends unless there is reason to believe that an offer of help will be forthcoming.

This tiny concession, which does nothing to dispel any doubts about the intentions behind the fund, was one of the very few changes made from the draft version of the manual, and even then is more one of wording than of substance.

Open Government' in Action

When Norman Fowler set up his review teams he made a great show of the importance of the openness of the review procedures and the essential place of consultation with interested bodies. In his speech to the Conservative Party Conference in October 1985, where the launch of the reviews was the centrepiece of his message, he referred several times to the value he placed on dialogue between government and informed opinion. 'I did not want a closed review behind the walls of Whitehall', he assured Conference, and went on: 'My aim has been to take the issues to the people and listen to their views. That is why ministers took evidence in public. Over 60 organisations gave their views, while overall we received over 4500 pieces of written evidence prior to the publication of the Green Paper.' Warming to his theme, he gave the following assurance that this massive undertaking would bear fruit:

> In this area, as elsewhere, we shall, of course, study very carefully the responses to the consultation process. That is why we issued a Green Paper for consultation. I make no apologies for doing that. To be prepared to consult and to listen is not a sign of weakness, it is a sign of strength. It is a mark of a government who trust the people, care about their opinions and work to find the best ways of serving their interests.

The message could scarcely be more strongly put. (Those with interests in areas other than social security will reflect for a moment on what he may have meant by 'as elsewhere'. If he was looking forward prophetically to the area of education reform or the poll tax then he was quite right, since the government behaved in exactly the same ways in its 'consultations' over those measures as it did with this Green Paper.)

We have already seen that the responses of the sixty organisations to which he referred condemned the social fund outright, a point which he omitted from his speech, though it was certainly known to him at the time. Whenever social security ministers were subsequently pressed to reveal the content of all this consultation they became remarkably coy. Their replies ranged from the downright obstructive, as in the following exchange in the House on 13 November 1985, exactly one month after Fowler's eulogy on the virtues of open government:

> *Michael Meacher:* Will you list the organisations in support of and opposed to [the government's proposals on] SERPS, housing benefit, income support, the social fund, child benefit and the death grant?
> *Tony Newton:* No.

to the rather more circumlocutory way of saying the same thing, as in Michael Portillo's reply to a similar question two years later, on 24 November 1987: 'We received 108 representations from interested organisations and individuals on the draft Social Fund Manual. The majority of these representations contained a variety of comments about the replacement of supplementary benefit single payments by discretionary grants and loans.' Since no one could doubt that, if there had been any remotely positive responses to the manual the government would certainly have invoked them, it is clear that the message coming from the 108 replies was wholly negative. We shall see just how 'carefully' the government did study these responses later; since it was not prepared to disclose the information let us examine these representations.

Responses to the Social Fund

The organisations that responded to the Green Paper and the subsequent draft manual included all those with extensive knowledge of the way in which social security affected the lives of claimants. There were three main groups: those that could be broadly grouped together as representing claimants; those representing the various professional groups that worked with claimants; and a third, small group of government-appointed advisory bodies. In addition to these three groups with specialist knowledge, the churches and the House of Lords also made their views known.

Groups representing the interests of claimants

A considerable number of organisations have the knowledge and experience to be able to speak on behalf of various claimant groups. During the passage of the 1986 Social Security Bill many of the larger organisations joined with other groups from local authorites and trade unions to form the Social Security Consortium in an attempt to co-ordinate opposition. There are thirty-four such organisations in the Consortium, including Age Concern, Disability Alliance – which is itself a coalition of many groups serving the interests of the disabled – Mind, National Council for One Parent families, Shelter, Youthaid, the major poverty lobby organisations such as CPAG, Low Pay Unit, Action for Benefits – which again is another coalition of a wide range of interested groups – the major consumer and voluntary groups, such as NACAB, the National Council of Voluntary Organisations, and leading local authority and professional associations such as the Association of County Councils and the British Association of Social Workers. No one could doubt the extent of the expertise of such a Consortium, or that it represents a very considerable weight of responsible and informed opinion in the field of social security.

In December 1987 the Consortium produced *Of Little Benefit*, a critical guide to the Social Security Act, which, *inter alia*, contained a critique of the social fund. Its conclusion was unequivocal:

> The Social Fund, along with the reduction in weekly benefits faced by some claimants, will inevitably lead to further impoverishment of already poor claimants. The replacement of grants by loans will mean large numbers of claimants living permanently below the minimum level set by Parliament. Claimants are expected to buy out of their weekly benefit items that used to be met by Single Payments, so the real value of their weekly benefits is in effect being cut.
>
> One result could be to drive claimants still further into the hands of moneylenders. Another will be to increase the demands made on charities and local authorities.

This critique was a distillation of many criticisms made by the constituent organisations in the Consortium. The responses of the individual organisations generally made similar points, condemning both the general principles of the fund and later the specific proposals in the manual. Typical of the objections to the whole concept of the fund is the following extract from a paper published

249

in September 1985 as a response to the Green Paper by the National Council for Voluntary Organisations (NCVO), which includes in its membership national and local voluntary bodies which, it claims, 'deal with hundreds of thousands of individuals claiming their rights to social security'. In a strongly worded attack on the proposals in the Green Paper it said:

> We cannot conceive of how it will be possible for the Social Fund to provide adequately for individual needs, if the Government limits at the start of each financial year the amount of money available through the Fund. What will happen if – and when – claims on the Fund exceed the cash provided by the Exchequer? If, for example, there is a severe winter, how will the Social Fund cope with the many pensioners who need help with their fuel bills?

The answer to the NCVO's question is that the fund would not have to cope with helping pensioners with their fuel bills, since such payments were expressly excluded; the pensioners would have to cope on their own.

The NCVO went on to 'view with profound disquiet the proposal for scrapping a system founded on legal entitlements, and replacing it by one founded on discretion', and to make the point that the reliance on a loan system would mean that 'many claimants could be trapped into living below the level of benefit set by Parliament'. After commenting adversely on other aspects of the fund it concluded with a general condemnation: 'All in all, the proposals for a Social Fund appear ill-conceived, and likely to create countless unforeseen problems for claimants, social workers, voluntary bodies, councillors and MPs alike.'

Another organisation that can claim extensive nationwide knowledge of how the social security system works in practice is the NACAB. Through its network of bureaux all over Britain it is able to call upon the experience and expertise of workers who deal with claimants caught up in the complexities and shortcomings of the administration of benefits. In the year of the Green Paper CABx in England and Wales dealt with over a million enquiries relating to social security matters, almost a fifth of all their work. NACAB's reply to the government was based on solid day-to-day familiarity with claimants and their problems. NACAB had no doubt that the social fund proposals were 'a step backwards'. As with most other commentators, it focused on four key areas of concern: the return to discretion, the use of loans, the fixed budget and the abolition of the right of appeal. NACAB was able to supplement its general criticisms with sharp comments from bureau workers, which gave clear expression to their concerns. Writing about the use of discretion one bureau worker drew attention to the impossible choices facing social fund officers:

> We find it totally unacceptable that any member of DHSS staff be expected to determine the priority between a battered wife returning to Edinburgh and claiming removal expenses, a couple who need clothes for their child going into hospital, a young mother whose clothes have been stolen from a washing line and a family needing further heating appliances.

NACAB could, of course, have added many more alternatives; the point is that these are exactly the kinds of choices which do face officers every day, and all within the constraints of a fixed budget.

Such was the strength of NACAB's misgivings that it concluded that no amount of tinkering with the proposals would make them acceptable: 'We strongly recommend that the proposals relating to the Social Fund be withdrawn, and the question of lump sum payments be looked at again.'

Time and again the same points were made by expert groups. The Disability Alliance spoke of the fund plunging claimants into a 'downward spiral of ever-increasing debt'; many references were made to the return to the Victorian Poor Law, with all its attendant shame, indignities and stigma; Age Concern wrote about the distress caused to the elderly when forced to seek charitable help. None could understand how it was possible to work a scheme designed to meet unforeseen needs within a fixed budget, and all deplored the removal of the right of independent appeal.

Once the draft manual was published these organisations could comment on the details of the fund. CPAG produced an examination of it, the gist of which is encapsulated in its title, *A Great Retreat From Fairness*. The analysis is merciless in exposing the inherent contradictions in the fund, and in laying bare its real

251

purpose – to save money at the expense of the poor. Expressing views echoed by the other groups representing claimants the CPAG report delivered an introductory broadside:

> Having seen the draft guidelines and directions, we can only say that we are even more opposed to the social fund than before. They confirm our scepticism at the promises that 'it will be able to respond to individual needs as they arise' (White Paper) and that 'the social fund will be flexible above all else' (John Major).

This is followed by a list of detailed criticisms, ending with a total denunciation:

> It is clear from reading the draft manual that the Government has ignored virtually all the reasoned arguments put forward by SSAC and others following the Green Paper. In this context, we believe that there is no room for constructive comments designed to make the social fund work better. Their impact is likely to be marginal on a scheme the fundamental parameters of which are so harmful to the interests of both claimants and the staff who will have to administer it.

After a full review of the proposals in the draft manual the report concludes: 'The draft manual makes our case for us. It makes it crystal clear that a cash limited, discretionary scheme of loans, paying grants in only limited cases, is incompatible with an equitable system of assistance that genuinely meets claimants' needs.'

The government's own advisers

The reference to the SSAC brings us to the second category of responses to the government's proposals, those of its own advisory bodies. The two with the most direct responsibility in this field are the SSAC and the Council on Tribunals. The latter is concerned with the conduct of various tribunals, including those hearing appeals on social security matters. Its comments were confined to the abolition of the right to an independent appeal. What the government proposed in its place was a right only to ask for a review of a social fund officer's decision, which would be carried out in the local office where the decision was made.

The Council on Tribunals was not in favour of such a scheme, and, in its annual report for 1985–6, said so in strong terms. It referred to the removal of the right of appeal as a 'highly retrograde step', and gave its reasons for thinking so. It was concerned that claimants would lose not only their right to an independent tribunal but, because of the intricacies of the con- stitutional issues involved, would have no redress either through a minister or very probably through the Ombudsman, so would have no other avenue of redress at all. The Council also pointed out that the number of successful appeals against DHSS decisions on single payments showed just how important it was to have an appeal system. Since 1981 almost a quarter of all such appeals had been successful, and the number of appeals was rising annually. In addition to these, many appeals were successful before they reached the tribunals because whenever an appeal was lodged the DHSS automatically reviewed the decision, which often resulted in a new decision in the claimant's favour. Thus both the appeals themselves and the threat of appeals had actually resulted in many refusals of payments being overturned, and the Council was very concerned that this opportunity would be lost to claimants under the social fund.

So great was the Council's concern that in January 1986 it issued a special report devoted solely to this matter. It was only the second time the Council had ever issued a special report in its thirty-year existence. The Council's conclusions were powerfully expressed, as one would expect from a body numbering four QCs and two professors among its membership:

> The people most affected by this proposal are among the most vulnerable in our society. Very good reasons are needed before the abolition of the right to an independent appeal in such circumstances, an appeal which has existed for over fifty years. It would probably be the most substantial abolition of a right of appeal to an independent tribunal since the Council on Tribunals was set up by Parliament in 1958. It is for these reasons that we are so critical of the proposal.

Whereas the Council on Tribunals was concerned only with one aspect of the proposals, the SSAC was appointed by the government specifically to advise it on all social security matters. As we have already seen, this did not prevent the government from completely ignoring its advice, but it could do so only at the risk of forfeiting its credibility in the eyes of the wider community. The SSAC is a highly respected, non-political body, consisting of members appointed for their impartiality and expertise. Its comments on the social fund therefore command respect across a wide spectrum of opinion.

The SSAC was one of the very few bodies which found anything to commend in the original proposals, albeit that this tentative acceptance was hedged about with many qualifications. As the government's intentions became clearer the SSAC's support receded. Once the draft manual was published its support was unequivocally withdrawn: 'As it stands, we do not believe the fund will work. Nor will it be fair to applicants.'

The SSAC invites comments from all interested organisations, and in part uses them to help it in its deliberations. In June 1987, in respect of the social fund, it reported that 'almost all the representations we have seen have been critical of the proposals. We agree with many of the criticisms that have been made.' There then follows the familiar catalogue of detailed objections to the principles and details of the fund, culminating in the conclusion that:

> we cannot support the social fund as it appears in the draft manual. It is dominated by a need to keep within the budget. It strikes what we regard as the wrong balance between loans and grants and between discretion and entitlement. We remain unconvinced that it will meet many of the genuine needs of some of the poorest members of society or command the confidence of agencies whose co-operation the manual itself sees as necessary.

In these carefully measured tones of an official government committee the entire basis of the social fund was dismissed out of hand. In a letter to its chairman, Peter Barclay, Nicholas Scott made it plain that the government had no intention of taking any notice of the SSAC's careful deliberations or of any of the other responses it had received. On receipt of this letter Peter Barclay,

CBE, senior partner in a firm of solicitors, chairman of the National Institute of Social Work, who had chaired an influential report on the future direction of social work in Britain, and his equally illustrious and respectable committee replied with an icy letter of repudiation. The full text read:

> At the Committee's meeting on 7 October [1987] we discussed your letter of 25 August and the Government's decision to proceed with the social fund substantially as planned. At the Committee's request I am writing to place on record that this decision is without our support.

In the urbane and civilised world of Whitehall that is as strong a public rebuke as it is possible to receive, and shows the enormity of the rift between the government and its advisers.

The professionals

There was opposition too from those who were expected to make the fund work. Whereas those who worked for the DHSS had little option but to carry out their duties, albeit reluctantly, other organisations whose co-operation was essential for the smooth working of the fund engaged in a rearguard action of non-compliance which was remarkable for its unanimity among a wide range of groups, many not noted for their open defiance of government.

Both the Civil and Public Servants Association (CPSA) and the Society of Civil and Public Servants (SCPS), the unions of the front-line workers in the DHSS offices, condemned the fund. In a letter to Norman Fowler, the SCPS, representing 25,000 executive and managerial staff, warned:

> You should be under no illusions about the depth of opposition to your proposals which are expressed and felt with conviction by members of this trade union. . . . We are in no doubt that your proposals represent a most damaging wholesale onslaught on the welfare state; we are convinced that . . . they will lead to widespread increases in poverty, and a sharpening of social division.

In a press release issued with the letter the union stated that the fund would not only damage claimants but would demoralise the already overburdened staff.

> The union concludes that the review will mean a worse system for claimants and a worse system for DHSS staff to administer. They are particularly concerned that it will be their members who will be expected to administer the much maligned social fund, based as it is on discretionary, cash-limited, recoverable loans, and their members who will be expected to act as judge and jury with no independent right of appeal for claimants. The unions have warned the Government that these proposals are unworkable and would lead to even further stresses and tensions in local offices – already at near breaking point due to staff shortages.

Because of the nature of the very personal judgements social fund officers must make it was envisaged that co-operation between them and other organisations having close contact with claimants would be essential. The desirability of this co-operation is a constant theme of the manual. Such was the opposition to the fund of all the agencies who might be expected to co-operate that instead they drew up plans for varying degrees of resistance. In a remarkable show of unity, all the organisations representing statutory workers in local authority social services departments and in the probation service produced responses to the fund that were total in their rejection of the principles upon which it was based. Having failed to make any impression on the government during the passage of the Social Security Bill through Parliament they advised their members to adopt a policy of non-cooperation, and to follow instead a policy of 'determined advocacy' on behalf of applicants.

It is important to be clear which groups were advising their members to take these oppositional stances. It was not just the unions and professional associations of the staff involved; it was also the employers' organisations and those representing the chief officers of the services. NALGO, the British Association of Social Workers and the National Association of Probation Officers were joined in their resistance by the Association of County Councils

(ACC) and the Association of Metropolitan Authorities (AMA), which between them represented the employers of all social services departments, and by the Association of Directors of Social Services and the Association of Chief Probation Officers. They refused to take part in any planning process, drew up codes of practice for their employees designed to minimise involvement with the operation of the fund, and some even produced pro-forma letters of protest for disappointed applicants to send to their MPs. As part of the 'determined advocacy' approach the ACC and AMA produced a practice guide that included the following advice to their employees in social services:

> If the application for a grant is turned down (even if a loan is offered instead), you should offer assistance to the person in challenging the decision. He/she can do this by;
>> applying for a review
>> contacting the local MP
>> complaining to the Ombudsman
>> alerting the press
>> seeking legal advice (e.g. a judicial review may be possible in extreme circumstances.)

Given the usual extreme reluctance of local authorities to encourage their employees to take such public action, indeed, given that many normally forbid them to do so in relation to their own policies, these are exceptionally confrontative measures to recommend.

The great and the good

It was not just the professionals who weighed in to the attack. The Bishop of Durham made the headlines when, on a Radio 4 interview on Good Friday 1987, he described the government's plans for the poor as 'verging on the wicked'. The Bishop of Southwark, pressed to say whether he agreed with this judgement, conceded that although 'wicked' might be a little strong he himself thought that 'iniquitous' was 'a better word'. Whatever the niceties of this theological distinction it is clear that he too did not approve of the government's social security policies. These condemnations were soon followed by the Roman Catholic Archbishop of Liverpool's censure of the government for fostering 'yuppie values', which he said was creating a hard and uncaring society, and the Bishop of Manchester wrote to the *Guardian* deploring Lawson's budget and the social security changes and referring to the 'immorality or injustice of what is happening'.

While these were the views of some of the more turbulent bishops in the church, the Board for Social Responsibility of the General Synod of the Church of England made a collective response in its reply to the Green Paper proposals. Making the familiar points about the problems likely to arise from the cash limits and abolition of appeals the Board concluded its comments about the social fund with: 'This seems to us a potentially unjust system which will create hostility and incomprehension.'

The House of Lords also expressed its displeasure and inflicted two defeats on the government during the passage of the bill through the upper chamber. The amendments sought to reintroduce the right of appeal and to create a more regulated structure for the social fund in an effort to reduce discretion. Back in the Commons the government rejected both.

The Government's Response

Norman Fowler had promised to 'study very carefully the responses to the consultation process'. Seldom can such impressive unanimity have been expressed by so many informed groups from such diverse perspectives as was contained in these condemnations not only of the principles but also of the detailed provisions of the social fund. The government's response was to ignore each and every objection. It made no concessions of substance in the principles or the details.

It went further; speaking at a meeting organised by the ACC in December 1986, John Major, a social security minister, brazenly claimed that 'the intellectual case for the social fund is compelling'. Speaking to a meeting of Conservatives in Cornwall in March 1988, Nicholas Scott dismissed the critics: 'The arguments against the social fund have avoided the real issues, relied heavily on scaremongering and ignored the real drawbacks of the existing system of single payments.' He commended the fund as a 'necessary, significant development of the way that society cares for people who need extra help'. And that was the outcome of the 'careful study'. The government and the Monday Club were right; everyone else was wrong.

The Social Fund Budget

Most of the criticisms of the fund had been voiced before the size of its annual budget had been known. When it was announced by John Moore in October 1987 the extent of the government's cynical hypocrisy about the ability of the fund to meet applicants' needs became clear. In the first year the budget was to be just over £200 million, of which only £60 million would be for grants, the rest for loans. This meant that the amount of money allocated for single payments had been cut from over £300 million in 1985 to £60 million in 1988. But for the massive cuts imposed in August 1986 single payments would have cost over £400 million by 1987; as it was they were still costing just under £200 million. This allowed the government to claim that the amount of money going into the fund was broadly in line with current expenditure on single payments. The crucial difference was that only 30 per cent of this sum was for grants. In the light of such a tiny budget all the talk of targeting on those with most needs and necessary flexibility in meeting needs was manifestly absurd.

The misery, while it would certainly fall on all claimants, would not fall equally. The DHSS allocated the grants budget according to a formula which meant that the cuts were distributed in a mysterious pattern across the country. In 1988 some offices received only about 13 per cent of the amounts they had paid out in single payments in 1986/7, others received 30, 40 or in one case even 50 per cent. Whatever the rationale for the formula the effect was to penalise the poorest areas to the advantage of the better off. Glasgow, Leeds, inner London, Sunderland, Middlesbrough and Newcastle each received some of the lowest allocations while Tunbridge Wells, Worthing, Guildford, Buxton, Epsom, Southport, the Isle of Wight and Exeter each received the highest – apart from Bognor, which received most of all. That Bognor should have been so favoured would undoubtedly have surprised George V, and he would not be alone in his bafflement. By any criterion the allocation defies comprehension; any criterion, that is, except political expediency.

The Effects of the Social Fund: Some Preliminary Pointers

The effects of the social fund are being closely monitored by the Benefits Research Unit at Nottingham University and the Social Services Research Group, and the full picture should become available in 1989. Initial findings suggest that the worst fears of the fund's critics have been realised.

Applications to the fund got off to a slow start, and although they picked up as the year went on figures given by Bill Taylor, the DHSS under-secretary responsible, showed that by November 1988 the loans budget had been spent at 81 per cent of the expected rate, while the budget for grants was running at only 49 per cent. If this level of take-up continued to the end of the year it would mean that only about £30 million in grants would have been made to applicants who until very recently would have expected to have received over ten times that amount in single payments.

In a parliamentary answer in July 1988 figures were given comparing the number of awards and the cost of payments under the fund for the first three months of its existence with the number and cost of single payments for the same three months under the old scheme one year before. These reveal not only the extent of the cuts but the marked change in the pattern of the awards. The only figures which are directly comparable are those for single payments and the social fund community care grants, since the other awards from the fund are in the form of loans which add nothing at all to the applicant's income. In the three months from April to June 1987 over 500,000 single payments were made at a total cost of over £40 million; under the new scheme in 1988 only 13,000 grants were made at a cost of £3 million. Those losing by the changes are the very poorest of all, since only those with virtually no savings qualified for awards under both schemes.

Even when allowing for the *loans* given by the fund the cuts are still savage. In the first three months only 117,000 loans were made, which takes the total number of grants and loans to less than a quarter of the grants made a year earlier. What also became clear was the huge increase in the number of awards being made to meet short-term crises. Whereas for the three months in 1987 only 3200 'urgent needs payments' were made to tide people over acute financial difficulties, in 1988 the number of crisis loans had shot up to nearly 69,000, suggesting a large increase in acute difficulties for claimants as a result of the loss of grants to cover rent in advance and deposits on accommodation. Moreover, whereas in 1987 the average amount of an urgent needs payment was £90, the equivalent amount in 1988 was less than half this, £42, suggesting that although more and more people were falling into difficulties the amount of financial help available to them was becoming smaller, and even that was available only in the form of a loan.

At a conference in January 1989 called to monitor the effects of the fund Richard Silburn, director of the Benefits Research Unit, reported that those being particularly hurt by the cuts were pregnant women, the mentally ill, people with fuel debts, women leaving refuges to set up a new home and those leaving institutional care. Embarrassed by the obvious failure of the fund the government simultaneously sought to blame the stance of non-cooperation taken by social workers and admitted that perhaps it had drawn the guidelines to social fund officers too tightly.

Explanations for the failure will come when those conducting the current monitoring exercise report their findings; meanwhile common sense would suggest that the low take-up of loans probably owes much to claimants' dislike of seeing their already meagre incomes further diminished. An insight into the reason for the low take-up of the grants was given by Pat Roberts, a very experienced medical social worker, who told of her attempt to secure a grant for an eighty-seven-year-old disabled woman needing help to repair her cooker to enable her to stay in her own home, by any interpretation of the rules a very high priority applicant. Writing in *Community Care* she said that the eleven-page application form had taken her an hour and three-quarters to complete, and she concluded that to succeed an applicant would need to have 'more than average tenacity; a higher education qualification in form-filling; a good welfare rights back-up service; lots of time'.

As with the effects of all the other 'reforms' it is becoming increasingly clear that what the critics foresaw would happen has happened. The poorest claimants have been severely disadvantaged by the introduction of the social fund and many have either gone without essentials, been driven to seek help from charities or followed the advice of the junior minister at the DHSS who suggested that the elderly should get their clothes from jumble sales. Small wonder that the government has chosen to release figures on the operation of the fund only by laying the information in the House of Commons library, which effectively means that they will not be available to the public, not be reported in Hansard or be made generally available by the DHSS. Even then the figures to be laid in the library will be in a form which will be difficult to interpret, which suggests that Nicholas Scott and his colleagues are less than proud of this 'necessary, significant development of the way that society cares for people who need extra help'.

12 A Poor Service for Poor People

If we sit back and do nothing, allowing the volume and complexity of the work to increase year by year, it is simply a matter of time before the service collapses. Indeed, there are signs that the collapse is already beginning in some of the more hard-pressed offices.

(Donnison, 1978)

It is with some regret that our conclusions remain exactly the same as those from our submission to last year's exercise ... that the administration and organisation of the [supplementary benefits] scheme are breaking down badly.

(NACAB's evidence to the SSAC, 1982)

The CAB Service has been advising the DHSS for the past three years that the services provided by their local offices were getting worse.

(NACAB, *Behind the Counter*, 1984)

A certain number of mistakes are unavoidable, but evidence of widespread dissatisfaction with the standard of administration is overwhelming.

(CPAG, 1984)

The social security system is at the point of breakdown in many local offices.

(Joint statement by SCPS and CPSA, 1986)

The DHSS had identified a significant level of

dissatisfaction with the quality of service in 1984 and 1985 and in general there was no evidence of any improvement since then.

(National Audit Office, 1988)

Concern about the quality of service provided by supplementary benefit offices has been a continuing theme throughout the 1980s. Such remedial efforts as have been made have been insufficient, and there is evidence to suggest that the quality of service has continued to deteriorate. At the present time the quality of service in London has become so bad that the DHSS has been accused of not fulfilling its legal obligations to claimants and has been the subject of a judicial review following action by several organisations concerned with claimants' welfare. In this chapter we consider the evidence about the quality of service provided by the DHSS, the consequences for claimants, the reasons for the continuing poor service and the government's strategies for improvements.

'In Some Places it is Very Good Indeed. In Some Places it is Absolutely Unacceptable'

As will be clear from the quotations above there is abundant evidence, spanning the last decade, testifying to the variable standards of service which supplementary benefit claimants can expect. The judgement that at its worst it is 'absolutely unacceptable' is that made by the DHSS's own regional organisational scrutiny team which reported in May 1988. It was echoing many other organisations that had reached the same conclusions.

The National Audit Office (NAO) had issued its report a month earlier with evidence which supported both the variability in the quality of service and the unacceptability of the service provided by some offices. Its survey of 1002 claimants revealed that 26 per cent rated the service provided by their local office as 'good', 41 per cent as 'fair' and 25 per cent as 'poor', a level of dissatisfaction which the NAO said 'must give rise to concern'. Claimants were asked whether they had experienced problems with the DHSS; 55 per cent had experienced 'none', 32 per cent 'some' and 13 per cent 'lots'. As the NAO points out, 'This suggests that around two million people receiving supplementary benefit at the time of the survey had experienced problems with the service provided during the previous twelve months.' Unemployed and single-parent claimants had experienced many more problems than pensioners: only 37 per cent and 38 per cent respectively had had no problems – for pensioners the figure was 84 per cent – and 19 per cent of both groups had had 'lots' as against only 1 per cent of pensioners.

The NAO report showed a wide range in the performance of local offices on a number of indicators. The best offices took an average of only two and a half working days to process claims for supplementary benefit while the worst took fifteen, and the evidence was that claims were taking longer to process in 1986/7 than they had in 1983/4. The time taken to process appeals from claimants ranged from five to sixty-two working days *on average*, which meant that many claimants would have to wait over three months before the DHSS sent its papers to the regional appeals office, where there would be further delay before a hearing date could be arranged.

The NAO noted a decline between 1983 and 1987 in the general standards of accuracy in dealing with claims. The national average for errors in calculating benefit is around 13 per cent; the NAO survey showed that offices' error rate ranged from 4 to 25 per cent – in other words, in some offices a *quarter* of all claims for supplementary benefit are *routinely* assessed incorrectly. It also estimated that 19 per cent of all visits to local offices were made by claimants whose payments had not arrived on time. Once at the office, 20 per cent of claimants estimated that they had been kept waiting for over two hours. The DHSS's own estimates showed that waiting times ranged from an average of one minute (*sic*) to an *average* time of three hours forty-one minutes. Notwithstanding that in 1983 the DHSS had recognised that local offices needed better facilities to make them more welcoming and attractive to claimants, the NAO survey revealed that five years later four out of five claimants were particularly concerned that they could be overheard when discussing private matters, 70 per cent were critical of facilities for children and almost half considered that there were inadequate toilet facilities. In most cases offices in inner cities, especially in London, fared worst whichever indicator of performance was considered.

This report is all the more important for being carried out by a body which is in no way identified with claimants or the organisations representing them. It was done on a large scale: 1002 claimants were interviewed and data was collected from eighty offices. From the bare presentation of the statistics it is clear that the quality of service in many offices is indeed unacceptable. The NAO estimated that about two million people had experienced problems of some kind. The reality of what this means for claimants is vividly shown in any of a whole series of reports compiled at intervals throughout the last decade by those organisations having daily contact with claimants. In particular NACAB has written a stream of reports drawing attention to the worsening situation. In the early 1980s comments about the poor quality of service could be brushed aside as merely the results of teething troubles associated with the change to the new system, which would vanish as local offices became more familiar with the complexity of the new regulations. Such optimism proved to be misplaced.

In a 1984 report, *No Benefit*, the London CABx claimed that as many as 70 per cent of claimants were not receiving their correct entitlement; half the claimants in the survey had not received their full entitlement due to delays by the DHSS, and delays were increasing; errors in assessing benefit occurred in 40 per cent of cases and many DHSS officers were still ignorant of the regulations. By 1986 the position had worsened to the point where, in *Out of Service*, the London CABx claimed that 'the system for administering supplementary benefits has virtually collapsed in many local offices'.

Out of Service formed the basis of the action against the DHSS, accusing it of failing in its statutory duties. Among the findings of the survey, which involved sixty-two CABx between them covering fifty-six DHSS offices in Greater London, were:

(a)   waiting time for callers was over an hour in 70 per cent of offices, with waits of over three hours not uncommon;

(b)   instances of claimants being turned away without

interview were reported by CABx all over London;

(c)   83 per cent of claimants reported 'frequent or very frequent' difficulty in getting through to the office by telephone;

(d)   obtaining replies to letters was felt to be 'virtually impossible', with 85 per cent of claimants reporting 'frequent or very frequent' difficulty;

(e)   nearly three-quarters of the offices failed in their statutory duty to process and pay claims within fourteen days and in 60 per cent of offices claimants had difficulty in obtaining an urgent needs payment to tide them over till benefit was paid;

(f)   85 per cent of the offices were reported to have 'virtually abandoned' making home visits to claimants, resulting in many elderly and disabled claimants losing benefits through lack of advice from the visiting officer;

(g)   nearly three-quarters of the DHSS offices in north London and half the offices in south London were reported to make errors in clients' benefits 'frequently or very frequently';

(h)   CABx believed that in 70 per cent of the offices the service had deteriorated; when the seven worst offices were reviewed ten months after the original survey the service was judged to have deteriorated still further.

Those are the cold statistics; what they mean for the million or so Londoners dependent on supplementary benefit can be illustrated by the following examples:

Kennington (Oval) DHSS was reported by two CABx to be still operating [October 1986] a restricted entry system for personal callers. Claimants usually queued from about 7.30 a.m. onwards till the doors were opened at 9.30 a.m. There was no guarantee that all those in the queue would be seen that day. . . . North Lambeth CAB reported that on some days only one person was available for interviewing. They had two documented cases of elderly people (85 and 90 years of age respectively) having to wait from 7.30 to 10.00 in order merely to be admitted into the waiting room.

Charing Cross CAB monitored the telephone calls they made to three DHSS offices between 19/6/86 and 24/9/86. . . . The average waiting time for calls was 4.5 minutes. In only one in five of all calls made did the CAB reach the relevant section. Nearly a quarter of these unsuccessful calls took more than ten minutes to get through.

For each enquiry it took an average of 2.5 calls to get through to the supplementary benefit section. In the case of 59 per cent of the enquiries, bureaux were unable to get through at all. Where they did get through, waiting time on the phone before they got through to the switchboard was 22 minutes per call.

Many claimants do not have a telephone and rely on public call boxes. It takes little imagination to see what this kind of service would mean for claimants, assuming they had been lucky enough to find a telephone in working order, in terms of money, exasperation and aggravation from the waiting queue.

These difficulties are not experienced only by Londoners, as an example from Coventry shows:

Man out of work, redundant. Claimed unemployment benefit immediately. Was advised could claim SB but told not to go down to office as people have to wait hours – better to phone and make an appointment. Man took advice – phoned DHSS six times in one day – told every time 'there are four people waiting in the phone queue already – do you want to hold?' He held for five minutes and put the phone down without getting through. Next day phoned office at 8.30 a.m. to book appointment. Told by switchboard after delay that the office staff did not start until 9.00 a.m. He phoned back at 9.00 a.m. exactly. Asked for appointment again. After a delay, was told by switchboard that the office staff did not start till 9.30 a.m. He phoned back at 9.30 a.m. Told they did not start till 9.45 a.m. He phoned back then – told they were not taking any appointments that day as they were so busy.

In May 1988 the *Guardian* carried an account of conditions at a

Paddington benefit office, making the point that, due to the waiting involved, claiming benefit was a full-time job.

Alfie Stranks, a 24-year-old living with his wife and baby in a hotel room, was outside the DHSS office by 7.00 a.m. At 3.20 they told him his papers were lost. 'I want to get a job, but it's hard when I spend two full days a week in here trying to get money that should be arriving by regular Giro,' he despaired.

The two public toilets inside the building are covered in filth. A used nappy sits on the sink in an office filled with little children but no changing facilities – although a mother and baby room has been hurriedly sorted out. Until a week ago, nobody was allowed out for refreshment once the doors were shut.

For some claimants the process of claiming benefit is degrading and humiliating, and reinforces the view that we as a society regard claimants as less than citizens. As if this were not bad enough, the poor quality of service they receive means that many are deprived of their full entitlement and so lead even more impoverished lives than they need. The latest official estimate for supplementary benefit not claimed is that in 1983 nearly 1.3 million claimants did not claim an average of £8.40 a week each. Even when people do claim they are not guaranteed their full entitlement; when such claimants seek help from CABx the mistakes may be rectified, but the CABx recognise that these are the lucky few. For some claimants the errors mean living with less money from week to week, for others going without payments to which they are entitled, for some it could even mean losing their homes. In the following example the claimant only just avoided losing his home through the intervention of the CAB; how many others were not so fortunate?

His benefit had been considerably reduced following a brief stay in hospital in August 1985. His mortgage entitlement was incorrect and no account had been taken of large service charges. Nevertheless, after several queries by the claimant he received two letters from the DHSS in March and April 1986 insisting the benefit was correct.

When he approached the CAB in April for help he had sizeable debts as a consequence of the error. The CAB sent letters to the DHSS and rang several times in the following month explaining the urgency of the situation only to be told that the papers could not be found or receive no replies to letters. The insurance company from whom the client had his mortgage intended to foreclose. Eventually, in mid-July 1986, the client told the CAB that through their intervention the benefit had been corrected and the arrears paid.

Further evidence about the quality of performance of DHSS local offices is provided in the annual reports of the Chief Adjudication Officer, one of whose functions is to monitor the quality of adjudication decisions in the DHSS and Department of Employment benefit offices over the whole country. A wide selection of cases is scrutinised to ascertain whether the adjudication officer's decision was correct. Broadly this meant seeing whether the decision was justified by the evidence as to the facts of the case, whether the law and regulations were properly applied and whether the correct amounts of benefit were calculated. In his first report, covering 1984, he found that 25 per cent of supplementary benefit cases failed this test, and concluded that 'the standard of adjudication cannot objectively be regarded as satisfactory'. The following year he concluded that things had become even worse, but in his latest report, for 1986–7, he noted an improvement, though in fact by this time the proportion of cases failing to pass the test had risen to 39 per cent!

Some decisions are more problematic than others, and when this is taken into account we see very wide variations in the error rates. Thirty-five per cent of all new claims for supplementary benefit were judged to have been handled incorrectly, as were 41 per cent of claims for single payments and a staggering 81 per cent of claims for urgent needs payments (though in these cases the adjudication officers generally appeared to err in the claimants' favour since the Chief Adjudication Officer complained about their unwillingness to see whether the claimant might not have found the money from other sources or at least have been made to repay it).

If a claimant lodges an appeal against a decision the DHSS carries out an internal review; in about a third of all such cases this resulted in the original decision being overturned, which, in the words of the Chief Adjudication Officer, 'to an extent reflects unsound adjudication at the first instance'. What must give rise to even more concern is the fact that in a quarter of these cases the review decision itself, which would have been subject to particularly careful scrutiny within the department, was found to be defective.

The Chief Adjudication Officer is at pains to point out that because decisions were not made correctly it does not follow that the claimants lost benefit; they may have gained, though with the exception of urgent needs payments that is less likely, or they may have been given the correct amounts but for the wrong reasons. Nevertheless, that such high numbers of defective decisions are made adds considerable weight to the evidence such organisations as NACAB and CPAG have consistently reported. There can be no doubt that the quality of service provided for claimants is generally far below that which would be tolerated for the customers of banks, of the Inland Revenue, or of any other public or private company, and that in London and some other big cities it is, as the DHSS's regional organisation scrutiny team admits, unacceptable. Poor people do receive poor service.

Why Do Poor People Receive Poor Service?

There are many reasons why this happens, some ideological, some organisational, some financial. It would be wrong to think that this government is alone responsible for the appalling treatment which many claimants must endure to secure their often inaccurate benefits. But governments can seek to alleviate the problems or to make them worse; there can be little doubt that this government has made them worse.

The poor have always been treated badly in Britain, and there is a long tradition of governments devising policies that deliberately seek to underline and reinforce the status of the claimant as a second-class citizen. In the early nineteenth century the Poor Law Amendment Act set out deliberately to wean the poor from a dependency culture to the burgeoning enterprise culture by denying 'relief' to the poor and incarcerating paupers in workhouses. It was no accident that these embodiments of the very essence of Victorian values became objects of such fear and loathing; they

271

were deliberately designed to be just that. Those who were forced by necessity to enter them were stripped of all dignity, families were split up and housed in different parts, pauper uniforms had to be worn, degrading tasks such as stone-breaking and oakum-picking had to be performed on pain of imprisonment, and inmates were not allowed to leave without permission. In short, they were treated little differently from criminals. This regime lasted until well into the twentieth century; certainly in the 1930s there are records of men not being allowed to leave to find work, and families were still being segregated. The principle behind these policies was known as 'less-eligibility', which meant that the lot of the pauper had to be seen to be worse than that of the lowest-paid 'independent labourer' to ensure that only the really destitute would seek help.

This ethos permeated those dealing with paupers until at least the Second World War. For example, a handbook entitled *Local Government of the United Kingdom* by J. J. Clarke, an expert on local government law, which by 1939 had run to twelve editions and was clearly intended to be and was used as guidance by local authorities (which at that time administered the Poor Laws through their public assistance committees), stated in the 1939 edition:

> The principles of poor relief may be summarised as follows –
> 1 . . .
> 2 The relief provided should be repressive, by making it morally repulsive, and severe in the treatment of the idle, immoral and vicious.

Not for J. J. Clarke the euphemisms of 'bringing the unemployed back into work' or 'weaning from dependence'; he told it how it was. Even Beveridge included in his scheme the idea that those on national assistance should be treated worse than those on the contributory benefits:

> [National assistance] must be felt to be something less desirable than insurance benefit; otherwise the insured persons get nothing for their contributions. Assistance therefore will be given always subject to proof of needs and examination of means; it will be subject also to any conditions as to behaviour which seem likely to hasten restoration of earning capacity.

A Poor Service for Poor People

That claimants must queue in the cold for hours before being admitted to shabby offices with no toilets or drinking water is merely the extension of the Poor Law tradition into the 1980s. It is designed to be stigmatising as a way of discouraging claims and reinforcing the degradation of being a pauper.

Public attitudes to the poor are the product of many influences, among which governments play only a part. Nevertheless, government action can affect how the poor are treated, which in turn influences the way they are perceived. A government which professes such enthusiasm for Victorian values, which has made such a public issue of the prevalence of fraud as distinct from the underpayment and non-take-up of benefits, and which has openly and unashamedly redistributed public money in favour of the rich and away from the poor is unlikely to set a high priority on providing good public services for the poor. On taking office, this government embarked upon a series of actions that were likely to ensure that the quality of service to the poor would deteriorate.

First, there has been the shift away from benefits based on insurance towards those based on means tests. Because the latter inevitably involve more complicated individual assessments they give rise to more difficulties, and most of the complaints about the quality of service provided by the DHSS are about supplementary benefits. A policy of shifting people from insurance benefits to supplementary benefits is bound to put more pressure on services to claimants.

Second, the numbers of people out of work in the 1980s have produced, inevitably, a huge increase in the number of claimants. Coupled with this has been an increase in the number of single parents. Whereas there were 3.2 million supplementary benefit claimants in 1979, there were over 5 million by 1986, the increase being wholly accounted for by claimants under pension age who in general have more changeable and complicated circumstances.

These increases have inevitably placed a heavy burden on the DHSS. The sheer size of its operations means that some errors, delays and poor decisions are bound to occur. In 1986/7, 65,000 staff in the 500 local offices dealt with 23 million callers. Over 40,000 staff dealt with supplementary benefits alone, handling 13 million visits by callers, 5.6 million claims for benefit, over 16

273

million reassessments of benefits, over 6 million claims for single payments and 1.6 million home visits. Perfection in an organisation of such size and activity is unlikely; it becomes impossible if the number of staff is deliberately allowed to fall behind the massive increase in workload, as has consistently happened.

The populist appeals made by the Conservatives at election time to run down the numbers of civil servants were followed by swift action, with cuts in the staff employed in the DHSS from 98,000 to 90,000 in the first five years. The huge rise in the number of claimants meant that it was impossible to make cuts in the staff dealing with supplementary benefits, but the increases in staffing came nowhere near matching the increase in the workload. Whereas the numbers of claimants rose by 78 per cent between 1979 and 1986, staff increased by only 29 per cent. The government justified the shortfall by claiming that some administrative changes, such as hiving off housing benefit to local authorities and introducing postal claim forms, had reduced the workload. However, the effects of the shortfall can best be seen by the worsening ratio of staff to claimants: in 1979 this stood at one member of staff to every 100 claimants; by 1986 it had increased to one to 125. The SCPS, one of the two main DHSS unions, summed up the effects:

> As a result staff in most local offices are faced with a choice; either they deal with claims thoroughly and allow a backlog to build up or they go through the claims as quickly as possible in order to cope with the increased number of claims but are forced to reduce the time spent on each claim to such an extent that each one is not considered properly.

It is not just the civil service unions that claim that the staff numbers are insufficient. In his report for 1985–6 the Chief Adjudication Officer reported:

> All nine Regional Adjudication Officers claimed that the criteria for determining staff numbers in relation to the increased volume of work falling on their respective sections during 1984 were unrealistic. RAOs used additional staff to a lesser or greater extent during the year in attempts to absorb the pressure, but even so it proved impossible to carry out many

routine tasks and delay was common on those which were undertaken.

This refusal to increase staffing levels to match the increase in workload has had the inevitable and wholly predictable consequence of lowering the quality of service to the public. From this one omission follow many others, all having the effect of making the service worse: home visits are reduced or suspended, preventing many claimants from receiving proper advice about their entitlement; staff are forced to take on duties without adequate training; the pressure on staff leads to more stress, staff therefore leave to be replaced by new and inexperienced staff (in 1985 the Chief Adjudication Officer reported that in many inner-city offices more than a third of adjudication officers had less than six months' experience); claimants' frustration leads to more abuse and a deterioration in staff–claimant relationships, and so on.

The drive towards greater 'efficiency', i.e. expecting staff to work harder and harder, has led not only to an unacceptable level of service in many parts of the country but also to great waste as the worsening conditions of work make it harder to retain or recruit staff. The DHSS's regional organisation scrutiny team made the point in their report in May 1988; commenting on the difficulties of recruitment and retention, they said:

> The consequences are low levels of experience and knowledge, which produce low productivity, which produces poor performance, which generates more callers and enquiries, which disrupt the flow of work, which further lowers productivity and so on in a vicious spiral. The constant need to train staff, many of whom do not stay long enough to become proficient, is a further drain on experienced staff and on resources and puts yet more pressure on the people directly providing the service.

A clearer condemnation of the pursuit of 'efficiency' through cutting staff would be hard to find. Add to this the fact that every 1 per cent of staff turnover costs the taxpayer £1.75 million in recruitment, training, supervision and lower productivity costs, and the policy stands condemned as self-defeating in monetary terms as well as in what it costs staff and claimants. The NAO found that the annual wastage rates of clerical posts ranged from

275

5 per cent in the best thirty offices to as much as 29 per cent in the worst thirty.

Other government initiatives have made matters worse. In 1981 it unilaterally abolished the system of linking civil service pay to 'fair comparisons' with similar jobs in the private sector, with the predictable result that pay rises not only fell behind those for comparable jobs but were often below the rise in the cost of living. Local management schemes were introduced to encourage managers to save costs, which some did by seeking to use fewer staff or lower grades to do the same amount of work. In some cases, notably in the Newcastle Central Office, management attempts to implement cost-cutting measures led to protracted strikes which cost far more than the measures were designed to save. There has also been a shift towards the use of casual workers and workers on temporary fixed-term contracts, which inevitably lowers the quality of service.

Computers to the Rescue

The government's plans for improving the service were set out in 1982 in a document entitled *Social Security Operational Strategy*. This described a strategy for the computerisation of the service over the following twenty years. Social security is clearly a prime candidate for computerisation, and once completed the whole process of calculating contributions and benefits should be done much more quickly and accurately. However, the cost of such a massive undertaking is to be met by staff cuts. Despite the stated aim in the document that the 'computer and communications technology should be used to cut administration costs and allow staff to concentrate on work for which human skills are essential', the programme envisages that the staff of the Department of Employment and of the DHSS would be cut from 100,000 to 75,000 by 1995 at a net saving over the period of £1.2 billion.

In May 1988 the DHSS's regional organisation scrutiny team prepared a report, *The Business of Service*, examining the problems facing local offices, came to much the same conclusions as everyone else, and recommended radical solutions. In their estimation the problems were so dire that, in their words, 'some places are already past the point of no return'. In support of this view they state that in the worst offices, mostly but not exclusively in London, it was taking twenty-five days to process new claims, callers were having to wait three or four hours – with average waiting times of ninety minutes – in 'sleazy' and 'forbidding' offices showing all the signs of long-term neglect and where privacy was impossible, error rates were 40 per cent, appeals were taking sixty days to prepare, telephones were not answered for long periods of the day and home visits had been abandoned. Almost universally staff claimed that they were under too much pressure, and that their rewards, particularly pay, were poor in relation both to their duties and responsibilities and to pay for similar jobs elsewhere.

The conclusions of the team were stark: the present structure is not the right one and without radical changes 'will never be able to deliver a reasonable standard of service overall'. They therefore put forward a fifteen-point plan aimed at restructuring the role and powers of managers, with more devolution to local cost centres responsible for their own budgets, establishing perform-ance criteria, and fostering a corporate identity (which they suggested paying consultants £100,000 to create). In other words, better management was to be the panacea that, in their view, would make 'everyone a winner'. (Those who work in other public organisations, such as universities and social services depart-ments, who have had their ills 'cured' by this remedy will instantly recognise the omens and advise the DHSS to settle for its ills rather than the proposed cure.)

For those offices past the point of no return the remedy of the scrutiny team was drastic: relocation out of the cities into new 'social security centres' situated in areas where recruitment and retention of staff would be easier (not to say cheaper, as no London weighting would be involved). These would handle all the proces-ses not requiring face-to-face contact with claimants, leaving a small office staff in the population centres to deal with callers. Computers and modern telecommunications would ensure that information would be readily available to this skeleton staff should they need to answer queries about the progress of claims etc. Twenty offices in London have been earmarked for the first phase of the strategy, to be moved by the end of 1989.

Not unnaturally, this cheerful optimism has been greeted with some scepticism by those who work in the local offices. They already have experience of this type of remote processing in handling child benefits, of which the National Union of Civil and Public Servants (NUCPS) and the CPSA comment that 'when callers ask what has happened to their claim, staff can seldom give a satisfactory answer. Telephoning the appropriate section is rarely productive.'

An Alternative Strategy: A Claimants' Charter

The unions representing staff who work in local offices are well aware of the shortcomings of their service and have been at the forefront in pressing for improvements. In 1986 they put a thirteen-point 'crisis programme' to the Secretary of State, followed in 1987 by a comprehensive alternative operational strategy document. The main feature of this strategy is that the only way to improve the service is to use the savings from computerisation to increase staffing levels, and in a carefully worked out blueprint they estimated that an additional 13,000 staff were needed to provide a 'user friendly' service. This was in sharp contrast to the planned *cut* of 8000 staff then envisaged for 1988. Their concept of what this user-friendly service would be is novel only in that it asks for social security claimants what most other people take for granted when they approach organisations, that is, a prompt, accurate, fully resourced service that can not only deal with claimants' concerns but can also involve them in the way the office is run by means of consumer councils and adopt a proactive open-door policy to inform people of their entitlements and encourage them to claim. Such aims seem a very long way from the proposed remote 'social security centres' servicing harassed and beleaguered inner-city garrisons.

Given different priorities, the opportunities offered by the computerisation of social security could transform the quality of service. If the government had meant what it said about using the staff released by the new technology to perform jobs best done by people, claims could be processed on time, letters and telephone calls answered, a proper system of home visiting or appointments with staff who had time to spend on claimants would be possible, more time could be given to claimants who are not literate or whose first language is not English, and more time could be devoted to the promotion of advice and information about benefits or in promoting take-up, much of it financed by the savings that will follow from the new technology. Such a service would do much to dispel the stigma that clings to claimants who know all too well that the reason they receive a poor service is because poverty is seen by some as a crime. Instead, computerisation is to be used to cut the amount of money spent on the service, and make massive staff cuts despite the indisputable evidence that the service for many claimants is already unacceptable. In addition, it now seems likely that claimants in inner cities are to be more or less abandoned in the untested hope that remote processing of claims will be so efficient that they will either no longer need to call at their local offices, or if they do their queries can be answered despite their papers being elsewhere. Given these priorities and these strategies, it looks as though the poor, and those who work for their benefit, will continue to receive a poor service.

13   Conclusion

No such thing as society.
No number other than one.
No person other than me.
No time other than now.
No such thing as society – just 'me' and 'now'.

(Neil Kinnock, speech to the Labour Party Conference,
Blackpool, October 1988)

There's no future for the ordinary person under this government.

(Letter to Neil Kinnock from a single parent, April 1988)

A Decade of Damage

In the past ten years a fundamental change has been made in the treatment of rich and poor in Britain. A decade ago there was a real chance not merely to continue the slow evolution towards principles of equity and efficiency in welfare but to accelerate it. Equal pay and equal rights legislation, although deficient, was in place; Europe was setting a powerful example of what could be done. It seemed that the argument on child care, and child and material benefits had been won and, with the reports of two significant government enquiries – the Finer Report on one-parent families and the Court Report on child health – also in the arena, the basis for a coherent family policy was established. Plans were finally being discussed for a disability income. Benefits and pensions were related to earnings, ensuring that people in work and out of work had a common stake in rising prosperity.

Conclusion

All this came to a halt in 1979. Ten years after taking office the Conservative government has radically changed the nature of social security in Britain. It has done so incrementally by stealth and by a fundamental 'reform'. The changes have flown in the face of almost all informed opinion, and have been consistent with other economic and industrial policies aimed at creating a society where to be old, disabled, unemployed or poor is to be regarded as a burdensome dependant on enterprising taxpayers, while to create wealth for one's own private use is held up as an example of the highest morality.

The overriding principle that has governed social policy in the last decade has been that of cutting public expenditure, reducing the amount spent on collective public provision in order to leave individuals 'free' to spend their own money as they choose. This has made possible the larger policy, the effect of which has been to redistribute wealth from the poor to the rich through Exchequer surpluses accumulated by savings on pensions and benefits, privatisation of national resources and assets. In one year alone, the savings from major cuts in pensions is now estimated to be £5 billion. Savings on all the cuts in national insurance and related benefits, accumulated over a decade, are now simply too complex to calculate, but there is no doubt that in the progressive and massive redistribution of wealth and power poor people have been made to pay dearly.

The main way in which this policy of 'rolling back the state' has been applied to social security has been by the erosion of Beveridge's concept of social insurance and its replacement by reliance on mass means-tested benefits. From this one policy, pursued relentlessly in relation to the elderly, disabled, sick and unemployed and from its parallel policy in the field of housing, where general subsidies have given way to means-tested housing benefits, have flowed most of the other social security problems that have dominated the 1980s. As a result, millions of people who could have drawn on contributory benefits or who would have had their rents and rates kept down by central subsidies have been forced to turn to supplementary benefits or to their town halls for housing benefits, and all the problems this book has identified have been made worse. There has been a deterioration in the standard of service provided as neither the DHSS nor the town halls have been able to cope with the massive increase in numbers who fell back on personal means tests.

One result of that policy is, as we have recorded, splinters in children's feet as mothers are told they must make do with three pairs of socks rather than shoes, families with no means of heating their food because they cannot afford to repair broken cookers, and old ladies ashamed in their own homes because they cannot afford curtains.

Nor has this been the only way in which money has been saved at the expense of the poor. The refusal to consider whether benefits are adequate, the refusal to give priority to ensuring that claimants know of and receive all the benefits to which they are entitled, the disproportionate emphasis on the prevention of petty fraud, the continual administrative offensives against the unemployed, the abolition of legal entitlement, have all closed down the escape hatches from poverty.

Autumn 1988: Decoding the Text and Reading the Signs

In the autumn of 1988 the government's past and future intentions toward people living on state benefits and pensions took on a sudden and chilling clarity. On 27 October it was revealed that child benefit would be frozen for the second year in succession and on 6 November it became clear that the Chancellor was considering extending means-testing into pensioners' universal benefits. Together they represent a single strand of thinking, final proof of the tone and style of a government that believes it can get away with anything. Whether we search the fine print and even the punctuation of the Tory party manifesto with regard to child benefit, or the confidential and therefore unguarded lobby interviews with the Chancellor, it is now clear that the government has no concern to protect what remains of a welfare state based on benefits as of right, or to recognise the extent and nature of poverty as it exists throughout Britain today.

To make good the losses of November 1985 and the freeze in April 1988, and to increase in line with inflation, child benefit should have risen to £8.35 in April 1989. Speculation began well in advance of the autumn statement to determine the government's intentions toward the benefit. Asked about her intentions, by Neil Kinnock in the House of Commons on 20 October, Mrs Thatcher made clear her concern for equity in the tax and benefit system by insisting that: 'This year . . . we directed £200 million in extra resources to families on income related benefits. . . . If the Rt Hon. Gentleman wants a general increase in child benefit it would also go to the topmost people on top tax.' The following day, John Moore developed the attack on child benefit, arguing that the benefit system should not be a 'decorative overlay – spread so thinly as to be ineffectual where it is really needed, and irrelevant where it is not'. The most comprehensive reply to this flawed logic came on 25 October 1988 in the form of an editorial in the *Financial Times*, which argued that:

> In the 1987 election manifesto the Conservative Party promised that child benefit 'will continue to be paid as now'. It is pure humbug to interpret that as a commitment only to the cash value of the benefit. A benefit is not the same benefit if inflation has meanwhile significantly eroded its purchasing power. If the Government wants to cut child benefit it should argue openly and explicitly for such a policy not allow inflation to do its work by stealth.

On the same day, to the outrage of the Tory back-benches, Kinnock called the Prime Minister a cheat on child benefit. It was a well-founded accusation. The uprating statement made by John Moore two days later brought not only the expected freeze in child benefit but, in addition, another illusionist's trick. Emphasising his intention to give 'direct help where it is most needed' he diverted £70 million of the £206 million saved on child benefit to child allowances on means-tested benefits; £136 million went back to the Treasury – *not* into the pockets of the poor. Thus, once again, poor families on child benefit paid for the 50p extra for the children of the very poorest.

The government's insistence that family credit is the best way to help children is clouded, however, by the fact that in January 1979 only one in three eligible families was claiming it, only half the government's estimated take-up. Amid mounting embarrassment Moore responded in March 1989 by reformulating the basis on which family credit entitlement was calculated to show that one in two families, not one in three, was claiming. An advertising campaign, costing £4.8 million generated a further 9,400 successful claims, producing an average benefit of £650 for every £510 spent on advertising, making it, as Robin Cook described it, 'Europe's least efficient benefit.' The government is not, however, easily persuaded by evidence. As Nigel Lawson put it on 4 November 1988, 'a lot of nonsense is talked about means tests'.

In that interview the Chancellor made clear his conviction that there was a case for 'restructuring' child benefit, but that, given the 'austere' nature of the interpretation of the manifesto, this could not easily be accomplished. His exact words were, 'We would not be able to go back on the manifesto because of the comma' (i.e. 'Child Benefit will continue to be paid as now, and direct to the mother'). The future of child benefit is, therefore, now an open question.

In the same interview Lawson also spoke of his future policy towards pensioners. In a very revealing aside he suggested that only a 'tiny minority' of pensioners 'have difficulty making ends meet'. This was amended in later radio broadcasts to a 'small minority', but when pressed in the House of Commons, Lawson, like the Prime Minister, replied with a catalogue of statistics arguing that pensioners' incomes were rising faster than ever before and that they were indeed better off. (The fact that so many of the younger pensioners are 'better off' reflects in part the increasing contribution that SERPS is now making to their overall income. This was, of course, not mentioned by either the Chancellor or the Prime Minister.) Lawson went on to argue that the implications of this growing wealth among pensioners and 'the evolution of the social security system' were to see 'whether we can do better targeting there, so that we can help that minority of pensioners who do genuinely have difficulty in making ends meet'.

No mention was made of the government's interest in developing an additional allowance for the very elderly; there had been no hint in the autumn statement, the obvious place for such a welcome innovation. Rather, Lawson referred journalists to the list of 'unpledged benefits' which can be reduced or abolished without reference to legislation. These included free prescriptions, the Christmas bonus, mobility allowance, child benefit, family credit, etc. Moreover, and for many journalists this was the final clinching argument, he agreed with them that back-benchers would have to be won over. They would have to be 'educated' to his view. This was in the context of the back-bench revolt on teeth and eye test charges, where the back-benchers were apparently 'educated' into supporting the government by threats of reduced hospital funding for their constituents.

No wonder, therefore, that the ten independent lobby journalists rushed into print convinced they had a major story of the further demolition of the welfare state. No wonder, equally, that they were all taken aback by the Chancellor's venom throughout the following week as he sought to discredit their stories, coming to the House of Commons reluctantly to tell back-benchers the good news that he had invented a new additional benefit but that he was unable to give them any further details because the work was not very advanced. Even the Conservative benches could be forgiven for being sceptical; coming from a government which had made forty-five separate cuts in national insurance benefits, siphoned off billions of pounds a year from pensioners and others by breaking the link with earnings, redistributed money from poor to rich on an extraordinary scale unique in Britain, this sudden conversion to inventing new benefits was hard to take seriously, unless to save the Chancellor's embarrassment.

Few people were taken in, especially since the subtext concerned the 'missing', 'blank' or 'recycled' tapes which the civil servants had at first offered to use to check the veracity of the lobbyists' accounts. The combination of incompetence, bluff and bluster, inevitably dubbed 'Lawsongate' for the inept attempts to conceal what might have happened, and Lawson's refusal to come to the House of Commons to 'clear his name' made for high parliamentary excitement during the last week of the 1987/88 session.

Other revelations equally significant for the future of social security were made in the autumn of 1988. The NACAB report showing that four out of five social security claimants coming to the CABx for help had lost money was published in November; the extent of poverty among disabled people was made clear in the second OPCS report on the disabled; changes were anticipated in the board and lodging regulations which will lead to greater homelessness among the young and all those in 'special needs hostels'. At the same time, the index used to uprate benefits was to be adjusted downwards, and the transitional arrangements for housing benefits were further cut back so that the modest expectations of claimants were even further reduced.

The evidence that the social security reforms have for many people made things worse not better, and of mounting, hidden poverty among the elderly and disabled, contrasts starkly with the Napoleonic refusal of ministers to admit the facts, or to concede that the Thatchercentric view of the world is anything other than correct. It is a view fully expressed in John Moore's speech on 21 October 1988, congratulating the government on its success in refocusing benefits

> dramatically to provide help where it is really needed and positive incentives for those who are able to participate in and contribute to the country's success. . . . What the Government has already done and what its policies will continue to do is to design and maintain benefits that give real help to the groups that society has clearly said it wants to help; low income families with children, disabled people, and pensioners.

The attempt to paint a picture of universal rising prosperity when mortgage rises far outstrip tax reductions, when basic pensions increasingly fall behind earnings and when rate rebates fail to match increases, presents no problems for a government for which language and statistics can mean anything it chooses to make them mean. If poverty is a political embarrassment, it can, like unemployment, be redefined. Just as 500,000 unemployed young people and women no longer exist on the unemployment register, so the poverty figures have been recast. In 1988 the *Survey of Low Income Families*, which has traditionally been used to provide numbers living on income support or on incomes up to 40 per cent above its level will no longer simply be subject to its customary delay; it will no longer be published at all. From 1988 the official comparisons will be only with people on 'average incomes'.

The debate about who is poorer than whom has now taken a

new and arcane turn. The government says that the lowest-paid 10 per cent of the working population is no longer as poor as it was. The poverty lobby says that the poorest third and the poorer half of the population are poorer than they were. It is a depressing and largely irrelevant debate when the picture of poverty is so clear. The fact is that the real incomes of the poorest are now worth less in relation to average earnings than they were in 1986. Then, a family on income support with two children lived on an income which was 43.1 per cent of average male earnings; in 1988 it was 37.1 per cent. In 1978 just over six million people (12 per cent of the population) were on income support; the latest figures show that there are now over nine million (17 per cent). Only half these new families, many of whom are of course unemployed, are there because the 'rates are more generous'. The government says it is spending 'more' on social security – 39 per cent more (£13 billion) since 1979. Of this increase, nearly half is due to increased numbers of pensioners, disabled claimants and single-parent families, a quarter to increased unemployment and a quarter to increases caused by the uprating of benefits.

Just as the statistics show a growing and persistent class of people who at the lowest end are becoming progressively poorer, so the evidence of the way in which the reforms have worked shows that the key objectives, targeting and simplification, have failed because the reforms were faulty at foundation. Family credit clearly does not reach all eligible low income families; neither does housing benefit. The debts, rent arrears and repossessions pile up. The social fund has swerved from underspending to 'overspending', which now brings to its meagre budget the threat of cuts; single parents are cut off, by regulation, from work; and the DSS pursues the scroungers with endless vigour while unemployment benefit errors have led to benefit underpayments of £89 million – an average individual loss of £15 a week. On top of that, recent studies show that the poll tax will, despite rebates, make 83 per cent of the poorest families worse off, and 71 per cent of the richest families better off.

Nevertheless, the attempt to persuade the people and Parliament that the snags can be ironed out in time goes on. Both morality and logic are overturned as the government argues that it was perfectly 'fair', for example, to give the richest 1 per cent of tax units in the country (200,000 people) £170 a week extra in tax cuts, but quite 'unfair' if the same people with children should receive an extra £1.35 a week to make up their losses in child benefit. The same logic insists that it is cheaper, more efficient and fairer to administer means-tested benefits than to provide universal benefits which really do go to all 'according to their need', which are known to be easy and cheap to administer, and the costs of which can be recouped through a system of fair and progressive taxation from those who are able to pay.

There are undoubtedly formidable problems in devising a social security system that is fair between different groups of claimants, provides a decent standard of living without destroying incentives to work and is within the limits of what the electorate will accept as right, sensible and affordable. We believe that the Social Security Act 1986 failed to solve them because it was the outcome of a process designed primarily at nil cost and to isolate and stigmatise the poor. The need for reform was not, ironically, in dispute. The need to improve supplementary benefit and family income supplement, to help the disabled and establish a more inclusive and fairer contributory system commanded political consensus. Moreover, the opportunities were there, in the form of the groundwork laid in the 1970s and the revenues from oil which, in part, could have strengthened the foundations of a fairer as well as a more productive society. What was not there was the political will to make genuine improvements.

'There Is No Such Thing as Society'

The changes made to social security have implications not just for the way in which we as a society treat those who at any one time are not able to provide for themselves or their families; they have a far wider significance as a statement of the values which lie at the heart of the kind of society we want to create. Social security gives concrete expression to a view of society which holds that we are all in this together, that your misfortune diminishes me, that together we can and must provide collectively for those who cannot for whatever reason provide for themselves. It is a view which is both

288

altruistic, based on the belief that we have an obligation to help one another, and selfish, since we cannot know when we too, will be in need. It is the antithesis of the view which believes that material success is everything, and that for the successful to succeed it is inevitable that the weak must go to the wall. To that extent, the sustained attack on welfare benefits and on the whole principle of collective provision through insurance and assistance has not just been an attack on the poor. The denial of collective responsibility, so openly proclaimed by the Prime Minister, is the celebration of a society whose essence was exactly caught by the television image of the rich young men in the City cheering like football hooligans at the news of Lawson's 1988 tax cuts. Later that year in her speech to the party conference Mrs Thatcher no longer relied solely upon the 'trickle-down' theory of helping the poor; her vision of the 'generous society' is now one where the poor are helped by the charity of the rich, though when that charitable impulse runs out, or cannot be sustained, there will now be fewer rights that can be claimed.

That loss of rights is the inevitable product of an ethic which is not merely 'me and now' but 'me against you' – and a determination to reduce citizenship to the ability to pay or the ability to survive without the necessary support. Once employment is abandoned as an objective of policy, and public services are seen as a drain on personal prosperity, social security takes on the role of a parasitical, deadening growth upon a healthy society. Moreover, since it represents a collective expression and a community of interest, it is at once a threat to narrow individualism as well as an alternative source of power. This view of social security spawns policies which have profoundly divided those out of work from those in work; the poorest from the near poor; the disabled from the severely disabled; the elderly with a little savings from the elderly with none; men from women; black from white, the 'north' from the 'south'.

A Decade of Deceit

This determination to wrench the social security system, and society with it, into a new shape was explicit not only in content but in the procedures of the reforms. The apparent commitment to the democratic process at the start of the reviews was revealed as openly cynical when a deaf ear was turned to all but those in tune with government ambitions. The great debate began with a trumpet blast from Norman Fowler heralding the advent of 'open government', but the commitment was short-lived. When the replies to the Green and White Papers arrived condemning almost all aspects of the reforms, not only were they ignored but the response itself was never revealed by the government. Indeed, no analysis was given of those in favour and those against the different proposals. The reason for this coyness is self-evident. Similarly, advice from the Social Security Advisory Committee was often ignored or, when it became clear that the SSAC was being inconveniently squeamish about the evidence of the damage likely to come from government proposals, simply bypassed.

But the government went much further than this in its departure from plain dealing. We have given examples in the book of a repertoire of devious practices ranging from economy with the truth to downright deceit. The government tried to mislead Parliament and the public over the scale of the losses claimants would suffer; witness the repeated claim that only 12 per cent would lose, or the Prime Minister's assertion that the 'overwhelming majority' would gain. This remark could have been made only from complete ignorance of the effects of the changes or out of a determination to conceal the real effects. The DHSS, which had already admitted that more would lose than gain tried to massage the figures to make it look as though there would be fewer people losing, as when housing benefit supplement was abolished one week before the changes. The government gave false undertakings to compensate claimants for their losses, as when it failed to compensate fully for the 20 per cent rates contribution. It offered its own back-benches concessions that were to a large extent illusory, as with the housing benefit transitional arrangements, and blatantly tried to fool them by its concession over the poll tax rebates which it knew, even as it gave them, it would try to claw back the following year. And, in the judgement of all honourable people, the government has simply overturned its election pledge on child benefit. It is a dishonourable record and, at times, a dishonest record.

When language is stretched beyond its common shared meanings and values, political exchange breaks down. The poll tax is sold to people, who *know* that it is fundamentally unfair, as increasing their 'personal control'. Means tests are justified as driving out 'dependency' when personal experience dictates that cutting insurance benefits, housing subsidies, or even student grants, makes it more difficult for families to free themselves.

That word 'freedom' is never far from the Prime Minister's lips. The uses to which she has put it have been truly remarkable. Tenants have been told they will be 'freed' from council oppression as they are sold off into the private sector, parents 'freed' from the dogmatic rule of the schools, employees 'freed' from the domination of the trade unions as their employment rights are removed, and more recently from the oppression of laws which prevent them working all night when aged sixteen, and of course claimants are to be 'freed' from dependency upon the DHSS. By reducing the power of the law to provide basic services and provide basic protection, by abolishing legal rights including rights to appeal, by taking administrative action against the unemployed, by usurping power with the excessive use of delegated legislation (which on scrutiny has often been proved to be outside the law) and by reducing and abolishing benefits the government has made a mockery not only of language but of the democratic process. Tenants' ballots, parents' ballots, the strategic pilgrimage of the backwoodsmen to the House of Lords, the deception of the members of the House of Commons, all have pressed language and democracy to the service of doctrinaire ends.

There is an Alternative

Out of this shabby story it is possible to see, by contrast, that there is an alternative view of society in which welfare is not seen as a drain on society but as central to its efficiency and to the strength of a modern democracy. Just as Beveridge cast his modern welfare state in the context of full employment, and the equal worth of every individual, our modern welfare state at the end of the century must be built on similar assumptions designed to deliver greater economic democracy precisely because it is built on more and better education, training and employment opportunities, a system that recognises new working patterns, the fact of fewer young workers, more women wanting to work and more elderly people wanting to stay independent for as long as possible. Other European countries are now moving fast toward high investment, highly sophisticated economies, knowing that in order to survive they must develop to the maximum the skills of all their people. If we do not follow that example, by increasing participation in education for the over-sixteens, developing employable skills and qualifications for young people between sixteen and twenty, increasing the volume and the quality of adult training, we will inflict the same cycle of low skills, low pay, unemployment and poverty upon successive generations.

A policy to combat poverty is a total economic and social strategy. It is in part based on the thesis that decent benefits contribute to the health and welfare of the economy. No one has illustrated this better than Churchill, who in a speech at Nottingham in 1909 described the beneficial effects of the old age pension:

> Nearly eight millions [pounds] of money are being sent circulating through unusual channels, long frozen by poverty in the homes of the poor, flowing through the little shops that cater to their needs, cementing again family unions which harsh fate was tearing asunder, uniting the wife to the husband and the parent to the children.

Thus, a benefit system which enables people to live in dignity and independence serves an economic as well as a humane function. National insurance has served those purposes and if

292

properly managed and funded will continue to serve them. But national insurance must take its place within a matrix of policies dedicated to creating a competitive, innovative economy with a confident and skilled workforce at all ages, with the prospect of lifelong education and training to give everyone the greatest chance of career flexibility and mobility. Policies to defeat poverty are therefore as much about equal opportunities to work, fair taxation and minimum wages as they are about entitlement to and levels of benefit; as much about children's and mothers' health and good child care as about the levels of child benefit. They mean promoting economic equality by targeting on *need over a lifetime* and not on *means*. They mean enhancing and not degrading self-respect.

Decent and rational policies for welfare strengthen democracy as much as they strengthen the economy. We have been concerned in this book to examine the way in which language, commitments, assumptions and promises have been made and deployed. At the heart of the change we want to see is not only a determination to deal with the truth in terms of what Britain can and wants to afford as a civilised nation caring for those who are unable to care for themselves, but also a new commitment to deal in the truth. This can mean taking responsibility for the full effects of policies on living standards, or it can mean taking account of the weight of expert and responsible opinion and dissent as to what can and must be done. It must take account of the limits to its own political mandate.

Sixty years ago R.H. Tawney offered his definition of democracy. It was, he said, not a form of government, but a type of society which involved on the one hand 'the resolute elimination of all forms of privilege which favour some groups and depress others, whether the source be differences of environment, of education or of . . . income', and, second, 'the conversion of economic power, now often an irresponsible tyrant, into the servant of society'.

Social security is not just for or about the poor. It is an expression of self-interest, social relationships and mutual responsibility. The relationship between society and democracy is, on any definition, indivisible. To play a part in society, without dependence or deference, means to be able to exercise full democratic rights. Those rights are as much economic as legal or political. Those who say that 'there is no such thing as Society' are in fact signalling another, more sinister message – their assumption that there is 'no such thing as democracy'. The urgent task facing everyone who cares about the future of society and of democracy is to prove them wrong.

Notes and Sources

Chapter 1

For general background to the impact of social security policy over the decade see Carole Walker and Alan Walker, *The Growing Divide* (CPAG, 1987). The Beveridge Report is essential reading: *Social Insurance and Allied Services*, Cmd 6404 (1942). On proposals for reform, pre-1980, see: the Supplementary Benefit Commission's annual reports 1975–8 – particularly the final report for 1978, Cmnd 7725. For the proposals for reforming the supplementary benefit system see DHSS, *Social Assistance* (1978) and 'Reform of the Supplementary Benefit Scheme', Cmnd 7773 (November 1979); for a response to this scheme, which, as modified, became law in the Social Security (No. 1) Act 1979/80, see Ruth Lister, 'Social Security: The Real Challenge', CPAG Poverty Pamphlet No. 38 (1978); and 'The no cost–no benefit review', CPAG Poverty Pamphlet No. 39 (January 1979).

For the quotations and background on the first round of public expenditure cuts and social security reforms during the period 1980–3, see the Chancellor's speech and the debate on the budget, Hansard, 26 March 1980, especially cols. 1457–9, and the Public Expenditure White Paper, Cmnd 7841 (March 1980). See House of Commons Library Reference Sheet 80/11 for a full list of background references on this bill and second reading of the Social Security Bill, 15 April 1980.

Estimates for the cuts in the social security budget have been calculated by the House of Commons Library.

For the increases in the social security budget between 1978/9 and 1987, see H.C. Deb., 8 April 1987, cols. 107–8W and Public Expenditure White Papers Cm 56 and Cmnd 9143.

For the role of the CPRS on family policy and pensions see Tessa Blackstone and William Plowden, *Inside the Think Tank*

(Heinemann, 1988), pp. 124–8. For the leaks giving details of the CPRS review of social policy, and inspired guesswork as to what the Green Paper might contain, see *The Economist*, 18 September 1982; *Guardian*, 15 February 1983; *New Society*, 24 February 1983; *The Times*, 21 November 1984; *Financial Times*, 6 February 1985; *New Statesman*, 8 February 1985; *The Economist*, 20 February 1985; *Sunday Times*, 8 April 1984.

Norman Fowler, interview in *New Society*, 27 October 1983, pp. 164–5, and speech to the Parliamentary Press Lobby, 13 February 1985.

On the conduct of the reviews and the exchanges between the review panels and the bodies giving evidence, see in particular 'The Social Security Reviews', *Poverty*, Winter 1984–5. For the reviews themselves the crucial documents are of course the three-volume Green Paper, 'Reform of Social Security', Vol. 1, Cmnd 9517, which gives a general history, rationale and account of the reforms themselves; Vol. 2 'Programme for Change', Cmnd 9518, which gives a more detailed account of the issues; Vol. 3, 'Background Papers', Cmnd 9519, which contained a series of factual papers on the distribution of low incomes etc. and a list of the membership, terms of reference and organisations giving evidence to the review teams. There was also the separate report on housing benefit, Cmnd 9520 (1985).

The government's proposals on the Green Paper were presented to the House of Commons on 3 June 1985, and further comment in the House of Commons occurred on 4 June 1985 (PMQs, Kinnock to Thatcher, cols. 150–1, 6 June 1985).

Responses to the reviews are simply too numerous to list, but the most significant are listed and analysed in the House of Commons Library Reference Sheet 85/6: Social Security Reform: Responses to the Green Paper, 12 November 1985. Individual quotations, e.g. the National Consumer Council, 'Of Benefit to Whom?', are from the published submissions.

On the White Paper and subsequent debates on the bill see: 'Reform of Social Security: Programme for action', Cmnd 9691 (December 1985); House of Commons Library Reference Sheet 86/3 on the Social Security Bill 1985/6; DHSS Technical Annexe, *Reform of Social Security* (HMSO, December 1985); statement by Norman Fowler, H.C. Deb., 16 December 1985, cols. 21–34.

For an analysis of the White Paper see in particular the Select Committee on Social Services, 'The Government's Green Paper "Reform of Social Security" ', H.C. 451, 17 July 1985. For important responses, see CPAG's 'Plain Man's Guide' to the White Paper (1986), the Institute of Fiscal Studies Commentary (1986), and the Policy Studies Review, 'Selective Social Security', by Richard Berthoud (1985).

The bill had its second reading in the House of Commons on 28 January 1986, col. 819, and in the House of Lords on 2 June 1986, col. 594.

For John Moore's major speeches on policy, see his speeches to the Conservative Party Conference on 7 and 12 October 1988, to the Conservative Political Centre on 24 September 1987 (the 'dependency culture' speech) and to the Institute of Directors on 8 June 1988 (the 'opportunity state').

The 'impact tables' were published on 26 October 1987.

The two major emergency debates on the impact of the changes were on 13 April 1988, H.C. Deb., cols. 173–220; 27 April 1988, cols. 351–406.

Chapter 2

Government estimates of the effects of the changes are contained in *Impact of the Reformed Structure of Income-Related Benefits* (DHSS, October 1987). Details of the proposals of the review team on housing benefit are in 'Housing Benefit Review', Cmnd 9520 (the report of the review team, DHSS, June 1985). Evidence to the review team from various organisations is summarised in P. Kemp and N. Raynsford, *Housing Benefit; The Evidence* (Housing Centre Trust, 1984). (For an account of housing benefit's disastrous beginning see P. Kemp, *The Cost of Chaos*, SHAC Research Report No. 8, 1984.)

The government's response to the review team's proposals is contained in the White Paper, 'Reform of Social Security; Programme for Action', Cmnd 9691 (DHSS, December 1965). Further information about the scheme can be found in *Hansard* in the debate on the draft regulations on 19 November 1987, in the main debate on the social security changes on 13 April 1988 and in the

Opposition Day debate on changes to the housing benefit scheme on 27 April 1988.

On the 20 per cent rates issue, see the Fourth Report of the SSAC (1985), paras. 4.23–4.28. The assurance that 'the most vulnerable groups' would be protected was given on behalf of the government by Lord Glenarthur in the House of Lords on 5 May 1987. The quotation from Norman Fowler comes from his speech during a debate in the House of Commons on 15 May 1987.

Information on the changes in tapers is contained in the answers to written parliamentary questions to Margaret Beckett on 5 November 1987 and to Frank Field on 25 November 1987. Information about the levels of income at which housing benefit ceases to be payable comes from the answer to a written parliamentary question from Margaret Beckett on 24 March 1988.

For Ridley's deceit see the *Guardian*, 19 April 1988.

Details about the numbers of claimants gaining and losing by the housing benefit changes are given in the answer to a written parliamentary question from Margaret Beckett on 18 December 1987. The information in reply to the question by Sir Brandon Rhys Williams was given on 4 February 1988.

Manchester City Council's press release is dated 19 April 1988.

Government figures on the effects of the changes to supplementary benefit are again contained in the impact tables. Details of the work of the Benefit Research Unit at Nottingham are available from the unit. Saul Becker and Stewart MacPherson, *Public Issues and Private Pain* (Social Services Insight Books in conjunction with the BRU) contains an account of their research in chapter 4. An account of the effects in Strathclyde is given in the *Scotsman*, 3 March 1988. The Oxford material comes from two reports from the Department of Social and Administrative Studies at the University of Oxford, both entitled *The Other Oxford*: that published in March 1988 is subtitled 'Who Gains and Who Loses?', that published in April 1988 is subtitled 'A Comparison with DHSS Estimates'.

The NACAB report is called *The Social Security Act: First Impressions* (November 1988).

For Moore's statement that he was 'very, very proud' see the *Guardian*, 16 April 1988.

Chapter 3

In the fight to maintain and improve the value of child benefit the CPAG has played a critical role. For the history and arguments for maintaining and increasing child benefit see the annual Budget Briefings put out in January and February each year by CPAG, and its literature for its most recent campaign for child benefit, 1987.

For 'The Battle for Women's Rights is Largely Won', see Prime Minister's speech to the Institution of Electrical Engineers, 26 July 1982.

For the most recent figures for the number of women in low pay see Low Pay Unit, *Britain Can't Afford Low Pay* (1988), pp. 10–12.

For Conservative support for child benefit in 1975, see Norman Fowler speaking on the Child Benefits Bill, H.C. Deb., 13 May 1975, cols. 341–2. See also the Conservative Party Green Paper, 'Proposals for a Tax Credit Scheme', Cmnd 5116 (October 1972).

The refusal to uprate child benefit for the first time was announced in Sir Geoffrey Howe's first budget, H.C. Deb., 12 June 1979. For successive attempts in the House of Commons to relate increases in child benefit to the rate of inflation, see the debates on 23 April 1980, H.C. Deb., cols. 484–8, 18 March 1982, cols. 500–12, 19 May 1986, cols. 74–5.

For the argument on child benefit as presented to the Review of Children and Young Persons see the evidence of the Adam Smith Institute and that of the CPAG, *Burying Beveridge* (1985).

For John Major's interview see *Poverty*, April 1987, pp. 6–8.

For Sir Brandon Rhys Williams's attack on the government see H.C. Deb., 12 January 1988, cols. 185–9

John Moore, speech to the Conservative Political Centre, 26 September 1987.

For the decision not to uprate child benefit in 1987 see H.C. Deb., 27 October 1987, col. 180. For comment see the *Guardian*, 28 October 1987 and the *Daily Telegraph*, 6 November 1987.

For the leaked papers on cabinet discussions on child benefit, see the *Independent*, 13 April 1988.

For parliamentary exchanges on the future of child benefit, see PMQs, Kinnock to Thatcher, 24 May 1988, cols. 189–90; and for the refusal to uprate child benefit in 1989, see H.C. Deb., 19 October 1988, col. 896W.

For CPAG comment on the family credit scheme, see *Burying Beveridge* (1985).

For the concession to pay family credit to the mother, see H.C. Deb., 14 May 1986, col. 149, and H.L. Deb., 23 June 1986, col. 40.

For an analysis of the interaction of family credit with housing and other benefits leading to marginal tax rates of over 70p in the £1, see H.C. Deb., 15 January 1986 col. 594 for the original assessments and 4 February 1988, col. 737. For a survey of lone parents and income support changes and comparisons with other countries see Joan Brown *Why Don't They Go to Work?* (SSAC Research Paper No. 2 1989); H.C. Deb., 30 November 1987, col. 464W. See also Report of the Social Services Select Committee, November 1988.

For figures on the cost of bringing up children, see David Piachaud, *The Cost of a Child* (CPAG, 1979) and *Children and Poverty* (CPAG, 1981).

Chapter 4

For general background on training policies, see White Paper, 'A New Training Initiative: A Programme for Action', Cmnd 8455 (December 1981); White Paper, 'Training for Jobs', Cmnd 9135 (1984); and White Paper, 'Education and Training for Young People', Cmnd 9482 (April 1985).

On training and benefit provisions in general, see the Family Policy Studies Centre, *Young People at the Crossroads* (1988); Kay Andrews, 'Income Maintenance for Young People in Education, Training and Unemployment in Britain', Australian Legislative Research Service Discussion Paper No. 5 (1984). Current statistics are most accessibly set out in the DES Statistical Bulletin 14/88, 'Educational and Economic Activity of Young People Aged 16 to 18 years in England from 1975 to 1988'. On the incidence of low pay among young people see Low Pay Unit, *Britain Can't Afford Low Pay. A Programme for a National Minimum Wage* (1988) and the *Employment Gazette*, October 1988, Tables 2.21–2.24.

For recent general comment and criticisms of the YTS training programme, see the MSC study by Duncan Gray and Suzanne King, 'The YTS: The First Three Years', Research and Development Paper No. 35. See in particular report commissioned by the Economic and Social Research Committee from David Ashton and Michael McGuire reviewed in the *Financial Times*, 21 November 1988 and Ian Jones, 'An Evaluation of the YTS', *Oxford Review of Economic Policy*, Vol. 4, No. 3, Autumn 1988, pp. 54–71. See also the review of a Leverhulme study by the University of Essex (*Guardian*, 2 December 1988) and of work by the National Institute of Economic and Social Research (*Financial Times*, 24 November 1988).

For the reaction of young people to unemployment and to the YTS, see the Youthaid Survey, *Nothing Like a Job* (1986); Dr Glynis Breakwell, 'Young People in and Out of Work', in *What Next* (ECSR, 1987); Susan McCrea, *Young and Jobless* (PSI, 1987).

For an account of cuts in benefit see the Youthaid Bulletin, May–June 1987, pp. 7–8, and the Unemployment Unit and Low Pay Unit, *Joint Briefing on the Social Security Bill 1987–88*. See also Youthaid, *Kicking Them While They're Down* (1987).

On the debate on compulsory training and its introduction by way of clause 4 of the Social Security Bill 1987/88, see the H.C. Deb., 21 June 1982, col. 23, in which Tebbit announced that the scheme would not be compulsory; and the debate on the social security reforms in which the question of compulsion was raised by Ralph Howells MP (Standing Committee B, 4 March 1986), cols. 543–59. For the SSAC's rejection of the loss of entitlement to supplementary benefits see the SSAC's Third Report, 1984, para. 6.19. Giving evidence to the Select Committee on Social Services, Tony Newton was clear on 26 June 1985 that there were no plans to remove benefit from sixteen- and seventeen-year-olds (Q. 200). For the official view of the arguments for compulsion, see the Department of Employment Press Notice, 23 October 1987.

See the evidence of the Social Security Consortium, 1986.

Lord Young, on *This Week, Next Week*, 3 May 1987.

For Youthaid's campaign to persuade Norman Fowler against the changes see Youthaid, letter to Norman Fowler on supplementary benefit, 26 June 1987; Fifth Report of the SSAC, 1986–7, Ch. 6 and Youthaid, *Kicking Them While They're Down* (1987).

Lop Pay Unit quoted in the *Independent*, 24 October 1987.

For current figures on homelessness in London, see Centrepoint Soho, *No Way Home: Homeless Young People in Central London* (June, 1988).

On the board and lodgings changes see NACAB, Board and Lodgings Briefing No. 2; West End Coordinated Voluntary Services, *Enforcing Vagrancy* (July 1986); Board and Lodgings Information Programme, *It's The Limit: An Exposé of Pricing in London's B & B Land* (1986); BLIP, *Disappeared: The Effects of the 1986 Board and Lodgings Regulations* (1987); Geoffrey Randall, Centrepoint Soho, *No Way Home*, op. cit.

See also the following *Hansard* references which set out the official changes in board and lodgings regulations: H.C. Deb., 29 November 1984, in which the 'increasing evidence of abuse' was referred to the SSAC; 21 March 1985, in which Tony Newton announced the government's revised proposals; the area limits and time limits for young people were debated on 2 and 4 April 1985; the new regulations to legitimise the changes found to be *ultra vires* in the courts were debated on 20 and 21 November 1985.

For the Prime Minister's assertions that there were enough YTS places and special provision for young people, see the exchange of letters between her and Neil Kinnock, 12 and 16 December 1988, and her response in the House of Commons to the suggestion that young people leaving care should also have some additional help, H.C. Deb., 6 December 1988, cols. 167–9.

On the impact of the proposals that young people under twenty-five should have lower rates of benefit, and on the subsequent modifications, see the SSAC Third Report, 1984, Evidence to the Review on Benefits for Children and Young People, paras. 6.18–6.20; and Fifth Report, 1986–7, Ch. 6 'Benefits for Students and Young People'. See also 'Counting the Cost', *New Society*, 6 September 1985, and 'Trapped by the Age Barrier', *Social Services Insight*, 30 January 1987, pp. 8–10.

For the campaign for a young householder's premium, see the Youthaid Bulletin, May–June 1987.

Chapter 5

On the current numbers of people in disablement and their characteristics, see the OPCS surveys, *Handicapped and Impaired*

People in Britain (1971), and *Disability in Great Britain*, Report 1 (September 1988); and SSAC, *Benefits for Disabled People: A Strategy for Change* (1988).

The case for reforming the present system of benefits for disabled people is given in the Disability Allowance, *Poverty and Disability: Breaking the Link* (1987). For assessments of how Conservative policies had affected disabled people, see the Disablement Income Group, *The Disastrous Years* (1981); Ros Franey, *Hard Times: The Tories and Disability* (Disability Alliance, 1983); *A Shameful Record: The Tories and Disability* (June 1987).

For the quotation from Hugh Rossi see the UK response to the International Year of the Disabled, 1982, reprinted in Disability Alliance, *Hard Times* (1983), p. 3.

For the conditions of eligibility for mobility allowance see the Disablement Income Group, 'Attendance Allowance and Mobility Allowance Reviewed', *Progress*, Vol. 14, Spring 1988, pp. 2–15.

For current numbers of people claiming disability benefits see H.C. Deb., 21 June 1988, cols. 547–8W.

For reforms to industrial injuries and statutory sick pay, see for example, White Paper, 'Reform of the Industrial Injuries Scheme', Cmnd 8402 (November 1981). See also the Consultative Document on the Industrial Injuries Scheme (DHSS, December 1985) and the response by the Industrial Injuries Advisory Council, February 1986; 'How to Add Insult to Injury', *Guardian*, 25 October 1986; and the debate on the scheme in the House of Commons on 20 May 1986, H.C. Deb., col. 223.

On statutory sick pay, see the Leicester Rights Centre, *Statutory Sick Pay: The Failure of Privatisation in Social Security*, and the University of Kent Nuffield Foundation Study, Press Notice, 31 October 1986. See also 'Sick Pay: Cheating the System', *New Society*, 3 July 1987.

For reaction of RADAR etc. on severe disability, see the exchange of letters between RADAR and the Secretary of State for Social Security dated 12 November 1983, 1 February 1984 and 19 February 1984, and Briefing of 22 February 1984.

For the way in which cause of injury determines rates of benefit, see Disability Alliance, *Poverty and Disability, Breaking the Link* (1987), pp. 22–3.

On the history of industrial injuries and the percentage basis for the award of benefit, see the Royal Commission on Civil Liberty and Compensation for Personal Injury (the Pearson Commission), para. 99.

For the parliamentary reaction to the cuts in invalidity benefit, see the second reading of Social Security (No. 2) Bill, H.C. Deb., 19 April 1980.

Calculations on the losses suffered up to 1983 are set out in Disability Alliance, *Hard Times* (1983), pp. 4–5.

For the cumulative losses in invalidity benefit up to 1987, see Disability Alliance, *A Shameful Record* (June 1987), p. 7.

For the announcement of the 'abatement' of 5 per cent in unemployment, sickness and invalidity benefit and the abolition of the earnings-related supplement, see Sir Geoffrey Howe's speech on his second budget, 26 March 1980, cols. 1459–61.

Figures for the losses on earnings-related supplement are set out in the Financial Memorandum to the Social Security (No. 2) Bill.

On the history of invalid care allowance, see White Paper, 'Social Security Provision for the Chronically Sick and Disabled', H.C. 276, 31 July 1974. See also the National Insurance Advisory Council, *Report on the Invalid Care Allowance Regulations* (1976), H.C. 271, 22 March 1976; and its report on the extension of the ICA to non-relatives, Cmnd 7905 (June 1980), and the Second Report of the Social Security Advisory Committee, 1982/83, which argued for the extension of the scheme to married women. See also the debate on the issue in the Social Security Bill 1984/85, 18 April 1985.

For the response of the disability organisations to the Fowler reforms, see Disability Alliance, *Reform of Social Security Response* (September 1985), and the DIG's response to the draft Social Fund Manual. See also chapters 59 and 60 of the *Disability Rights Handbook April 1987–April 1988*, which describes the parliamentary campaign to improve provision for the severely disabled under income support. For other responses to the Green Paper, see the Association of Directors of Social Services, 'The Disabling Effects of the Green Paper', *Community Care*, 27 June 1985. See the major debate on disabled people introduced by Alf Morris MP on 17 February 1987, H.C. Deb., col. 788. On the issue of a higher rate of benefit for the severely disabled, see Tony Newton's evidence to the Social Services Select Committee (H.C. 451), 26 June 1985, and the final report, paras. 36–7; see also SSAC Fourth Report, para. 3.15. For the government's proposals see H.C. Deb., 23 July 1986, cols. 399–400; and the DHSS Press Notice, 11 December 1986.

On the creation of the Independent Living Foundation, see DHSS Press Notice, 9 February 1988, and the *Independent*, 10 February 1988 and the Disability Rights Bulletin, Summer 1988.

For the surveys on disabled people see NACAB, *Losers and Gainers* (March 1988); and the *Scotsman*, 3 March 1988. For the debate on the impact of the changes on disabled people, see Hansard, 13 April 1988, cols. 173–180 and the *Daily Mirror*, 10–15 April.

For the minister's response in advance of the OPCS study, see the *Independent*, 29 July 1988 and for an impact study on the changes, see *Disability Rights Handbook*, April 1989–April 1990.

Chapter 6

For a concise account of the history of the old age pension, see M. Bruce, *The Coming of the Welfare State* (Batsford, 1968), chapter 5 'The Turning Point: Social Reform 1905–14', pp. 154–227.

Estimates for the increase in the value of pensioners' incomes and the range of incomes are based on the Family Expenditure Survey 1986. See also the *Observer*, 6 November 1988, and *Economic Trends* (July 1987). Figures on the estimated contribution from SERPS are set out in Retirement Pensions by Annual Statistical Enquiry, Sept 1988. Table RP11; Hansard, 13 December 1988 and 11 April 1989. On pensioners' incomes in general, see *Employment Gazette*, May 1987, p. 246, and June 1988, p. 233. For European comparisons, see H.C. Deb., 7 February 1985, col. 685W. For those on supplementary benefit and not claiming, see H.C. Deb., 30 October 1986, col. 232W.

For morbidity and mortality figures, see the King's Fund *et al.*, *Promoting Health Among Elderly People* (1988).

The figures for the numbers of pensioners, based on Government Actuary calculations, were reprinted in the Green Paper, para. 5.2.

Calculations on losses caused by the break with earnings have been calculated by the House of Commons Library. See also

H.C. Deb., 21 October 1988, col. 1031; on European comparisons see H.C. Deb., 19 March 1985 and the ESSPROS Social Protection Eurostate 2 86 Series F; on the value of the pension, see House of Commons Research Note, 'The Value of the Pension Since 1974', No. 347 (1987).

The Select Committee on the Age of Retirement took considerable evidence on the implications of changing the age of retirement. See the full report and appendices, H.C. 26 I and II (October 1982).

See SSAC Second Report, 1982–3, para. 6, and Fourth Report, 1985, para. 2.12.

On the early exchanges on the costs of SERPS see the Government Actuary's Quinquennial Review 1982 (H.C. 451) updated in DHSS, *Population, Pension Costs and Pensioner Incomes* (June 1984). In 1982 the SSAC thought these fears were misplaced. Cf. its Second Report for 1982–3, para. 6.6.

Figures on occupational pensions are from the Seventh Report of the Government Actuary's Department, p. 6.

For the 'pensions time bomb', see *The Times*, 25 January 1984.

On the origins of SERPS see 'Better Pensions', Cmnd 5713 (September 1974). On the background to abolition, see Tessa Blackstone and William Plowden, *Inside the Think Tank* (Heinemann, 1988), pp. 127–8.

For the projected figures and costs, see the Government Actuary's Report on the Social Security Bill 1986, Cmnd 9711 (January 1986), pp. 14–22. Full argument set out by the SSAC's Third Report, 1984, Ch. 3 and Fourth Report, 1985, paras. 2.5–2.10, 'The abolition of SERPs. Is the case proven?'

For the Bernard Benjamin quotation see the Independent Pensions Research Group, *Stealing our Future* (January 1986), p. 7.

See the Union Coalition for Social Security, Press Release, 17 February 1986. Among those who protested against the abolition of SERPS were: Legal and General, the National Consumer Council, the National Council for Voluntary Organisations, the Society of Civil and Public Servants, Age Concern, EOC, the Tory Reform Group and the TUC.

For the debate on the advice of the Government Actuary, see his letter in the *Guardian*, 17 June 1985. See also 'Fowler's SERPS Plans Rejected by Advisers', *Financial Times*, 15 June 1985; 'Fowler

Ignored Expert Advice to Keep SERPS', *Guardian*, 13 June 1985; *Pensions Today*, October 1985; 'Researchers Doubt SERPS Burden', *Financial Times*, 1 July 1985; 'Should We Afford SERPS', *New Society*, 12 July 1985; 'Pensions: Voyage to the Unknown', *Observer*, 28 July 1985; 'Concern at Plan to End SERPS', *Financial Times*, 14 September 1985; 'Actuaries and Voluntary Groups Oppose Plan to Abolish SERPS', *Financial Times*, 16 September 1985, 'Government Actuary "Did not Mislead" on Pensions', *Financial Times*, 22 October 1985.

Sir Douglas Wass, former Permanent Secretary of the Treasury, 'Pensions Will Still Have to be Paid For', *Observer*, 18 August 1985.

For reaction to the White Paper, see, for example, Independent Pensions Research Group, *Stealing Our Future* (January 1986), and the Union Coalition on Social Security, 17 February 1986 and the SSAC's Fifth Report, 1986–7, para. 2.6.

On the current value of SERPS, see H.C. Deb., 12 January 1987, col. 124.

On the long-term costs of pensions, see the Government Actuary's Quinquennial Review 1982 (H.C. 451) updated in DHSS, *Population, Pension Costs and Pensioner Incomes* (June 1984). In 1982 the Social Security Advisory Committee thought these fears were misplaced: cf. its report for 1982, para. 6.6.

On the overall impact of recent government policies on elderly people, see Help the Aged, *Pensioned Off* (October 1988).

Chapter 7

For information on changes in the employment count, see various articles in the *Employment Gazette*, e.g. October 1986, p. 422, November 1986, pp. 462–3, and relevant bulletins from the Unemployment Unit, e.g. Winter 1986, and its *Statistical Briefing Supplement* (June 1988). On this and other general matters concerning the unemployed, see David Taylor, 'Living With Unemployment', chapter 8 in Alan Walker and Carol Walker (eds.), *The Growing Divide* (CPAG, June 1987).

The quotation from Richard Berthoud is from Policy Studies Institute, *Selective Social Security*, (1986), p. 2, quoted in 'Living With Unemployment'.

The report by Sir Derek Rayner is *Payments of Benefits to*

Unemployed People (1981), a joint publication by the DHSS and DoE. Prof. A. B. Atkinson (LSE) and J. Micklewright (Queen Mary College, London), *Turning The Screw; Benefits For The Unemployed 1979–1988* is an excellent résumé of changes in benefits for the unemployed, together with estimated costings.

For more information and the source of the estimates of the effects of the tightening of the contribution qualifications for unemployment benefit see the report of Standing Committee E on the Social Security Bill, 3 December 1987.

For a full account of the disqualification rules and their effects see Dominic Byrne and John Jacobs, *Disqualified From Benefit* (Low Pay Unit, February 1988). For the official guidance, see the *Adjudication Officers' Guide*, Vol. 10.

The quotation from Michael Portillo comes from his reply, dated 29 February 1988, to the letter from the Director of NACAB.

For further information about the operation of the disqualification rules and the arguments about the changes to thirteen and twenty-six weeks, see the report of Standing Committee B on the Social Security Bill, Wednesday 30 April 1986, and the report in *Hansard* of the debate to approve the draft statutory instruments on 1 March 1988 respectively.

The DoE circulars on 'avilability testing' are LO CODE 7 CIRC 26, 6 October 1986, and LO CODE 7 CIRC 26 (Rev.), December 1987. These contain an appendix outlining action to be taken by administrative officers in response to claimants' answers to specific questions. For discussions of the operation of the tests, see the reports in *Hansard* of the statement by Kenneth Clarke, Minister for Employment, on 28 October 1986, and the adjournment debate on 22 July 1987. Figures in the text are taken from these reports.

For discussion of fraud control, see Geoffrey Beltram, *Testing The Safety Net*, Occasional Papers on Social Administration No. 74 (Bedford Square Press, 1984), pp. 100–8, and Roger Smith, 'Who's Fiddling?; Fraud and Abuse', chapter 9 in Sue Ward (ed.), *DHSS in Crisis* (CPAG, 1985).

The account of the work of the Regional Fraud Squad's activities at Hove, and the written statement by the claimant were provided by Simon Montgomery, who was working in the Hove office at the time.

For an account of Operation Major, see *Fraud and Operation Major: An Assessment* (CHAR, 1983).

On low pay, see *Britain Can't Afford Low Pay* (Low Pay Unit, October 1988). On the deterioration of wages and conditions of employment, see Dominic Byrne, 'Rich and Poor; The Growing Divide', chapter 4 in *The Growing Divide*, op. cit.

Chapter 8

The opening quotation is from the *Annual Report of the Supplementary Benefits Commission* (1978), Cmnd 7725, para. 1.4. For a full discussion of the issue of adequacy of benefits, see chapter 8 of the SSAC's Sixth Report, 1988.

Beveridge's calculations of the scale rates are contained in his report, *Social Insurance and Allied Services* (HMSO 1942, reprinted 1966), pp. 76–90.

The evidence about what has happened to benefit rates since the Beveridge Report comes from Green Paper, 'Reform of Social Security', Vol. 3, Fig. 1.1, p. 7, and from David Piachaud, 'The Growth of Poverty', chapter 3 in A. and C. Walker (eds.), *The Growing Divide* (CPAG, 1987).

The regulation quoted which sets out what the scale rates are deemed to cover is regulation 4(1) of the Supplementary Benefit (Requirements) Regulations. On the change to income support there was no longer any need to define what the rates were to cover since additional extras and single payments to meet exceptional needs were abolished, thus removing the need to define the baseline against which payments could be designated as 'additional' or 'exceptional'; there is therefore no current statement of what income support payments are deemed to cover.

The work of Prof. Jonathan Bradshaw and Jane Morgan is published as *Budgeting on Benefits* (Centre for Family Policy Studies, 1987), and as an article under the same name in *New Society*, 6 March 1987, pp. 17–19. There is also an article by them and Deborah Mitchell, 'Evaluating Adequacy; The Potential of Budget Standards', *Journal of Social Policy*, April 1987, Vol. 16 Part Two, pp. 165–81, which discusses the value of this approach.

The reported research by the Policy Studies Institute is Richard Berthoud's *The Reform of Supplementary Benefit* (PSI, 1984). Both the passages quoted are on p. H4 of the Working Papers Summary of Findings (emphasis added). The quotation from Geoffrey Beltram's book is in *Testing the Safety Net*, Occasional Papers On Social Administration No. 74 (Bedford Square Press, 1984), p. 125. His chapter 8 deals extensively with the issue of adequacy of benefits. The J. Mack and S. Lansley book is *Poor Britain* (Allen & Unwin, 1985).

The quotation from the Green Paper dismissing the need to consider the adequacy of benefits is in Vol. 2, para. 2.50.

Chapter 9

The conditions under which claimants could be given a single payment to meet exceptional needs not covered by the weekly supplementary benefit payment are set out in the Supplementary Benefit (Single Payments) Regulations 1981, as subsequently amended. Regulations 4, 6, 28 and 30, referred to explicitly in this chapter, can be found in *Supplementary Benefit and Family Income Supplement: The Legislation* (Sweet and Maxwell, latest edn 1987). This contains an excellent commentary by John Mesher, barrister and Reader in Law at Sheffield University, which provides many useful interpretations of the regulations taken mostly from the decisions of the social security commissioners. All the regulations have now been superseded by the social fund.

Another excellent source of comment on these and all other social security law and regulations is the *Welfare Rights Bulletin*, published by CPAG.

The examples in the chapter are all taken from the published decisions of the social security commissioners; they are identified by their numbers, given below. In the order in which they appear in the text they are: R(SB) 19/82 (prohibition on the payment of damages); R(SB) 47/83 (burst water tank); R(SB) 21/84 (raincoat, dress and shoes); R(SB) 10/82 (borrowed overcoat); R(SB) 24/83 (borrowed bed, wardrobe and electric fire); CSB 568/81 (gas fire not the same as coal fire); R(SB) 19/82 (carpet not the same as PVC); R(SB) 33/84 (wellingtons not the same as shoes); R(SB) 26/83 (vandalised flat); R(SB) 15/81 (claimants may not give presents); R(SB) 7/82 (boots falling to pieces); R(SB) 36/83 (reimbursement for bedclothes); R(SB) 12/85 (widow's decorating materials); CSB 38/81 and R(SB) 9/82 (regulation 30 not an absolute discretion); R(SB) 5/81 ('shoes that let in water. . .'); R(SB) 2/82 (defective shoes); R(SB) 9/82 ('other available means must be proved'); CSB 113/1985 (unable to keep up payments); R(SB) 4/86 (payment for safety clothing). The report of the mother's claim for repairs to the broken fence is in *Welfare Rights Bulletin*, No. 57, p. 5.

For an account of the effects of the August 1986 cuts, see Ruth Cohen and Maryrose Tarpey (eds.) *Single Payments: The Disappearing Safety Net* (CPAG, February 1988). The quotation about the young couple from the North-East is taken from this report, p. 15, as are the examples of the application of regulation 30, pp. 25–6. For further evidence of the effects of the cuts, see Gill and John Stewart, *The Beginning Of The End?* (National Welfare Rights Officers Group, 1988).

For the government's arguments for the August 1986 cuts in single payments and the response of the SSAC ('We received a large number of representations, almost all of which were extremely critical of the government's proposals'), see 'The Supplementary Benefit (Miscellaneous Amendments) Regulations 1986 etc.', Cmnd 9836 (HMSO, July 1986). The reference to regulation 30 being a 'significant safety net' is in para. 59.

Chapter 10

The quotation at the head of the chapter is from Janet Allbeson and Roger Smith, *We Don't Give Clothing Grants Any More* (CPAG, 1984), p. 54, which is an account of the cuts in clothing grants and their effects on claimants. The figures relating to the numbers of single payments are quoted on p. 53. The quotation about claimants' juggling 'food, fuel, clothing and rent' is on p. 56; that from the grants officer of the FWA is on p. 55.

The report by the DHSS review team is *Social Assistance: A Review of the Supplementary Benefits Scheme in Great Britain* (DHSS, July 1978). Chapter 5 deals with the adequacy of the scale rates to meet basic needs, and the quotation comes from para. 5.7. Chapter 9 deals specifically with the problem of single payments (then called 'exceptional needs payments'); the comment that it would not be possible to discontinue the payments without causing hardship is from para. 9.40.

The quotation from Geoffrey Beltram is from *Testing the Safety Net*, op. cit., p. 119.

The regulation governing single payments for clothing is regulation 4 of the single payments regulations. The main ones relating to furniture discussed here are regulations 9, 10 (and later 10a) and 13.

The comment from the commissioner about the meaning of abnormal rate of growth is quoted in *Welfare Rights Bulletin* No. 56, pp. 5–6.

The commissioner's decision relating to the underwear, two bras and a jumper is R(SB) 6/81; those relating to the clothes for a job interview are R(SB) 21/84 and C(SSB) 67/85. The decision setting out the complexities of the regulations is R(SB) 2/82. As always, John Mesher provides an excellent commentary on them in *Supplementary Benefit and Family Income Supplement: The Legislation*, op. cit., and the quotation from him is taken from p. 274 of the 1986 edition.

The report of the Social Security Policy Inspectorate is *Single Payments For Furniture* (SSPI, 1985). The figures relating to the number of wrong decisions and high success rate of appeals are from para. 1.37 and 1.38. The statement that the grants had been 'properly spent' is in para. 4.10. The three quotations used from the report are from paras. 4.5, 4.6 and 4.8.

The government's case for the cuts in August 1986, and the response of the SSAC, are contained in 'The Supplementary Benefit (Miscellaneous Amendments) Regulations 1986 etc.', Cmnd 9836, op. cit., from p. 9 of which the figures are taken, as are the quotations at the end of the chapter (see below).

The effects of the cuts are graphically documented in Cohen and Tarpey (eds.), *Single Payments: The Disappearing Safety Net*, op. cit., from where the quotations and examples are taken. Evidence of the scale of the cuts is on p. 6; the example about the old Liverpudlian woman is on p. 9; evidence about the cookers is on p. 32; the potentially 'exploding' cooker is on p. 40; the quotation from the local authority is on p. 26. Evidence about the effects of the maternity cuts is in chapter 6. The case of the stolen pushchair is on p. 40, and the two final quotations come from p. 12 and p. 67.

(For a similar account of the effects of the cuts see also G. and J. Stewart, *The Beginning of the End?*, op. cit.).

Comments by the SSAC are from Cmnd 9836 (see above); the comment that the representations were 'critical' is from p. 33; the comment that carpets and curtains would be regarded as essential is from p. 39, and the final long quotation is from p. 45.

Chapter 11

For the report of the 1978 review team see DHSS, *Social Assistance* (July 1978). The quotation about the code of practice is in para. 3.15.

The discussion in the Green Paper on the social fund can be found at paras. 2.60 *et seq.* and 2.96 *et seq.*

For brief details of the analysis of the responses of the major organisations to the Green Paper in general, including the social fund, see *Reform of Social Security; A Checklist of the Responses of 60 Key Organisations*, compiled for CPAG by Angela Hadjipateras (November 1985).

The quotation from the draft Social Fund Manual about the need not to exceed the budget is from para. 4016. Other paras. used are 4051 (prohibition on keeping a waiting list); 3002 (the possibility of having the need met by someone else); and 6050 (the quotation about other possible sources of help). The restatement of this in the revised Social Fund Manual is at para. 4058. The prohibition on a reapplication within six months is in the Secretary of State's Direction No. 7, and the exclusion of heating costs and deposits are in the Secretary of State's Directions No. 12 and 23; these directions are contained in the Social Fund Manual, published by the DSS.

The quotation from *Of Little Benefit: An Update* (Social Security Consortium, December 1987), is from p. 18.

The quotations from the National Council for Voluntary Organisations are from *The Future of Our Welfare State* (September 1985), pp. 3 and 4.

The quotations from NACAB are from p. 41 ('a step backwards', and the recommendation that the proposals be withdrawn) and p. 34 ('We find it totally unacceptable . . .') of *Reform of Social Security: Programme for Change* (NACAB, September 1985).

The quotation from the Disability Alliance is taken from Reform of Social Security: Response (Disability Alliance, September 1985).

The quotations from Ruth Lister and Berth Lakhani, *A Great Retreat From Fairness* (CPAG, May 1987) are taken from pp. 2 and 13.

For the full comments of the SSAC see *The Draft Social Fund Manual: Report by the SSAC* (June 1987). The quotations are taken from paras. 2, 4 and 45.

The quotation from the SCPS is taken from a letter sent by the union to Norman Fowler dated 15 October 1985.

The quotation about 'determined advocacy' is from *Social Fund: Position Statement and Practice Guide* (ACC and AMA, January 1988), p. 17.

For the views of the Bishop of Southwark see the *Guardian*, 9 April 1988; for those of the Archbishop of Liverpool see the *Guardian*, 16 April 1988, and the letter from the Bishop of Manchester was published on 30 March 1988. For the response of the Board for Social Responsibility of the General Synod of the Church of England see its report entitled *Reform of Social Security* (August 1985). The quotation is from para. 9. The debate in the House of Lords was on 30 June 1986.

The quotations from the speech by Nicholas Scott are taken from his address to the AGM of the North Cornwall Conservative Association, 25 March 1988.

Details of the allocation of the social fund budget to DHSS local offices were given in a written answer in *Hansard* on 4 November 1987, cols. 764 *et seq.*

The report by Bill Taylor of the details of the low take-up was given in the *Guardian*, 14 November 1988, p. 4, which also reported the comments of Richard Silburn about those most affected by the cuts.

The parliamentary answer comparing the first three months of the fund with the similar period a year before is in *Hansard*, 18 July 1988, col. 485.

The quotation from Pat Roberts is taken from 'Simplicity Itself . . .', in *Fundamentals*, a *Community Care* Supplement, 21 July 1988.

Chapter 12

The quotations at the head of the chapter are taken from:

(1) *Social Work Today*, 19 September 1978.

(2) NACAB, *Monitoring of the New Supplementary Benefits Scheme; 1982 Exercise*, p. 34.

(3) NACAB, *Behind The Counter; DHSS Local Offices*, June 1984, para. 26.

(4) Janet Allbeson and Roger Smith, *We Don't Give Clothing Grants Any More* (CPAG, May 1984), p. 23.

(5) CPSA and SCPS, *DHSS Crisis Programme* (December 1986), para. 1.

(6) National Audit Office, *DHSS: Quality of Service to the Public at Local Offices* (April 1988), para. 5.

The quotation that in some places the service is 'absolutely unacceptable' comes from *The Business of Service*, the Report of the Regional Organisation Scrutiny (known after its chairperson as the Moodie Report) (DHSS, May 1988), p. 1.

The quotation from the NAO report (see 6 above) is from para. 3.

The quotations from *Out of Service* (see 8 above) are from pp. 4, 31 and 34 respectively; *Out of Service*, Greater London CABx, 1986.

The example from the Midlands is taken from a return to the NACAB information retrieval section.

The quotation about Alfie Stranks is from the *Guardian*, 6 May 1988, p. 5.

The example about the incorrect mortgage entitlement is from a return to NACAB information retrieval section.

The information about the poor standards of adjudication is taken from the *Annual Report of the Chief Adjudication Officer* for 1984–5 and following years (DHSS). The quotation about the unsatisfactory standard is in para. 3.8 of the report for 1984–5; the information about incorrect adjudications is in App. 8, and the information about reviews is in para. 3.14 and App. 7, para. 99.

The quotation from J. J. Clarke is on p. 584.

The quotation from the Beveridge Report is from para. 369.

Information about the cuts in the numbers of staff in the DHSS comes from SCPS, *Jobs Blueprint: The Alternative Operational Strategy* (1987), p. 8, as does the quotation about the effects of the increased workload.

The quotation from the Chief Adjudication Officer's report is from App. 12, para. 1 (1984–5).

The quotation about recruitment and retention from the *Business of Service*, op. cit., is from para. 30, and the information about the costs of staff turnover is from para. 31.

The quotation from *Social Security Operational Strategy* (DHSS, 1982) is from para. 125, and the forecast of staff cuts from para. 106.

The quotation from NUCPS and CPSA is from their joint document, *Trade Union Response to Interim Report of the Regional Scrutiny* (February 1988), p. 5.

For the alternative operational strategy and claimants' charter see *Jobs Blueprint*, op. cit.

Conclusion

Monitoring of the social security changes is being undertaken by several bodies, including the Nottingham Benefits Research Unit, the Department of Social Administration at Oxford, and the Social Services Select Committee. Some useful published references include the following:

For a list of changes to the Social Security Act see Hansard 3 July 1989, c.10.

On the impact on young people, see the Scottish Council for the Single Homeless, *Lossline*, (April 1991); Martin Fairclough, *From Government Claims to Real Effects of the 1986 Social Security Act. A study of the experience of Bristol Claimants and Welfare Rights*, (Bristol, 1989); Association of County Councils, *No Benefits for Barry* (April 1989).

On unemployment benefit errors, see *30th Report of the Committee of Public Accounts*.

On the Social Fund, see *Monitoring the Social Fund: One Year On*, Interim Report of the SSAC, (April 1989); and the Annual Report on the *Social Fund 1988–1989*. For comment, see the *Guardian*, 17 July 1989.

Notes and Sources

On the impact of the poll tax see CPAG, *A Charge on the Community: The Poll Tax Benefits and the Poor* (1989).

On the living standards of poor people, see Richard Berthoud (PSI), *Crime, Debt and Poverty* (1989); the Low Pay Unit, *Ten Years On: The Poor Decade* (1989); and the Social Services Select Committee, *Public Expenditure on Social Security*, HC 315, 12 April 1989.

Index

319

Index

capital limits: housing benefit, 34, 36, 38, 140–1; supplementary benefit, 42; unemployment benefit, 151

carers, 105–6, 110

carpets, single payments, 199–200

Castle, Barbara, 127

Central London Social Security Advisers, 87

Central Policy Review Staff (CPRS), 9, 50, 128–9

Centre for Policy Studies, 133

Centrepoint Night Shelter, 86, 87, 88–9

Charing Cross, 268

charities, 208, 246

Chief Adjudication Officer, 270–1, 274–5

child benefit, 3; advantages of, 52–3; Fowler review, 15–16; frozen, 54, 59, 282–4; future of, 58–9; government promises, 56–8; Green Paper, 19, 20, 22, 55–6; increases below inflation level, 6–7, 55; opposition to, 54–5

Child Poverty Action Group (CPAG), 56, 189; on family credit, 60; on family premium, 66, 67; and the Fowler review, 15, 39–40; and quality of service, 263, 271; and single payments, 212, 216–17, 232, 234, 235–6; and the social fund, 243, 249, 251–2; survey of supplementary benefit, 184

children: disabled, 110; Fowler review, 10, 14, 15; as individual luxury, 51; living standards on supplementary benefit, 182–5; rates of supplementary benefit, 67

Children and Young Persons Act, 208

Church of England, 20, 258

churches, and the social fund, 248, 257–8

Churchill, Sir Winston, 292

Citizens' Advice Bureaux (CABx): on the disqualification rules, 153, 154–5, 161; and quality of service, 263, 266–70, 285; and single payments, 211, 232, 234; and the social fund, 250–1

citizenship rights, 92

Civil and Public Servants Association (CPSA), 255, 263, 278

Clarke, J. J., 272

clothes: single payments, 209–10, 214–19, 235; supplementary benefit levels, 182–3, 185

Collins, Basil, 14

Community Care, 261

community charge *see* poll tax

Community Programme, 71

computers, 276–9

Confederation of British Industry (CBI), 20, 134

Conservative Manifestos: *1979*, 124; *1983*, 9–10, 125, 129; *1987*, 56, 58, 79, 283, 284

Conservative Party Conference (1985), 247

Conservative Political Centre, 171, 183

Conservative Research Department, 99

Index

Conservative Womens'
Conference (1986), 146
Cook, Robin, 30, 34, 38, 117, 284
cookers, single payments, 231–3
Council on Tribunals, 252–4
Court of Appeal, 219
Court Report, 280
Coventry, 268
Crewe, 162
criminal injuries compensation,
96
crisis loans, 163, 241, 246, 261
Crossman, Richard, 3, 127
Currie, Edwina, 19

death grant, 10, 17
debt, and single payments,
194–6, 208–9
'decency threshold', 51–2, 169
Department of Employment,
80, 148, 155, 159, 165–7, 270,
276
'dependency', 291
Department of Health and
Social Security (DHSS): A
Code, 189; benefits for young
people, 79–80; board and
lodgings payments, 83, 84–7;
and child benefit, 55, 58;
clothing grants, 214–19;
Fowler reviews, 14–16; fraud
control, 164–9; great debate
on social security, 10; and
homelessness, 88–9; housing
benefit, 39; Independent
Living Foundation, 113;
maternity benefits, 69; and
mortgage interest payments,
35; privatisation of sickness
benefit, 105; quality of
service, 263–9; and the
Rayner review, 148; reform

of supplementary benefit,
43–4; single payments,
190–1, 253; social fund,
255–6; and supplementary
benefit levels, 185–6
Department of Social Security
(DSS), 241–6
diet, special needs payments,
41, 108
Disability Alliance, 101, 105,
108, 111, 112, 113, 249, 251
disabled: additional benefits,
108–10; benefits, 95–8;
carers, 105–6, 110;
Conservative manifesto
promises, 95; housing benefit,
114–16; Independent Living
Foundation, 113, 118;
introduction of severe
disablement allowance,
106–7; losers and gainers,
112, 113–19; numbers of, 94,
97; privatisation of sickness
benefit, 103–5; reform of
benefits, 99–103; review of
benefits, 10, 107–12; special
needs payments, 41
disablement benefit, 102–3
Disablement Income Group
(DIG), 107, 112, 113
discretionary payments, single
payments, 205–13
dismissal, unfair, 171
Disqualified From Benefit, 153
Donnison, David, 177, 179, 183,
184, 186, 189, 263
Drake, Jacqueline, 106
Dunwoody, Gwynneth, 161

earnings, link with long-term
benefits and pensions cut, 7–8,
99, 100, 121, 123, 124–5, 136

Index

'earnings-disregard', 67–8

earnings-related benefits and pensions, 3, 99–100, 101, 126, 127

Edinburgh, 39

education, 81

Eliot, T. S., 158

emergency payments, 42

Employment Act (1988), 79, 156–7

employment protection, 171

Employment Training (ET), 75, 156–7, 171

Enforcing Vagrancy, 85–6

'enterprise culture', 169–72, 271

Epsom, 259

Equal Opportunities Commission (EOC), 52, 60, 66–7, 69, 106, 137

European Commission, 71

European Communities Council Directives, 106

European Court, 106

European Decency Threshold, 51–2

European Economic Community, 72

evicted tenants, 222–3

Exeter, 259

Factories Act, 153

Fair Wages Resolution, 170

family: political significance, 50–1, 52–3; supplementary benefit changes, 66–73

family credit, 71; aims, 59–60; gainers and losers, 48, 62–5; Green Paper, 17, 19, 21, 22; and housing benefit, 36–7;

payment mechanisms, 60–1; Social Security Act, 27; take-up rate, 70, 283–4, 287; taper, 61

Family Expenditure Survey (1985), 146

Family Finances Survey, 182

family income supplement (FIS), 3, 19, 54, 59, 60

family premium, 66

Family Service Units, 184

Family Welfare Association, 216–17

Field, Frank, 23

Financial Times, 19–20, 283

Finchley, 26

Finer Report, 280

First World War, 92

food, supplementary benefit levels, 182

Fowler, Norman: attempted abolition of SERPS, 129; and child benefit, 53, 55; cuts in single payments, 236; and family credit, 60–1; and housing benefit, 31; and 'open government', 247, 290, 291; and the responses to the social fund, 258; social security reviews, 10–16, 22–3, 24; supplementary benefit levels, 187; treatment of disabled, 107; treatment of unemployed, 146–7, 149, 156, 157

France, 72, 123

fraud control, unemployed, 164–9

'freedom', 291

funeral grants, 241, 244

furniture, single payments, 219–21, 223–33

322

Index

general elections: June 1983,
9–10, 125; May 1987, 31, 56,
283
Glasgow, 140, 259
Godden, Felicity, 117
Government Actuary, 14, 20,
131, 132, 138
graduated contribution pension
scheme, 127
A Great Retreat From Fairness,
251–2
Greece, 123
Green Paper on the reform of
Social Security (1985); aims,
16–19; and child benefit,
55–6; on disability benefits,
108–10; disregard of equal
rights for women, 71; on
maternity benefits, 69; and
'open government', 247;
pensions policy, 123, 125–6;
privatisation of sickness
benefit, 104; proposed
abolition of SERPS, 121,
129–31, 133; responses to,
19–21; social fund proposals,
66–7, 243, 250;
supplementary benefit levels,
187; widow's benefits, 137–8;
on young people, 89
Guardian, 9, 14–15, 26, 167,
258, 268–9
Guildford, 259

Hambro Life, 14
Hansard, 262
Harris, Amelia, 94, 98
Hayhoe, Barney, 14
Health and Social Security Bill
(1983), 107
Health Visitors Association,
237

heating: single payments,
231–2; and the social fund,
245, 250; special needs
payments, 41, 108
Hencke, David, 14–15
High Court, 84, 197
homelessness, young people,
82–9
House of Commons:
administration of
supplementary benefit,
189–90, 212–13; and child
benefit, 56–8; and disability
benefits, 99; and family credit,
60, 62; and Fowler's 'open
government', 247–8; and
homelessness, 88; responses
to the social fund, 258; and
the review of disability
benefits, 114, 117; Social
Security Bill, 22; and young
people's benefits, 91, 93
House of Lords, 22, 31, 61, 111,
248, 258
household expenses, single
payments, 219–33
housewives, non-contributory
invalidity pension, 106
Housing Act (1988), 40
housing benefit: adjustments,
38–9; board and lodgings
payments, 82–9; capital limit,
34, 36, 38, 140–1, cuts in, 24;
and the disabled, 114–16;
effects of changes, 35–8;
further cuts, 40; gainers and
losers, 48; Green Paper, 10,
17, 18–19, 21, 22;
introduction of, 8; levels,
29–30; pensioners, 121,
139–43; and rates, 29–32, 39;
review of, 27–30; and

323

Index

Index

Leeds, 259
Letchworth CAB, 85
life expectancy, 122–3
Lister, Ruth, 245
Living From Hand to Mouth, 184
living standards, 11–12, 177–88
loans *see* social fund
local authorities: charges to disabled, 101; and housing benefit, 34
Local Government of the United Kingdom, 272
London: board and lodgings payments, 84; homelessness, 86, 87, 88–9; quality of service, 264, 266–7, 277; social fund, 259
London Weekend Television, 186
lone-parent premium, 66
low pay, 169–71
Low Pay Unit, 76, 81, 153, 155, 169, 249
Lynes, Tony, 67

McAvoy, Thomas, 141–2
Mack, J., 186–7, 188
Major, John, 56, 94, 252, 258
Manchester City Council, 38
Manpower Services Commission (MSC), 78
maternity allowance, 69
maternity benefit, 10, 69–70, 100
maternity grant, 17, 69, 70; single payments, 233–5, 237; social fund, 241, 244
maternity rights, 102
Mates, Michael, 33
Meacher, Michael, 152, 248
means tests: Green Paper, 17, 20; housing benefit, 28–9, 34; shift towards, 70–1, 273

Mesher, John, 222–3
Micklewright, J., 148–50
Middlesbrough, 259
milk, free, 60
Minchell, 168
Mind, 249
Mirror, 117
mobility allowance, 4, 96, 97, 98, 100
Monday Club, 19–20, 31, 243, 259
Moore, John, 49, 183, 286; and child benefit, 57, 58, 283; cuts in single payments, 236; and disability benefits, 117, 119; on the 'enterprise culture', 171–2; and family credit, 61–2; housing benefit adjustments, 38–9; social fund proposals, 259; Social Security Bill, 23
Morgan, Jane, 181–2
mortgages: interest payments, 18, 35, 149, 181; tax relief, 34–5
Mother and Baby, 234

NALGO, 256
National Association of Citizens' Advice Bureaux (NACAB): and the disqualification rules, 153, 155; on housing benefit reforms, 44–5; on income support, 47–8; and quality of service, 263, 266, 271, 285; and single payments, 232; and the social fund, 249, 250–1; survey of disabled benefits, 114; on treatment of young people, 85, 92; widow's benefits, 138

325

Index

National Association of Probation Officers, 256
National Audit Office (NAO), 264–6, 275–6
National Consumer Council, 20
National Council for One Parent Families, 249
National Council of Voluntary Organisations (NCVO), 249, 250
National Health Service (NHS), 52
national insurance, 101–2, 292–3
National Superannuation and Social Insurance, 98
National Union of Civil and Public Servants (NUCPS), 278
New Earnings Survey, 169–70
New Society, 10, 129
New Workers' Scheme, 171
New York Times, 128
Newcastle, 259, 276
Newton, Tony, 14, 86–7, 90, 156, 248
Newton Abbot, 162–3
No Benefit, 266
non-contributory invalidity pension (NCIP), 98, 106
North Lambeth, 267–8
Nottingham University, 43, 46, 260
nursing homes, 83

Observer, 21, 73, 144
occupational pensions, 126–7, 130, 133–5
Occupational Pensions Scheme Joint Working Group, 14
Of Little Benefit, 249
Office of Population Censuses and Surveys (OPCS), 94, 114, 119, 122, 286
Old Age Pensions Act (1908), 120
Ombudsman, 253
one-parent benefit, 3
'open government', 247–8, 290, 291
Operation Major, 168
Orme, Stan, 7–8
Out of Service, 266
Oxford University, Department of Social and Administrative Studies, 46, 47

Paddington, 269
Parry Roberts, T. G., 14
part-time workers, and supplementary benefit reforms, 45
Peacock, Alan, 14
pensioners: housing benefit, 121, 139–43; income, 122; income support, 122; living standards, 284; numbers of, 123; quality of service, 265; special premiums, 41; supplementary benefit, 44–5, 46–7, 137; women, 51
pensions: earnings-related, 126, 127; Fowler review, 10, 14; Green Paper, 20, 21; introduction of, 120–1; occupational, 126–7, 130, 133–5; personal, 133–5; reform of SERPS, 126–37; relation to average earnings, 123; value of, 124–6
personal pensions, 133–5
Piachaud, David, 67, 180
Pitt, William, 53
Plowden, William, 128–9

326

Index

Index

parent premium, 66;
opposition to, 21–2; pensions
policy, 126; proposals, 17,
31–2; reform of SERPS,
134–5; on young people, 90
widowed mother's allowance,
138
widows: benefits, 137–8;
SERPS, 127–8
widow's allowance, 137
widow's pension, 138
Williams, Shirley, 77
Wilton Park conference, 14–15
Wolfson, Brian, 157
women: as carers, 105–6; causes
of poverty, 51–2; disabled, 94,
97; disqualification from
unemployment benefit, 153;
equal rights, 71; life
expectancy, 123; maternity
benefits, 69–70; SERPS,
127–8, 134; supplementary
benefit changes, 66–73;
widow's benefits, 137–8

Women's National Commission,
60
'workfare', 157
workhouses, 120, 147, 271–2
Worlock, Derek, Archbishop of
Liverpool, 258
Worthing, 259
WRVS, 208

Young, Sir George, 54
Young, Jimmy, 57
Young, Lord, 79
young people: board and
lodgings payments, 82–9;
homelessness, 82–9; official
view of, 74; supplementary
benefits, 77–93; training,
75–7, 78–82; unemployment,
74–82
Young Workers' Scheme
(YTS), 42, 74–5, 76, 78–82,
89, 156–7, 170–1
Youthaid, 77, 79, 81, 91, 92–3,
249